FIVE
CORE
METRICS

The Intelligence
Behind Successful
Software Management

⌂DH *Also Available from Dorset House Publishing*

For More Information

✔ Contact us for prices, shipping options, availability, and more.

✔ Sign up for *DHQ: The Dorset House Quarterly* in print or PDF.

✔ Send e-mail to subscribe to *e-DHQ,* our e-mail newsletter.

✔ Visit Dorsethouse.com for excerpts, reviews, downloads, and more.

DORSET HOUSE PUBLISHING
An Independent Publisher of Books on
Systems and Software Development and Management. Since 1984.
353 West 12th Street   New York, NY 10014   USA
1-800-DH-BOOKS   1-800-342-6657
212-620-4053   fax: 212-727-1044
info@dorsethouse.com   www.dorsethouse.com

FIVE
CORE
METRICS

The Intelligence
Behind Successful
Software Management

Lawrence H. Putnam *and* **Ware Myers**

DORSET HOUSE PUBLISHING
3143 BROADWAY, SUITE 2B
NEW YORK, NEW YORK 10027

Library of Congress Cataloging-in-Publication Data

Putnam, Lawrence H.
  Five core metrics : the intelligence behind successful software
management / Lawrence H. Putnam, Ware Myers.
      p. cm.
Includes bibliographical references and index.
  ISBN 0-932633-55-2 (soft cover)
  1. Computer software--Development--Management. 2. Computer
software--Quality control. I. Myers, Ware. II. Title.
  QA76.76.D47P8675 2003
  005.1'068--dc21

                              2003046157

All product and service names appearing herein are trademarks or registered trademarks or service marks or registered service marks of their respective owners and should be treated as such.

Cover Design: David W. McClintock
Cover Illustrations, from Figures 7-03 and 7-04: Elisabeth Thayer

Distributed in the English language in Singapore, the Philippines, and Southeast Asia by Alkem Company (S) Pte. Ltd., Singapore; in the English language in India, Bangladesh, Sri Lanka, Nepal, and Mauritius by Prism Books Pvt., Ltd., Bangalore, India; and in the English language in Japan by Toppan Co., Ltd., Tokyo, Japan.

Printed in the United States of America

Library of Congress Catalog Number: 2003046157

ISBN 13: 978-0-932633-55-2   12   11   10   9   8   7   6   5   4

Acknowledgments

We want to thank our colleagues who have been most helpful in providing their insights and opinions concerning the material in this book. They have been generous in sharing examples from their experience and a rich lore of stories from their consulting work in a wide variety of different companies, industries, and environments. Our thanks go to Doug Putnam, Larry Putnam Jr., Lauren Thayer, Kate Armel, Michael Mah, Ira Grossman, Bill Sweet, Stan Rifkin, Jim Greene, Anthony Hemens, and Hans Vonk.

Many of the figures in this book were specially prepared by people at Quantitative Software Management or were inspired by figures presented in QSM training materials. These resources were greatly appreciated. In particular, Doug Putnam revised and adapted many of the figures; his help was invaluable. Elisabeth Thayer drew the gnomes that appear on the cover and are used in figures to illustrate some of the key ideas. Again, we are thankful for all these efforts on our behalf.

Many people think that the role of editor and publisher is merely to check the spelling and to correct the grammar. Not so! The work done at Dorset House by Nuno Andrade, Vincent Au, Wendy Eakin, and David McClintock, in suggesting many meaningful changes to the text, has improved the style, consistency, integration of the ideas, and readability. We are deeply indebted to them for their diligent work in tending to these matters.

Finally, we thank our consulting and tools clients with whom we've worked over the past decade or so. These professionals have demonstrated the efficacy and value of good metrics programs leading to useful estimates up front, to control of projects under way, and to quantified benefits of process improvement initiatives. They have succeeded in making these ideas work.

Contents

FIVE
CORE
METRICS

The Intelligence
Behind Successful
Software Management

Introduction

Processes, methodologies, and methods for developing software have become the center of much activity in recent years. Today's practices for developing software are much more effective than those historically employed. However, these practices are complex, and they rely heavily on software tools. Neither processes nor tools are easy to adopt. Mastering them takes *time* over a period of years, and the measurement of improvement year by year keeps the ever-changing goal in management's sights.

Moreover, a process improvement effort does not rest solely on the enthusiasm of a solitary developer here or there. It encompasses the entire software organization and even its clients, in-house or out. A program of this magnitude depends on the understanding and support of the management structure—not only at the beginning, when enthusiasm runs high, but also over the long haul.

But what can sustain such interest, if not wild enthusiasm, over time without end? Let us look to the history of business for guidance. Double-entry bookkeeping did not arrive with the first Homo sapiens, tens of thousands of years ago. It was invented rather recently—in fourteenth-century Venice. Bookkeeping is said by some to be the epitome of dullness. Yet for six centuries, the principal output of the accounting process—the profit metric—has maintained the interest

3

and excited the daily effort of businesspeople. It is a way of keeping score in the great game of business.

Software development is part of this great game. At some point, profit tells the participants whether the software game is going well. Unfortunately, profit comes rather late in the game. The project may have crashed and burned long before the bean counters' profit-and-loss statement reveals that the company is wallowing in loss.

Therefore, software development organizations need a more immediate measure of how they are doing. This measure is especially needed to motivate senior management to persist in its support of process improvement. We need this measure to enable project managers and the developers themselves to persist in their efforts to control software development. We need it to enlighten clients and users.

Some approaches use periodic assessment to motivate improvement, such as the Capability Maturity Model (CMM) of the Software Engineering Institute (SEI) and specification 9001 of the International Standards Organization (ISO). The attention they have gained supports our belief that many managers feel the need, not only for the guidance that these models provide, but also for the assurance that assessment offers.

Unfortunately, assessments are of necessity periodic, years apart. When performed, an assessment does indeed give a jolt to the pursuit of process improvement, but in the long intervals between assessments, motivation falters. Further, assessments are imprecise. They depend upon the judgment of the assessors, who may be swayed by the artifices of those assessed.

Metrics, in contrast, are continuous, that is, weekly or monthly—as often as measures are made. They are reliable, since they rest upon counting definable elements of software production. They meet the need for immediate control at the project level. They also meet the need to measure process improvement. Being accurate and frequent, they quiet management's nerves—or excite management to action—every week or month.

Many observers proclaim passionately that people are important. Measures don't solve problems, they say, people do. Metrics just get in the way, they add. We agree that people are important—leadership is better than dictatorship, and people still have to solve the problems encountered in software development. Metrics, when poorly chosen, inaccurately collected, and unwisely applied, do upset people and impede problem solving. But measures that are well chosen, accurately collected, and wisely applied do intensify the motivation that improves the process within which people solve problems.

Software development, to be effective, needs an appropriate process. A process, to endure successfully in a world of limited resources and time, has to be measured, evaluated on those metrics, and often redirected as a result. Its relationship to scarce resources is gauged through metrics. The common complaint of overstimulated developers—"Just get out of our way"—fails to grasp these fundamentals.

Our intent in this book is to show that just a few key metrics—five, in fact—are enough to meet these needs. These five metrics provide the equivalent of the historic profit metric that energizes business, but they provide it much sooner—during development, instead of after release. Consequently, the metrics have more of a chance at critical points to motivate senior management and senior stakeholders to continue their support. Simultaneously, the metrics encourage acquisition managers, project managers, and the developers themselves to pursue the often frustrating path of process improvement.

Before describing the structure of this book, we pause to describe the experiences from whence this research sprang.

The Evolution of the Metrics

The ideas expressed in this book are the outcome of Larry Putnam's research and work in software development, first in the Army and then with twenty-five years of operating the consulting firm Quantitative Software Management, Inc. (QSM) of McLean, Virginia. Larry's final years in the Army were particularly productive in developing these concepts:

> My Army career roughly coincided with the early decades of the computer age. In a series of assignments, between periods with the troops, I became familiar with the ability of the pioneer computers to perform huge, tedious computations. It was this experience that prepared me to apply computer power, later on, to the metrics of software development.
>
> Early on (between 1959 and 1961), in one of the physics courses I took at the Naval Postgraduate School, I had to do some tedious calculations to a precision of twelve decimal places. The only tool available to us for that kind of work was the desktop mechanical calculator, and I had to hire time on it in town. Tedious experiences like that made computers very appealing when I first encountered them.

Computing Nuclear Weapons Effects

My first encounter with nuclear weapons effects was at the Army's Special Weapons Development Division in the Combat Development Command at Fort Bliss, Texas, where I was stationed between 1961 and 1964. The computer we used was a Bendix G15, which was the size of a refrigerator and had about as much power as a programmable calculator has today. One of my jobs was supervising the preparation of the Army's nuclear weapons selection tables, which commanders used to pick the right weapon for a particular tactical operation. As the weapons developers upgraded the weapons, the Army had to recalculate these tables, each of them several hundred pages in length.

At first we programmed the G15 in Assembly language. Later, I had an opportunity to program the machine in a higher-order language, ALGOL. These were very small engineering programs of perhaps fifty-odd lines of code.

A few years later (in 1966), I needed to do some blast calculations to support the course on nuclear weapons effects I was teaching at the Defense Atomic Support Agency in Albuquerque, New Mexico. Next door, Sandia Laboratories had just received a Univac 1108, the largest scientific computer then available. They had not yet fully loaded it, so they offered time to users on the base, providing the applicants did their own programming. They offered a FORTRAN course for this purpose, and I took it.

As you may expect, when the night operators fed my first deck of IBM punch cards into this giant computer, it immediately kicked me off. The FORTRAN course had failed to teach the procedures for job control cards! After about ten tries, I got my program past that hurdle, only to run into syntax errors in my own program. It turned out to be a lengthy period before I got my program to compile, run, and generate the data I wanted. In the back of my head, however, I lodged a firsthand appreciation for the perils of big-time computer programming. Also lodged there, fortunately, was some ability to apply mathematics and statistics to difficult problems. That would come in handy later.

Computer Budgets in the Pentagon

In 1972, after I'd completed a tour in Vietnam and two years commanding troops at Fort Knox, Kentucky, the time came for duty in Washington. The personnel people, in their inscrutable way, divined that I was eminently qualified to take charge of the Army's automatic data processing budget. I was going to deal with the budgetary process for the Army's procurement of computers and funding of software development programs.

The Army was spending close to $100 million per year developing software to automate its business functions—payroll, inventory management, real property management of bases around the world, mobilization plans, force deployment plans, command and control structure. It was virtually everything that had anything to do with business and logistics. The hardware on which these programs were to run cost another couple hundred million dollars.

As I began this tour, I knew little about software beyond the FORTRAN, ALGOL, and Basic programs I had written. Most of the initial work on these Army business functions had been coded in Assembly language. The Army Computer Systems Command was redoing this Assembly code in higher-order languages, principally COBOL. We were in the midst of completing 50 to 70 systems in the range of 50,000 to 400,000 lines of COBOL when I began to hear those ominous words, "overruns," and "slippages."

I really became aware of the Army's problems with software the first time I went to the budget table across from the people in the Office of the Secretary of Defense. We were looking at the next fiscal year and the five years that followed. To take an example, when the Standard Installation Division Personnel System first became operational the year before, its project organization had 118 people. For the next year, we had projected the count to fall to 116, then to 90 for each of the next five years. Those were numbers that had come up from the field.

"What are these ninety people going to do?" the budget analyst from the Office of the Secretary of Defense asked, reasonably enough. "Isn't the system finished?"

Well, there was a big silence in the room. I was new. I didn't know the answer. I looked to my right, then to my left, at the long-term civilian employees who had come into the Pentagon with the first computers. They were the acknowledged experts, but they were strangely quiet. Finally, the lame answer dribbled out: "maintenance." Nobody on the Army side of the table could satisfactorily explain what that meant.

"Look, this is a ten-million-dollar item," the budget analyst finally said. "Unless I can get an answer, I'll have to delete it. It's getting late, so let's adjourn for today and reconvene at nine A.M."

We scurried off and called the Army Computer Systems Command, which was responsible for the Personnel System. We waited by the phone into the evening. Finally, the response came, again some lame comment about maintenance, but we knew it would not make sense to the budget people. And it didn't. By 9:15 the next morning, we had lost $10 million.

After the budget meeting, as I walked down the halls of the Pentagon with my boss, a major general from the Corps of Engineers, he mused, "You know, Larry, this business of trying to plan the resources and schedule for software projects is very mystifying. It wasn't like that in the Corps of Engineers. Even early on in a project—the big dams, the waterways—we always had some feel for the physical resources we would need: how many dump trucks, the number of cubic yards of concrete, the power shovels, the people. From numbers like these, we could make a crude estimate of schedule and costs."

We reached the elevators, and he fell silent until we got off on our floor.

Then he continued: "Any time I try to get similar answers on software, I get a dialogue on the architecture of the computer itself, or a little explanation of bits and bytes, or some other irrelevancy. Never anything about how long the work is going to take, how many people it is going to require, what it will cost, or how good it will be at delivery. That's the kind of information we need at our level, here in the Pentagon. That's what we need to come to grips with this business of planning and managing software development."

At this point, he turned and went into his office. He didn't seem to expect any immediate answer from me, but his comments set me off on a line of thinking that has lasted to this day. How do software systems projects behave? Can we model this behavior with a few core parameters? Is there a way to get the answers that senior managers want?

A couple of weeks after this budget disaster, I stumbled across a small paperback in the Pentagon bookstore. It had a chapter on managing R&D projects, by Peter Norden of IBM.[1] Norden showed a series of curves, such as the one in Figure I-1, that depicted the buildup, peak, and tail-off of the staffing levels required to move a project through research and development and into production. He pointed out that some of these projects were for software, some were hardware-related, and some were composites of both.

What struck me about the function, which Norden identified as a Rayleigh curve, was that it had just two parameters. One was the area under the curve, which was proportional to the effort applied. (In the case of software projects, effort is proportional to cost.) The other was the time parameter, which related to the schedule.

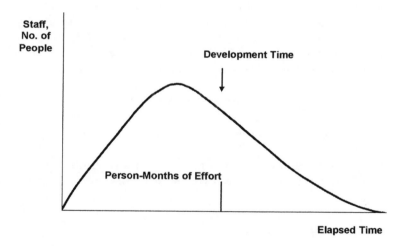

Figure I-1:   *A Norden-Rayleigh curve showing the number of staff and the amount of effort required by development projects over time.*

I found that I could easily adapt these Rayleigh curves to the budgetary data I had on the Army software projects. We had the number of person-years applied to each project in our budget, for each fiscal year of each project. So, I quickly plot-

---

[1]Peter V. Norden, "Useful Tools for Project Management," *Operations Research in Research and Development,* ed. B.V. Dean (New York: John Wiley & Sons, 1963).

ted all the software systems that we had in inventory and under development. From the plots, I could establish the parameters of the Rayleigh curves. Then, from these parameters, I could project the curves out to the end of the budgeting cycle. Within a month, I had about fifty large Army development projects under this kind of control. I was able to do credible budget forecasts for those projects—at least for five years into the future.

The next time the budget hearings came around, a year later, we were in the downsizing phase at the end of the Vietnam War. Budget cuts were endemic, and we were asked to cut the application of effort on a number of existing systems. The turnaround time was short; we had twenty-four hours to report on the impact such cuts would have.

Now that I had the Rayleigh curve and an understanding of that methodology, I was able, using a pocket calculator programmed with the Norden-Rayleigh function, to quickly make estimates of what would happen if we reduced the projections for several of the projects. It was easy to show that the aggregate of these cuts would wipe out the Army's capability to start any new software projects for the following three years.

We did not lose any money at that budget meeting.

Applying the Rayleigh Concept to New Projects

Naturally, the next important question was,

> How do I use the equations that stand behind the Rayleigh curve to generate an estimate for a new project?

More questions followed:

> It's nice to pick up those that are already under way, but is there some way I can find the time and effort for a new project? Is there a way to build a budgeting and staffing profile for getting the work done?

I looked into that. Right away the notion arose that somehow we had to relate the size of the Rayleigh curve—the time and effort it represented—with the amount of function the project was to create. To measure the functionality, we had to ask, How do the people building software for the Army—its in-house developers, like the Army Computer Systems Command and its contractors—think about the functionality they are creating?

I found out that they thought about the lines of code they had to write. They talked a lot about the number of files they were creating, the number of reports they were generating, and the number of screens they had to bring up. I saw that those types of entities were clearly related to the amount of functionality a project had to create. I would have to relate these functional entities to the schedule and effort needed to get the job done.

Here, my experience with analyzing nuclear effects data came into play. I knew that I had to

- *measure* a number of samples of the activity
- find the *pattern* in these measurements[2]

The next year-and-a-half to two years, I spent about a third to half of my daily Army schedule analyzing data. The first set of data was a group of about fifteen to twenty systems from the Army Computer Systems Command. I attempted some mathematical curve-fitting, relating the size of those systems in lines of code, files, reports, or screens to the known development schedules and the associated person-months of effort.

The first approach was to use a simple regression analysis of functionality, expressed in lines of code, as the independent variable; person-months of effort served as the dependent variable. I used the same approach with schedule.

Next, I did some multiple regression analysis in which I related effort to combinations of lines of code, files, reports, and screens. The statistical parameters that came out showed that these relationships might be useful for predictions, but they were not extraordinarily good fits. Certainly, more work and investigation were needed before any conclusions could be drawn.

By this time (1975 to 1976), I had been in contact with other investigators in this area. Judy Clapp from the Mitre Corporation had done some studies on ten to fifteen scientific and engineering systems that were being built for the Electronics Systems Division of the Air Force Systems Command at Hanscom Air Force Base. C.E. Walston and C.P. Felix at IBM Federal Systems Division had published a paper in the

---

[2]Lawrence H. Putnam and Ware Myers, *Industrial Strength Software: Effective Management Using Measurement* (Los Alamitos, Calif.: IEEE Computer Society, 1997), p. 5.

IBM Systems Journal,[3] having amassed a database of about seventy-five projects that gave a good feel for a range of different parameters related to software. All of this information was very useful toward establishing relationships between lines of code, pages of documentation, time, effort, and staffing.

In trying to do this analytical work, I had to go back about twenty years, to my academic training at the Naval Postgraduate School, to refresh my memory on statistical analyses, working with data, and drawing logical inferences and conclusions. I had to do a lot of relearning to polish skills that had become very rusty from years of neglect.

The Rayleigh Concept Leads to the Software Equation

One promising experiment employed multiple regression analysis to relate the size of the systems in lines of code to the schedule and the person-months of effort applied. I did these curve-fits first with the Army data, then with the Electronics Systems Division data, followed by the IBM data. I was lucky in that I got some very nice fits in about twenty of the Army data systems.

Concurrently, I did some theoretical work on integrating Rayleigh curves. I tried to establish the parameters of integration from a little bit of the historic data from the Army and IBM. I found good consistency in generating the key parameters for the Rayleigh equation:

• the work effort (area under the curve)
• the schedule parameter (distance along the horizontal axis)

These different, independent approaches to getting a parameter-estimating equation were leading me in the same direction and producing similar results. What ultimately fell out is what I now call the *software equation.* It related the amount of function that had to be created to the time and effort required. It originally looked like this:

Quantity of Function = Constant x Effort x Schedule

[3]C.E. Walston and C.P. Felix, "A Method of Programming Measurement and Estimation," *IBM Systems Journal,* Vol. 16, No. 1 (1977), pp. 54–73.

In the process of fitting a curve to the data representing a number of systems, I made three significant observations:

1. A *constant* was generated.
2. Effort and time were both raised to *powers*.
3. *Effort and time* were present in one equation.

Constant. The fact that a constant was generated in the process of curve-fitting is not in itself significant. A constant is always generated in this process. When you generate a line or a curve from data on a number of instances, you will find that you need a constant to balance the ensuing equation. The point of importance here is that this constant is not invented to balance the equation. It is an outcome of the historic data. Consequently, it has some kind of relationship to the data from which it originated.

Parenthetically, we should note that this constant is not the single, unchanging number its name implies. It is actually a parameter. Although in any given instance, such as a particular project, it is a single number, it may be different for each project, depending on the associated facts.

I thought a lot about what this relationship might represent, what the physical meaning of this parameter might be. Somehow, it seemed to be related to the efficiency of the development organization or the level of technology the organization was applying to its development practices. That is, where expert opinion believed an organization to be more advanced, a larger parameter was at work. That is, organizations that expert opinion believed to be more advanced fell heir to a larger parameter.

The first name I used to describe this empirically determined parameter was Technology Factor. I used that term in the first papers I published with the IEEE Computer Society, between 1976 and 1977. I have continued to use that parameter to represent the efficiency of the software development organization. Over the years, I have renamed it several times:

- Technology Factor
- Technology Constant
- Productivity Constant
- Process Productivity Parameter

The latter is probably the most descriptive term for the real relationship of this mathematical parameter to the software development process.

Powers. In the process of curve-fitting, I found that exponents were associated with both the time and effort parameters. The presence of these exponents means that the software equation is nonlinear. This, in turn, signifies that the software development process is not simple or linear; it is complex, or nonlinear. Well, in view of the difficulty we have always had with it, that complexity is not a great surprise!

Effort and time together. The curve-fitting brought effort and schedule together in the same equation. In other words, they influence each other. They are not independent entities. This conjunction leads to some possibilities in project planning, such as the "time-effort trade-off" that we will explore at length in Chapter 11. The additional fact that both effort and time carry exponents has further implications as well.

This work was the genesis of my software equation, which we still use today. Though originally derived by statistical analysis, the data I analyzed was itself real. Since then, the QSM software equation has been applied to tens of thousands of projects that were also real. The result: It has proven to be a very good measurement and estimating tool for more than twenty-five years.

The QSM software equation is a macro model that links the amount of function to be created to the management parameters of schedule and the effort required for production. The empirically determined constant, or process productivity parameter, represents the productive capability of the organization doing the work. This equation brings together four of the management-oriented measures that the major general from the Engineer Corps yearned for, now some thirty years ago.

The presence of the process productivity parameter suggests that the software equation provides a very good way to tune an estimating process. If you know the size, time, and effort of your completed projects, you can calculate your process productivity parameter. Then you can use this calculated parameter in making an estimate for a new project. So long as the environment, tools, methods, practices, and skills of the people have not changed dramatically from one project to the next, this process of playing back historic data can serve as a very useful, simple, straightforward calibration tool.

Second Key Relationship: Manpower Buildup Equation

The other relationship that emerged in these studies was the direct one between time and effort. Clearly, these two were parameters in our Rayleigh equation. But was there anything we could learn from the basic data as to the relationship between the two? Again, more curve-fitting. There was a distinct relationship:

Effort is proportional to schedule cubed.

This relationship had been noted and discovered earlier by Felix and Walston and several other investigators who had done research in software cost estimating.[4]

This finding was especially important because it gave me the basis for making estimates. I had two equations and two unknowns (time and effort). The software equation involved size, time, effort, and the process productivity parameter. The second equation linked effort with development time. With two equations, one could solve for the two unknowns.

The second equation, of course, also required some parametric determinations. We found a parameter family that seemed to relate to the staffing style of the organization. Organizations that use large teams of people tend to build up staff rapidly. Rapid buildup produces a high value for the ratio of effort divided by development time cubed.

Organizations that work in small teams generally take longer to complete development. Small teams are typical of engineering companies that tend to solve a sequential set of problems one step at a time. For such companies, I saw that the relationship of effort divided by development time cubed produced a much smaller number for the buildup parameter. This observation told us that organizations adopted different staffing styles. This parameter was actually a measure of the manpower acceleration being applied to a software project.

It became evident in studying these different types of organizations that large-team organizations tend to finish their projects a little bit faster than small-team organizations. The latter took a little bit longer to complete their work, all other things being equal. This finding suggested some sort of trade-off between team size and how long it takes to get the work done.

---

[4]Ibid.

The Rayleigh Curve As a Process Control Vehicle

The other significant idea that I started working on during my Army years was the notion of using the Rayleigh curve as a process control vehicle for projects while they are under way. The curve projected the planned staffing and effort. As the project progressed, actual staffing and effort could be compared to the plan. Managers could observe deviations from the plan and initiate prompt corrective action.

An extension of the control idea was to take real data as it was happening on a project. If this data differed from the original plan, something had to change. The purpose was to calculate the actual process productivity parameter being achieved. Using it, a new Rayleigh curve could be projected to a new completion date. The new curve would let you dynamically predict effort, cost, and schedule to completion.

I did some early curve-fitting investigations but ran into some problems and snags that for a time prevented this idea from being fully realized. Nevertheless, there was enough work and enough positive results to suggest that the process control application should be pursued.

It had become evident, however, that not many people were interested in dynamic control. Most organizations were having so much trouble coming up with the initial forecast that the idea of learning how to control an ongoing project was not high on their priority list. Trying to reach good solutions in dynamic measurement and control was premature. (However, I did eventually work out the project control aspects, as we report in Chapter 13.)

And now, the book itself, reflecting the experience of another quarter of a century, is divided into four parts. Part I, What Software Stakeholders Want, begins on a positive note with the view that some software organizations are doing very well. They are doing well because they have integrated key metrics into their development process. These practices give them predictability.

Part II covers the five core metrics needed for effective control: schedule time, effort, functionality (as expressed in size), reliability, and productivity. Because these five metrics are related to each other, developers can use known values to predict the others. This provides a base for estimating. Then, they can control the progress of their projects against those predictions. Further, with these measures, they can track improvements in the way they develop software.

Part III is given over to the application of metrics at the project level. This set of chapters applies the metric concepts to the estimation and control of a single project. Estimation and control are important because software development does not in reality begin with programmers sitting down to write code. There are such preliminary maneuvers as finding out what to do. That "what" is the essential basis of the time, effort, and other resources needed to eventually write code that implements the "what" successfully.

Part IV extends the employment of metrics to control that resides above the project level. The general idea is that the acquirers of software development capability can employ these metrics to guide their relationship with development organizations. Higher levels of management can use them to manage a portfolio of projects and to guide their employment of reusable components. Organizations can gauge improvement by tracking these metrics.

Part I
What Software Stakeholders Want

Software stakeholders—the clients, management, and developers—want predictable operations. A fair percentage of software organizations are now achieving this goal. They are an existence proof, as the scientists say, that orderly software development is within reach. That is not to say that reaching it is easy, only that it is possible.

 What do we mean by predictable? We mean that a project organization at a certain level of *productivity* can accomplish the required *work* within a planned *time* frame, by expending a planned amount of *effort.* We mean that the result of the work, the product, will attain the planned level of *reliability.* These five factors (shown in italics) can be measured and are, therefore, *metrics.* It is evident that measurement stands astride the path to predictability.

That path in software development is called a *process.* In some organizations, the process may be the result of careful thought. In other organizations, that process may merely have grown like a weed: "It's the way we do things around here." In either case, for the path to be predictable, the organization has to be able to repeat the process. Thus, metrics are needed to measure the process and make its repetition predictable.

The prediction, then, is based on the metrics. Management has to allot the work (measured by a metric) in relation to the resources available (measured by metrics). The staff wants to keep the work within the limits of its capacity (another metric) because then staff members can plan to have a life outside of work. The client wants a predictable outcome because it has to fit the outcome into its own plans. To be successful, software development has to integrate metrics with process. That integration is *the intelligence behind successful software management.*

We turn in the first chapter of this Part to some organizations that are using metrics successfully.

Chapter 1
Some Software Organizations Are Doing Very Well

Metrics are being used successfully in many software organizations, including the one in a large telecommunications supplier that we have studied. In the year before this supplier woke up to the benefits of metrics, between 1993 and 1994, ten of its twelve completed projects—that's 83 percent—exceeded budget and schedule (see Figure 1-1). The cost of this excess was more than $15 million. Alarmed by this sad record, the organization instituted a regime of measuring key project variables. But it did more than measure, of course. It began to use the measurements to control its projects.

In the organization's first year of using measurements to guide action, the percentage of projects that were out of control dropped by 30 percent and excess cost was reduced to about $6 million. In the second year, nearly all of the projects then in progress were under full control.

Guided by measurements, a company can greatly improve its ability to develop software, just as that telecommunications supplier did. Employing measurements, a company marketing a software development concept can establish that its product is a superior one. That is what Netron, Inc., based in Toronto, did. It had already installed its technology in several-hundred client companies, beginning in 1981. The technology was working well. The clients were happy with it. The question Netron faced in the marketplace was, How can we persuade the rest of the world?

Netron called its technology *frame engineering*. The merit of frame engineering is that it enables projects to attain a very high degree of component reuse. Briefly, a frame is an adaptable building block. It contains instructions for converting the contents of the frame into source code, ready to be compiled. These instructions are executed by a frame processor. It is a pre-compiler working at what Paul Bassett, the inventor of frame engineering, calls "construction time," as opposed to "run time."[1]

Experience of a Large Telecommunications Supplier

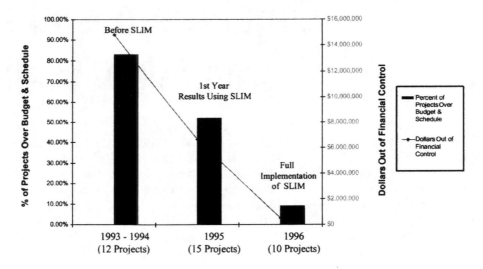

Figure 1-1:   *The introduction of quantitative methods, also known as Software LIfecycle Management (SLIM), enabled a telecommunications supplier to reduce the frequency and magnitude of its software project overruns dramatically.*

Frames are relatively large components. Netron supplies a few hundred standard ones. With standard frames alone, an organization developing business systems can reach 70 percent reuse. In addition, clients may develop their own frames, specific to their particular business functions. By developing its own specialized frames, an organization gets into the 80 to 90 percent reuse range. Reuse on this scale greatly increases the efficiency of the development process.

---

[1]Paul B. Bassett, *Framing Software Reuse: Lessons from the Real World* (Upper Saddle River, N.J.: Prentice Hall, 1996).

To demonstrate this efficiency, Netron asked nine of its client companies to provide basic metric data—size, duration, effort—on fifteen business-system projects. Ira Grossman and Michael C. Mah, partners in QSM Associates, Inc., applied the methods described in this book to that data. The fifteen frame-based projects were all way above the average of QSM's proprietary database of project metrics, as shown in Figure 1-2.[2]

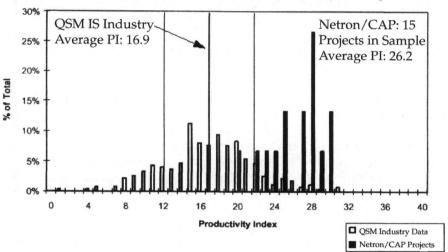

Figure 1-2:   *The productivities of the QSM database projects (white bars) are distributed over the entire productivity range, while Netron's frame-based projects (black bars) lie near the upper end.*

To be specific, we note three facts suggested by the comparison shown in Figure 1-2:

- The average (process) productivity of the fifteen frame-using projects was 9.4 times the average of 2,800 projects recorded in the QSM business-systems database.
- All but one of the frame-based projects had higher productivity than 84 percent of the projects in the database.
- Nearly half the frame-based projects (47 percent) had higher productivity than 95 percent of the database.

---

[2]The QSM database provides core metrics on the more than 6,300 projects reported by software organizations since 1983. The database is further described in Appendix B.

The productivity index (PI)—actually the *process* productivity index—is derived from three common metrics: size, effort, and schedule time. Therefore, we can also express the meaning of this index in the more common currency of schedule and effort:

- The schedules of the frame-based projects were, on average, 70 percent shorter.
- Their effort (or cost) was 84 percent less.

For those who feel more comfortable with the conventional measure of productivity, source lines of code per person-month,

- Thirteen of the projects achieved SLOC/PM in the top 20 percent of the QSM database.

Netron was happy. The metrics gave the organization firm numbers to show prospective clients.

We were also happy! Figure 1-2 demonstrates not only that Netron's clients were doing very well, but that many of the organizations reporting metric data to QSM's database were also doing very well. That is the thesis of this chapter: Some software organizations are succeeding with metrics-based management.

Unhappily, the figure also reveals that some organizations (other than Netron's clients) are not doing so well. However, as the experience of the telecommunications supplier and Netron's clients reveals, individual organizations can take steps to increase their productivity and to move up the scale shown in Figure 1-2.

Maturity Assessments Reflect Hope

In the late 1980's, the Software Engineering Institute at Carnegie Mellon University, under contract with the Department of Defense, introduced the Capability Maturity Model. That model defined five levels of software maturity, with Level Five being optimal:

1. Initial
2. Repeatable
3. Defined
4. Managed
5. Optimizing

Exactly what these levels represent would involve going into detail not pertinent to our immediate purpose. Rather, let us just note that the Software Engineering Institute felt that there were five levels of software capability. The Department of Defense and its organizations and contractors agreed with this analysis. They have made considerable efforts since then to improve their software capabilities and, indeed, some organizations have lifted themselves two or three levels. These level assessments are made by teams of assessors, evaluating how many of the 28 evaluation criteria an organization has achieved. These evaluations, based on assessment-team judgment, appear to correlate, at least approximately, with QSM's process productivity index, as shown in Figure 1-3.

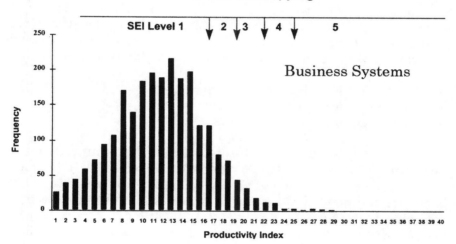

Figure 1-3:   *The process productivity index, based on metrics, and the capability maturity level, based on assessment, do reveal a common theme: Software development organizations have different levels of capability.*

Similarly, ISO 9003 of the International Standards Organization reflects the same faith—that less-capable software organizations can advance to greater capability by adopting the dictates of a standard. Perhaps you never doubted this reality in the first place—that software organizations operate at different levels of capability. Organizations are composed of people, and many observations and tests demonstrate that the various capacities of people, when measured, provide scores along a range, with most of the scores clustered near the average. The capability of software organizations is similarly distributed, as Figures 1-2 and 1-3 show.

Nevertheless, a good many software organizations seem to have made little effort to advance in capability. About half of those assessed so far are mired in Level One.

Has Software Development Mired Down?

Back in the 1980's and early 1990's, we took great satisfaction from the apparent improvement in the productivity of software development organizations. For instance, one of QSM's client companies, a business systems developer, had a sustained record of improving its process productivity by 16 percent per year for more than a decade. It was the only organization doing that well, but it did demonstrate what was possible. At that time, the average gain in process productivity (per year) for organizations reporting to the QSM database was

- 10 percent, for business systems
- 8 percent, for engineering systems
- 6 percent, for real-time systems

By 1997, however, Howard Rubin, chairman of Hunter College's Department of Computer Science, reported that productivity (as measured in source lines of code per professional per year) had dropped 59 percent over the previous two years.[3] Rubin's finding was based on questionnaires returned by companies that chose to respond to his request for productivity data. Our analysis of the QSM database indicated that productivity had dropped 40 percent during the same two-year period.[4]

In 2001, analysis of the QSM database by Douglas T. Putnam, vice president of professional services, showed that process productivity increased from 1982 to 1997 but declined in the period from 1997 to 2000 (see Appendix B). Of course, the QSM database, large as it is, encompasses only a small part of the entire software development industry. Nevertheless, the possibility of a decline in software productivity is alarming. Can there be reasons for this decline?

---

[3]Howard Rubin prepared the 1997 Worldwide Benchmark Report for the Meta Group, Stamford, Connecticut. The report itself contains more than 2,000 pages in five volumes, but Rubin published a summary of it in *IT Metric Strategies*, April 1998, pp. 1-12, Cutter Information Corp., Arlington, Massachusetts.

[4]Lawrence H. Putnam and Ware Myers, "QSM Database Shows Drop in Productivity," *IT Metric Strategies*, May 1998, pp. 13-16, Cutter Information Corp., Arlington, Massachusetts.

There were three great influences at play during the final years of the second millennium. One was the assignment of increasing numbers of programmers to the Y2K problem. The second was the growth of the Internet. The third was the implementation of large-scale applications such as enterprise resource planning and business-to-business commerce.

The first of these influences, Y2K, was technically simple, but the level of productivity with which companies pursued it was difficult to measure. The other two influences increased the interconnections between individual projects, thus increasing complexity. The ensuing complications may have caused the decline in process productivity by challenging the abilities of software professionals and the methodologies and tools they were then using.

Since the mid-1990's, there has been a considerable enhancement of methodologies and tools. Organizations that are not keeping up are probably experiencing a decline in productivity. We cite just one fact:

> Software organizations distribute themselves about the mean, roughly along a normal curve—the bell-shaped curve of statistical theory, as Figure 1-3 demonstrates. The statistical distance between an organization that lies one standard deviation below the mean (16th percentile) and an organization that operates one standard deviation above the mean (84th percentile), measured in terms of process productivity, is a factor of 10.[5]

Way Down Low

Some software development organizations are getting "things" right, as the right-hand stretch of Figure 1-3 shows us. The great majority, however, are mired in the lower reaches of productivity in the left-hand part of the figure. Way Down Low is where most of us have to start.

For instance, QSM recently consulted for a Capability Maturity Model Level One organization embarking on a big redo of its inventory of medical systems. This is the way that organization was conducting estimation on software projects:

- They know the size of the team they want to put on a project. (Staff)
- They know the schedule specified by higher authority; accepted it as gospel. (Months)

---

[5]Lawrence H. Putnam and Ware Myers, *Measures for Excellence: Reliable Software on Time, Within Budget* (Englewood Cliffs, N.J.: Prentice Hall, 1992), p. 33.

- They multiply the two together, to get the effort. (Staff-Months)

Then they get into the project. Soon they see how far behind they are. They panic. They throw more and more people into the breach, trying to meet the schedule. They now see that it is impossible. Even in panic mode, the project is still impossible.

Unfortunately, deadlines that are handed down and treated as gospel are quite common in the industry. For instance, the manager of software development at a Wall Street firm told a *Wall Street Journal* reporter, "We don't have the luxury of determining our schedules. They're 'told' to us. Then, given this time frame, we try to tell the client what we can build. In the end, we wind up working lots of overtime—because they want *everything*."

Over the last quarter-century, we have encountered this behavior frequently. We still do. And that is Way Down Low, where far too many software organizations still languish. And that is where they have to start if they are to move up. The competition never sleeps.

Intelligence Can Guide Us

Whether it's a single company making use of metrics or nine companies finding out from measurements how much difference a new technology made, metrics can tell us that we are *doing things right*. Metrics provide and enable the following:

- dependable estimates of project effort, schedule, and reliability
- control of the project during its course
- ability to replan an errant project along the way
- master-planning the assignment of resources to all projects within the organization
- monitoring process improvement from year to year

Furthermore, an organization can apply these same metric capabilities to the oversight of development subcontractors and outsourcing contractors.

But first we must ask, What do we mean by *doing things right?* We mean that, fundamentally, we are turning out software products in less development time, with less effort, at a better reliability level. What are those "things" we are trying to do right? If we do some "thing" and then make some measurements, the metrics tell us whether it was the right "thing" to do. Moreover, advancing metrics confirm our confidence in the value of continuing to do that "thing."

By now, enough organizations have done some "things" and tracked favorable metrics as a result that we have a pretty good idea of what the "things" are. In fact, the "things" plus the metrics to measure them constitute "the intelligence behind successful software management." What are the most important of these "things"?

Process. At a minimum, a software organization needs a process that it can repeat the next time. Repeatability lies at the heart of estimating and bidding. More importantly, it enables a project to meet the expectations of its own and the client's management. Beyond repeatability lie two more stages. The first is the employment of guides to improve the process, such as specifications and the Capability Maturity Model. The second is the move to a process standard, such as the Unified Software Development Process (described further in Chapter 3).

Standardization. We hesitate to bring the dreaded word standardization into play. Many software people regard the writing of code as more an art than a science. Indeed, at a certain point, there is art in it. But Shakespeare did write in the English of his day, then an emerging standard. Artists of software can work in standards intelligible to other artists, as well as to their other co-workers, managers, and certain of the client representatives. One of these "standards," dating from as recently as 1997, is the Unified Modeling Language (UML). It gives developers a "drawing" medium to work in. It enables them to recall their own work months later. It enables developers to read each other's work. It provides a permanent record of the work accomplished.

Software tools. An important outgrowth of standardization is software tools. When everybody does his own thing in his own way, you can't reduce that proliferation of half-formed methods to tools. Tool builders have to have a large market (in other words, some degree of standardization) to support their cost of development and marketing.

The software product. Before management can intelligently assign staff to a project and forecast the schedule it will take, it needs a clear grasp of what the product is to be. That preliminary task itself takes some staff and time, so people in a hurry sometimes bid before they have product functionality, commonly known as "size," as the basis for a more reliable bid. In other words, an effective software process provides for certain phases before formal construction under a bid (or other costing arrangement) begins.

Risk. A software product of some size and novelty involves risk:

- Critical risks: Elders determine that the product is within the current state of the art and within the capabilities of the project organization available.

- Significant risks: Elders establish that the project can surmount these risks within the schedule and effort planned.

These "things" and the metrics that measure them are what we mean by "the intelligence behind successful software management."

Chapter 2
A Finite Planet Makes
Measurement Essential

It seems, in the grander scheme of things, that we humans live on a rather small planet with limited resources. That fact of life has shaped our evolution.

- In the hunter-gatherer culture of a few tens of centuries ago, the nearly nonexistent technology of the period could support only a few million people.
- We can only go without food, drink, warmth, sanitary facilities, and other necessities for rather short periods of time.

Thus, from the beginning of our evolutionary history, we have been up against the limits of time and resources. It is built into our genes to be careful about both.

Beginning about a million years ago, our forerunners found that stone tools could ameliorate this harsh equation. With the help of tools, they could get a little more of what they had to get to stay alive.

Out of the tribulations of these million years has come the market economy. At a fundamental level, this economy calls for us to minimize time and effort and to improve productivity, in order to get to market with a competitive product. This handful of what we will identify as metrics—time, effort, productivity—descends from our evolutionary history. It is not the invention of some mean-spirited metrics guru who is trying to spoil the fun in which we creative programmers would otherwise frolic.

Rather recently, in terms of evolutionary millennia, we reached the point where we found that software—another kind of tool—could further ameliorate our unceasing quest for food and drink. Unfortunately, at the advanced living standard software developers have attained, they have so far removed themselves from the problem of accessing food and drink that they tend to forget this evolutionary history. They disregard the reality that, like everyone else on this planet, they are beholden to these few metrics.

These few metrics, in turn, become a tool. For instance, soaring downhill on skis is great fun. Trudging back up the slope for another run is great drudgery. So, someone invented the ski lift, a tool, letting electricity do the work that used to be the task of human legs. Now we just enjoy the view on the way back up the mountain.

Similarly, conducting software development in harmony with a few metrics makes it possible for software developers to enjoy their work. And beyond work, to enjoy the rest of their lives—their families, their recreation. The intelligent use of metrics in this area of life makes it possible for developers to accomplish their work in something near a standard workweek, and thus have time for the other interests of a rounded life. The effective deployment of metrics is not something in opposition to the interests of developers. In fact, it is something in their best interest.

The reality is that poor use of measurement systems in software development accomplishes neither the objective of allotting work in relation to resources or of keeping work within the limits of human capacity. What do we mean by "poor use of measurement systems"? We mean not only failure to use measures, but failure to use measures that are themselves effective and that are effectively related to each other.

These failures are, broadly speaking, of two general types.

- Some managements set the scope of a software project and the date of completion in terms of management goals, such as the date the corresponding hardware is to be finished, with little consideration of the size and capability of the software team that is available to develop the software. In other words, these managements make little use of software development metrics.

- Other managements do place a numerical value on the scope of the work to be done. That is, they ask experienced developers to estimate the number of lines of source code they expect the project to produce. That is fine, but then they err in estimating the level of productivity the project will achieve. One form of this error is to take programmer productivity to be so many lines of source code per month. That is an unreliable metric, as we shall show in Chapter 5. Another approach to estimating productivity is to have experienced managers and developers judge what it is by evaluating a dozen or more factors. That way, too, is subject to considerable error. It is the best managers can do until they have a record of metrics on completed projects from which they can measure what it actually was (to which we devote Chapter 7).

Beyond the measures lies the further obligation of tying them to the process of software development. Our task is to find the metrics that are effective in measuring and controlling the process. We introduce that task in the remainder of this chapter and devote much of the rest of the book to elaborating it.

What Makes Metrics Effective?

Finding the right metrics is the initial goal. Finding the correct relationship between them is the second necessity.

What the Right Metrics Are

The right metrics are those that enable software development to operate successfully in a market-oriented economic system. There are five of them. We call them the core metrics:

1. quantity of function, usually measured in terms of *size* (such as source lines of code or function points), that ultimately execute on the computer
2. *productivity*, as expressed in terms of the functionality produced for the time and effort expended
3. *time*, the duration of the project in calendar months
4. *effort*, the amount of work expended in person-months
5. *reliability*, as expressed in terms of defect rate (or its reciprocal, mean time to defect)

The five core metrics should be standardized, certainly within the scope of a single project, preferably within the company, ideally across the entire software world. Solid definitions make cross comparisons possible. Uniform definitions facilitate education, training, and the mobility of people.

How the Core Metrics Relate

We can represent any kind of work activity by a statement such as the following:

> People, working at some level of *productivity*, produce a quantity of function or a *work product* at a level of *reliability* by the expenditure of *effort* over a *time* interval.

Software development is a work activity; this work relationship applies to it. The statement shows that all five core metrics are interconnected. That is, when you push on one, the others feel it. In practice, that means that all five should be considered together. As we shall see in later chapters, time and effort have an especially profound influence on each other.

The practical problem, then, is to reduce each core-metric concept to a clear definition, to find units that express this definition, and to express their relationships in a set of working equations.

This challenge has baffled much of the software community for several generations. We will discuss it in Chapter 4 and in detail in the rest of this book. In the next section, however, we take an initial look at three of the approaches currently in wide use.

The Management of Software Projects Is Very Difficult

Software development presents management with a double challenge. One is the management of the individual project—acquiring the needed funds and a schedule of sufficient length and then carrying out the work successfully within the limits set by them. Beyond that first challenge is the necessity to improve the *process* of carrying out the work.

The software world, of course, has been aware of these twin challenges and has developed many aids, going all the way back to programming languages, compilers, editors, and the like. In the 1980's, computer-aided software engineering (CASE) had a period of popularity. At present, we group the approaches to these challenges in three categories.

Specifications

The Department of Defense, the International Standards Organization, and others have published specifications with the goal of making software development work better. In general, these specifications list scores of practices thought to be desirable.

Specifications, however, are weak in providing the means through which organizations can attain these goals. The key weakness, from the point of view of the core-metrics idea, is that such specifications usually fail to quantify the goals. They lack a means of measuring progress toward the achievement of the generalities they espouse. Experts can write volumes expounding them and project people can read and read—until their minds reel. Still, lacking effective means of measurement and of tying metrics to process, management, and staff have little to encourage their continued effort. They will not be sure that their efforts are getting them anywhere.

Capability Maturity Model

The Capability Maturity Model lays out a path for organizations to follow to improve their software development capability. The path is divided into five levels, described further in Chapter 19. Each of the levels, above the lowest one, is characterized by "key process areas." For instance, the second level, called "Repeatable," has key process areas for software project planning and software project tracking and oversight. However, "the CMM does not mandate how the software process should be implemented; it describes what characteristics the software process should have," according to Mark C. Paulk, the current supervisor of the Model at the Software Engineering Institute, Carnegie Mellon University.[1] That feature of the CMM leaves organizations free to implement metric aspects of project planning and tracking in ways that may not be wholly satisfactory.

Organizations are assigned to levels by teams of professional assessors. This approach suffers from several blemishes:

- Judgment is an unreliable substitute for attributes that are subject to actual measurement.
- Evaluations are too infrequent—normally years apart—to provide much of an incentive for those who are being evaluated to persevere.

---

[1]Mark C. Paulk, "Software Process Proverbs," *Crosstalk* (January 1998), pp. 4–7.

- The evaluation process is expensive—the evaluation team works from several days to several weeks on each assignment.

It is our experience that, above all else, executives, managers, and developers themselves need reassurance, at frequent intervals, that they are improving. They need encouragement to continue their efforts to improve. The Capability Maturity Model's "pats on the back" come years apart, not day in and day out as measurement can provide.

Process

Specifications and Capability Maturity have to be implemented through some kind of software development process. Of course, there are, at present, almost as many processes, defined or undefined, as there are software development organizations. Some of the best-known processes are described in Chapter 3.

From the standpoint of a single organization, it ought to be able to repeat whatever process it has. Repeatability of process enables an organization to project effort and schedule on the next project.

From the standpoint of the software world at large, there is merit to having a single process. Artifacts (or drawings or models) could be standardized around that process. Educational organizations could train to that process. Software-tool builders could design tools for that process and these tools could be better, less expensive, and more widely applicable. Developers could transfer between projects, divisions, or companies more easily.

Again, the process has to be measurable—for estimating and bidding purposes, for control during development, and for gauging improvement over a series of projects.

Measure What Has Been Done

The answer to the very difficult problem of managing software development is the establishment of metrics that are correctly related to each other. For now, we observe that a satisfactory model requires at least three relationships:

- The first relationship will contain both time and effort, so that it takes into account their very substantial effects on each other. It will also contain terms for pro-

ductivity and size, a measurement reflecting the amount of work or functionality.
- The second relationship will also contain time and effort. (In estimating, time and effort are unknowns, and it takes two equations to find two unknowns.)
- The third relationship will deal with reliability (the defect rate).

We named productivity as occurring in the first relationship. Its value comes from past projects. For completed projects, the values of the other terms—time, effort, and size—are known. Productivity is obtained by a simple computation. Since it is derived from measured attributes, it is as precise as those measurements. Moreover, it may be expressed in many levels, and this can provide users with a frequent sense of achievement as those values increase.

Productivity may be calculated not only at the end of each project but during the project as well—as soon as enough has been completed for the metrics to be valid. In a well-run organization, we hasten to add, in-project checks are employed not as a whip to the people but as a guide to running the project within the time and effort planned. If the original plan turns out to be inadequate, these checks serve as a guide to replanning the time and effort allocations.

The third relationship contains the attributes affecting the number of defects, namely, the size, productivity, time, and effort. In effect, defects occur at a rate derived from historic data, but the core metrics at which each project operates modify this rate. For example, a larger project generates more defects. High productivity results in fewer defects. Allowing for adequate time reduces defects, and so on.

These Five Metrics Work Together

A software project is a unified endeavor. The five core metrics are tied together as Figure 2-1 suggests. In sub-figure *a*, we see that effort takes place over time, in the form of some kind of curve, such as the Rayleigh curve. Sub-figure *b* depicts the occurrence of errors during development. Both these sub-figures represent the same project, that is, the same functionality (features or size) at the same productivity level. Sub-figure *c* shows the rate of code production (functionality) associated with this effort-and-defect profile. They are all synchronized in elapsed time. The magnitudes of the curves can change if productivity, staffing, or the schedule are changed.

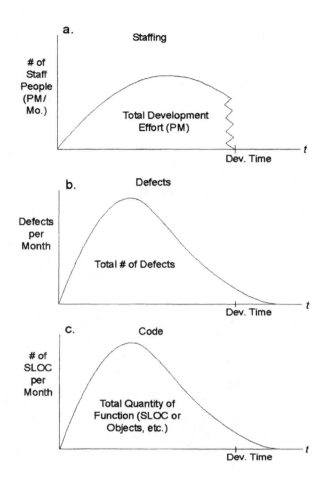

Figure 2-1: These three figures demonstrate that the five core metrics work together. (a) Staff is added to a project over the time of its schedule. The area under the curve is proportional to the effort (person-months, or PM). (b) During the early part of the project, the growing staff commits errors at an increasing rate. The area under this curve adds up to total defects. (c) Points on the third curve represent the rate at which code or function is produced. The area under this curve is the total of code or function produced. Reducing the functionality (features or size) of the product reduces effort and defects. Improving productivity (probably over considerable time) would have the same effect. The opposite result occurs if we experience increasing functionality, features, or size, or if we experience falling productivity.

That brings us back to the point with which we started. Only by working more effectively can we, all of us, extract a higher standard of living from the raw materials that this planet provides. This means producing more for each hour we spend working.

Software has become the preeminent tool to help us reach that objective. Producing more software of better quality for each hour that we spend developing software is the multiplier that enables us to reach the overall goal. You can see why it is so important that we do it—software development—right. You can see why we have to have a system of metrics to do it right.

Chapter 3
Integrate Metrics with Software Development

People are important, and people have to solve the intricate problems encountered in software development. It is equally true that collaborative leadership is better than command management, especially in knowledge work, for people do not solve problems on command—at least not well. It is also true that a software development process, clumsily applied, can get in the way of what people are trying to do. Moreover, we might as well admit—for it is true—that when metrics are poorly chosen, inaccurately collected, and unwisely applied, people get upset. When people are upset, they solve problems poorly. To put it in a nutshell, people solve problems; metrics provide the schedule time and staff allowance within which people solve problems.

Thus, when pertinent metrics are applied effectively, people become more productive. Metrics make the process of software development more reliable and efficient. The challenge is to work metrics into that process. This chapter begins the exploration of the typical phases of development and the ways metrics can be integrated into the process.

Metrics Meter Limited Resources

As we pointed out in the previous chapter, software development, like everything else on this third rock from the sun, operates on a planet of limited resources that measures time by rotations of its globe. Every rotation carries costs because the people doing the work like to eat every day. That is, we mean to say, neither staff power nor schedule time are free goods.

The reliability of the product isn't free either. People work over a period of time to produce software. That software may be of high reliability—with few defects—because the people had sufficient time to avoid or correct the defects. However, software released with many defects merely transfers that working time, usually multiplied one hundred-fold, to the users, the help-line crew, and the maintenance staff.

Staff, schedule time, and the number of defects represent three of the five core metrics. The fourth core metric is the amount of function contained in a software product. It is commonly measured in lines of source code or in function points. The fifth core metric is the productivity level—or process productivity—of the project. But when do we measure the five core metrics: size, productivity, time, effort, and reliability?

In the beginning, the software project is just a gleam in some dreamer's eye, and there is nothing to measure. At the end, we have a product and can count the lines of code, but at that point, the count is of little value. Measurements would have come in handy earlier, when we were trying to estimate the time and effort. It is evident also that we need metrics at many in-between points. That is, between the start and the end of the software development process. We need to have metrics integrated into that process. The work has to be measured and evaluated on those metrics, and often redirected as a result.

Thus, development operates through process. Process, in turn, operates through resources. The key resources, time and effort, are scarce. In consequence, they have to be metered out to projects. That metering is properly the province of a measurement system, or metrics for short.

That is the nub of the metric side of the argument. Unfortunately, developers in the trenches often see the situation quite differently. They see a rather amorphous project, full of problems that may take a long time to penetrate. They see a schedule imposed by upper management or clients with little grasp of the problems still to be unearthed. They see a staff of inadequate size with junior members inexperienced in the problems to come. To them, that too-short schedule and inexperienced staff are the "metrics" imposed on the project. And, of course, in that situation, these "metrics" are what pass as the outcome of management's stab at the time and effort metrics.

That word "stab" is the key to a happier metric future. Suppose that instead of "stabbing" more or less blindly at the metrics, management were able to reach these metrics as the outcome of an intelligent methodology. That is, the time and effort metrics were well suited to the needs of the developers. The productivity level at which the staff can function was well established. Under this scenario, developers could be happy with the metrics offered with the project.

It is evident that developers are unhappy, not with metrics per se, but with lousy metrics. In a world of finite resources, metrics have to be an integral part of an effective software process. But they don't have to be lousy.

What Is the Process?

An early representation of the software development process was the waterfall model, summarized in the first column of Table 3-1. Many understood the model to prescribe a one-way path through the workflows of software development: requirements capture, analysis, design, and so on, as shown in the table. In truth, that understanding was based on the first diagram of workflows in Winston Royce's landmark paper, "Managing the Development of Large Software Systems." If readers of the paper had turned the page, they would have seen that the second diagram shows feedback arrows from each workflow to the preceding one. "As each step progresses and the design is further detailed, there is an iteration with the preceding and succeeding steps," Royce wrote.[1] Really, a quite modern attitude! Despite Royce's iterative view, many software people still consider his model to be a sequential, single-pass flow of work—not an iterative process.

 The U.S. Department of Defense (DoD) divided the software problem into four phases: feasibility study, high-level design, main build, and operation and maintenance. These phases were convenient for managing contracted parts of the development. With little hard knowledge to go on, the first two phases could be handled as level-of-effort contracts. By the time the high-level design was completed, the knowledge was on hand for a fixed-price contract.

Developed in 1999, the Unified Process brought together the previous processes or methodologies of Ivar Jacobson, Grady Booch, and James Rumbaugh, each already a well-established methodologist. Although divided into four phases like the Department of Defense's version, the phase names are quite different. The four phases are named not in terms of their content, but in terms of their position in

[1]Winston W. Royce, "Managing the Development of Large Software Systems," *Proceedings, IEEE WESCON* (August 1970), p. 2.

the development sequence. Within the Elaboration phase, for example, the Unified Process locates a number of activities involved in getting ready to build the system in the next phase.

Table 3-1:   *The waterfall model of software development, originating in the 1960's, listed what we now call workflow activities. It was followed by the four phases of the Department of Defense process. The Unified Process, pulled together in 1999, redefines the four phases and assigns them new names to make clear that they are something different. In the final column, a survey author, attempting to come up with a generic set of names, confuses workflows and phases.*

	Waterfall[2]	**Dept. of Defense**[3]	**Unified Process**[4]	**Generic**[5]
I	Requirements	Feasibility Study	Inception	Initiation
II	Analysis	High-Level Design	Elaboration	Conceptual Requirements
III	Design	Main Build	Construction	Analysis
IV	Coding	Operation, Maintenance	Transition	Design
V	Testing			Construction
VI	Operations			Deployment

The generic set, shown in Table 3-1, presents a combination of sequence names, such as Initiation, and workflow names, such as Analysis, that is confusing. The confusion arises from our long immersion in the waterfall model. If you are going to go through the workflow activities (those listed in the first column of the table) only once—in waterfall fashion—process and workflows are the same. However, in the more modern sense of the spiral model or iterative development, which assume repeated passes through workflows instead of a single pass, there is a distinction between process and workflows. For example, if a team decides that it needs to develop a prototype in the first phase, it has to go through an abbreviated version of requirements capture, analysis, design, and coding to get to the prototype. In other words, part or all of the workflows may occur in any phase. There is a

---

[2]Royce, loc. cit., pp. 1–9.

[3]Lawrence H. Putnam and Ware Myers, *Measures for Excellence: Reliable Software on Time, Within Budget* (Englewood Cliffs, N.J.: Prentice Hall, 1992).

[4]Ivar Jacobson, Grady Booch, and James Rumbaugh, *The Unified Software Development Process* (Reading, Mass.: Addison-Wesley, 1999).

[5]Ellen Gottesdiener, "OO Methodologies: Process & Product Patterns," *Component Strategies* (November 1998), pp. 34–44.

distinction between phase and workflow, and the Unified Process grasps this difference.

In the following sections, though, we describe each phase of the software development process in terms of the Unified Process model, and we note that the DoD model, or some version of it, is widely employed.

Phase One: Inception

It would be nice to know, before spending a few million dollars, that the proposed system is technically feasible and that there is a business case for it. In the very beginning, when all you have is a high-level executive waving his arm broadly and saying, "Wouldn't it be super to have a single system that integrates all our operations?" you can't estimate time and effort. You don't have enough information to make even a rough estimate of the size of the necessary software.

You first have to take three preliminary steps: You have to break the grand vision down into something concrete enough to study; you have to define what is within the system and what is external to it; you have to figure out if your organization can produce this system that you have roughly defined.

Is the system technically feasible at the current state of the art? This question seems to arise in areas such as the Department of Defense, the Federal Aviation Administration, and other organizations where well-meaning but not technically based leaders dream dreams that reach beyond what is immediately possible. This question also arises in new areas, sometimes called "green fields," in which we have not previously done a project. In more mundane fields, feasibility of many applications is more certain. It is enough to realize that the project is a follow-on or that the developers have worked in this application area before. That experience helps us feel certain that the work is at least feasible.

Even if a proposal is technically feasible, though, it may not be appropriate for our particular organization at this time. We may lack certain skills needed by the project. Our organization may not have access to the needed funds. The product may not be consonant with our company's core competence. We explore these issues and others in greater depth in Chapter 9. In the meantime, Figure 3-1 illustrates the position of Phase One at the beginning of preliminary work on the project.

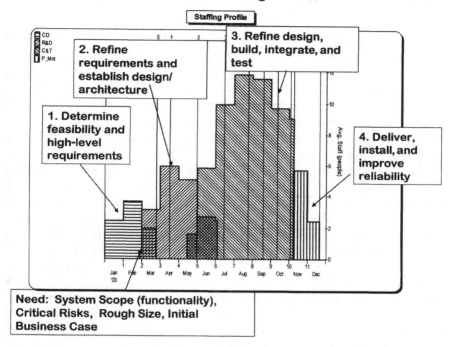

Figure 3-1:   *The Phase One (Inception or Feasibility) team does enough work to justify the move into Phase Two.*

Several of the key decisions made in the first phase should rest on a background of reliable metrics. Even the rough estimate of system size that is possible in this phase depends upon having readily available knowledge of the size of past systems. Coming up with the very rough estimate of construction time, effort, and cost involves having some knowledge of how to turn the size estimate into this very rough estimate.

Phase Two: Elaboration

In order to bid on a business basis, you need to extend further your knowledge of the project. You need to know with considerable precision what you are going to do. That is the purpose of the Elaboration phase. This phase has three goals:

- Extend the requirements to the point of blocking out most of the architecture.
- Block out most of the architecture.
- Identify the risks that, if not mitigated, could result in excess costs.

Before you can proceed with the architecture, you have to have a good grasp of the key requirements. It is these requirements on which you base the architecture. You do not have to capture all the details of the requirements in this phase. In familiar areas, it may be sufficient to block out known subsystems. In less familiar areas, you may have to carry the architecture to a lower level of structure.

Are there aspects of the architecture you understand so poorly that you cannot count on implementing them within the time and effort estimates toward which you are aiming? If so, you have to explore these aspects further. For example, you may have to find an algorithm, or even code one, to assure that it can be done. You may have to carry this portion of the project through complete requirements capture, analysis, design, implementation, and test, to a working prototype, to be certain not only that it can be done but that it can be done within business constraints. The latter, of course, are metrics of some sort.

When does your estimate become good enough? During this second phase, as you find out more about what it will take to implement the system, your size estimate becomes more precise. Your corresponding time and effort estimates become more accurate. You carry the architecture, design, and risk reduction to the point at which your estimate meets two criteria. First, it falls within the plus and minus limits normally associated with practice in your field of business. Second, it is within some probability of successful completion. Note that both of these criteria are based on metrics!

Figure 3-2 summarizes what the Phase Two team needs to accomplish.

Just where, during the progress through Phase Two, the size estimate becomes good enough to base a bid on, is not a settled issue. Under pressure from management, customers, and the market, this phase is often ended prematurely before enough is known to support a valid bid. Of course, for organizations with little in the way of a background in metrics, a lack of knowledge of the system being bid makes little difference. They were just guessing anyway. For the organization using metric methods, the size estimate midway through this phase still has too large a margin of error. Its estimates of time and effort at this point will have a comparably large range of uncertainty. Bidding such numbers leads to all the troubles with which we are familiar in the third phase, Construction—time and effort overruns, poor quality, even cancelled projects.

Resource Planning Model

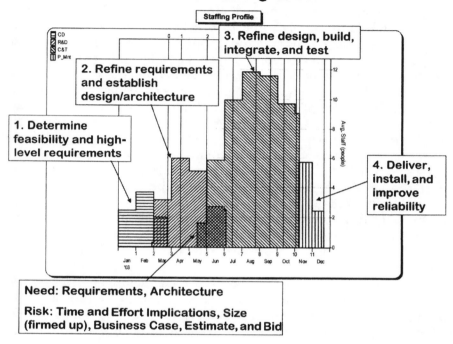

Figure 3-2:   *The Phase Two, Elaboration, team carries the exploration of the project to the point of supporting a bid.*

As long as bids are based more on executive intuition than on metrics, it makes little difference where you end the second phase. For organizations that are using better estimating techniques and learning how to make more precise estimates, it is more important to carry the second phase to the point of having an accurate size estimate.

Well, that sounds reasonable, you may be thinking. Then, on further thought, you ask, "Who is going to finance this up-front work?" Business units sometimes like to think they are passing costs to some other business unit. Between companies, the one requesting a bid likes to think it is passing the cost of what it ought to absorb to the software contractor. Similarly, within a company, a department needing software sometimes tries to pass the cost of planning that software to the software department. If these little "successes" result in inadequate attention to Phase Two, it is the using company or department that eventually suffers from the poor software that results. Thus, whoever finances Phase Two, the using organization needs to make sure that the financing reaches the goal of providing the schedule and effort funding required to complete Phase Three, Construction, successfully.

Extending Phase Two long enough to reach these goals may delay the beginning of Construction. Psychologically, this deferral can be hard to take. We all like to see that construction is under way. People like to count lines of completed code. However, when construction is started prematurely, developers may try to proceed under an inadequate bid, that is, in too short a time with an inadequate staffing level. That is bad from both a business standpoint and a technical standpoint. In mid-construction, developers realize that the architecture does not entirely satisfy the requirements, that unmitigated risks upset the schedule, and that necessary changes are costing more money than is available.

One way to reduce these problems is to keep the project length within bounds. Don't try to set up a five- or ten-year project that will solve all your problems for all time. Too many factors—requirements, environment, reusable components, hardware, and operating system platform—are certain to change over such a long period of time. Instead, try to set up a flexible architecture within which you can set up a series of short projects. You should probably hold most projects within a two-year time scale. The trick is to design an architecture that is extendable into subsequent releases and generations of the product.

In this second phase, Elaboration, a measurement system is even more critical than in the first phase. It is this phase that, by definition, concludes with a business bid. A bid is the supreme metric that governs the project through the Construction Phase and the Transition Phase. But a bid does not spring into existence from nothing, like lightning from the brow of Zeus. Rather, it is built up from lesser metrics, like size, productivity level, and reliability.

Phase Three: Construction

As we mentioned at the beginning of this chapter, *people solve problems;* metrics don't. However, metrics can help people solve problems. There have to be *enough* people over time, and that is a metric known as effort, measured in staff hours or staff months. There has to be a sufficient period of time and that is another metric, schedule time, measured in weeks, months, or years. Moreover, users of software generally want the people to solve the problems adequately—we might hang the sobriquet "quality" on that desire. There are many aspects of quality, some not readily reducible to a number. Reliability is quantifiable, however, and reflects to some extent the other aspects of quality. In the form of defect rate (or its reciprocal, mean time to defect), reliability is the third key metric.

Therefore, the time and effort implicit in the business bid provide the problem-solving people with the effort and time they need in the third phase to construct software to an acceptable level of reliability and quality. Ergo, metrics are critically important to the success of the third phase.

In addition, metrics play a second role in the Construction Phase: control. That is an ominous word—nobody likes to be controlled. We would all like to be free spirits! But remember, we live in a world of limited resources, and *control* is what keeps us safely within those limits.

Given the initial estimated metrics for effort (staff-months), schedule, and defects at the end of the second phase, we can project the rate at which effort will be expended and defects will be discovered during the Construction Phase. We can also project the rate at which *function*, such as lines of code, will be completed. In addition to projecting the average rate of occurrence of these metrics, we can project bands above and below the average.

We have now established the basis for "statistical control" of the key variables in the Construction Phase. Statistical control means that we count up the actual number of staff members, the actual lines of code produced, and the actual number of defects found during each week and see if these actuals fall within the statistical-control band. If they do, the project is proceeding according to plan. If an actual falls outside the control band, it is out of control. Work is not going according to plan. Something is probably wrong. It is a signal to look for the problem.

Under statistical control, we discover the problems as they happen, every week. They are fresh. The people who were involved are still around. The traditional alternative is to discover such problems in system test. At that point, there is little project schedule left. Some of the people are gone, while others no longer remember very clearly what they did—perhaps months ago—that now turns out to be wrong.

The Construction Phase is where most of the work of software development is accomplished. It is where most of the money is spent. Metrics are important in this phase for two reasons: to provide adequate resources and time for the task, and to confirm that the resources are being utilized according to plan.

The alternative is to fly by the seat of your pants. That does not work in the air. In a cloud, the seat of your pants is deceptive. Instrument-flight instructors preach, "Depend on your instruments, not your pants." We preach a similar message: "Depend on your metrics, not your hopes and fears."

Phase Four: Transition

The Construction Phase ended with system test conducted in-house, resulting in a system state known as initial operational capability. However, the system has not yet operated in a user or customer environment. That is the province of the Transition Phase. This phase oversees the movement of the product into the user environment, which may differ slightly from the in-house environment.

In a broad sense, there are two types of products. The first, the shrink-wrapped product, goes to many customers. As a start, the vendor may conduct a beta test (usually toward the end of the Construction Phase) with a representative selection of those users. The second type of product goes to one customer, often for installation at one site, sometimes at several sites. The customer usually conducts an acceptance test in its own environment.

In general terms, there will be two types of feedback from the user environment:

- Defects will turn up, either due to the new environment or because they were undetected during the in-house tests. The software organization has to correct them. In some cases, it may be possible to hold them for the next release.
- The software may fail to meet some of the needs the users now identify. Again, the software organization may be able to modify the system to accommodate these needs, at least those that it can readily add within the current structure. In other cases, the modification will be added to the list for consideration in the next release.

The amount of effort and schedule time needed by the Transition Phase depends upon the extent to which users encounter new needs and defects. If requirements were carefully captured in the early phases, if users were consulted during analysis and design, if users tried out operating prototypes, if they viewed operating increments early in the Construction Phase, and if this early feedback resulted in modification of the initial requirements to accommodate needs discovered along the way, then few new needs should turn up in the Transition Phase. At best, however, a software organization will find it difficult to estimate the amount of modification work that will feed back from users. Keeping a record of what happened on previous projects can serve as a guide.

If a project has followed good inspection and testing practices, the system will reach initial operational capability with fewer remaining defects. However, there are metric methods for estimating the number of defects that do remain at this point. Then, as the users operate the system in their own environment, they gradually unearth these defects. They or the system builder correct the defects and revise the estimate of the number still remaining. Using this methodology, it is possible to make a rough estimate of the amount of rework to be expected from defect discovery.

On the whole, however, the core metrics—size, effort, time, productivity, and defect rate—are less applicable in the Transition Phase than in the earlier phases. The best guide is the experience of navigating previous projects through this phase. On that basis, the software organization can allocate a certain amount of time and effort. It can then make modifications and correct defects within that budget while trying to defer more time-consuming modifications to the next release or to the maintenance budget.

Chapter 4
"I Want Predictability"

"What do you want for Christmas?" I asked a neighbor of mine in northern Virginia, at a little pre-Christmas good-cheer gathering. He is the chief executive officer of a mid-sized company.

"Well," he responded with a smile, "I've got a couple hundred neckties, and I don't even 'suit-up' every day anymore." Then his smile faded. "You know what I really want? I want software development to be predictable."

He knew I had a software company, but we had never talked about it before.

"I want my software people to be able to predict the cost and schedule of every job they undertake," he went on. "I want them to be able to predict the reliability of the product. I guess I would even like to have some glimpse beforehand of its quality."

"Funny you should say that," I said. "That's the business I'm in."

"You know, in every other part of my business, the executives in charge are able to do those things. They forecast their budgets, and they come pretty close to them. If they are bidding on an outside job, they come up

with a price and a delivery date, and I can count on their coming close to those numbers. Not so, my CIO. He seems to be operating in the dark."

"Yes, we've found that about one third of the soft-ware projects on which we have collected data exceeded their budgets or their schedules by more than thirty per-cent." I started to pull up more statistics from memory.

Just then, the pretty lady from down the street shoved an empty glass between us. "Would one of you gentlemen be kind enough to push through that crowd at the bar?" she asked. That was code for "Don't be so seri-ous at our holiday party."

"Delighted," I said, forcing a smile as I took the glass.

"Stop by my office," the CEO called after me as I dis-appeared into the crowd. —L.H.P.

The Software Situation Is Serious

"Software development projects are in chaos," The Standish Group International reported.[1] Only 16 percent of projects are "completed on time and on budget, with all features and functions as initially speci-fied." Thirty-one percent are cancelled during development. Fifty-three percent are completed short of the original goals for schedule, budget, or functionality.

In other words, if software projects were bridges, about one third would fall down during construction; about one half wouldn't get all the way across the river; and only one sixth would carry traffic. The ferrymen would not have to worry about planning a career change.

Unfortunately, as software takes over more and more business and governmental tasks, *we* do have to worry. Some of us even retreated into the woods as the dreaded changeover to the Year 2000 approached, fearful that the software on which modern life depends would fail. For-tunately, it didn't, though its successful operation came at a tremen-dous fixing cost.

The Standish Group estimates that there are 175,000 projects each year in the United States alone, costing $250 billion. The cost of fail-ures and overruns eats up a large fraction of that huge sum. No one can put a price tag on the cost in agony of the people involved, but we suspect that young people are avoiding the software field and older ones are leaving it. American companies increasingly depend on devel-opers from overseas who may be more willing to endure the agony.

---

[1] *Charting the Seas of Information Technology,* The Standish Group International (Dennis, Mass.: 1994), p. 12.

Department of Defense Calls for Predictability

In *Guidelines for Successful Acquisition and Management of Software-Intensive Systems*, the Software Technology Support Center states, "In light of these plans for funding Defense modernization through improved management, there is widespread agreement—among DoD, the defense industry, and the Congress—that our process for determining weapon system requirements and acquiring software-intensive systems often is costly and inefficient. One major problem stems from the wide-scale unpredictability of the acquisition process. In a speech to the 1993 Software Technology Conference, Salt Lake City, Utah, Lloyd K. Mosemann II, Assistant Deputy Secretary of the Air Force (Command, Control, Computers, and Support), astounded the audience by saying:

> *"It might surprise you, or perhaps even shock you, for me to say that the Pentagon does not want process improvement, it does not want SEI Level 3, or reuse, or Ada, or metrics, or I-CASE, or architectures, or standards. What the Pentagon wants is predictability! Predictable cost, predictable schedule, predictable performance, predictable support, and sustainment—in other words, predictable quality."[2]*

In the years since 1993, Mosemann, now senior vice president of corporate development at Science Applications International Corporation, has not relented. In another keynote speech to the Software Technology Conference 2002, he again emphasized, "the underlying need within the defense community is for *predictability*." (His italics.) Referring to the employment of best commercial practices, he concluded: "The government needs to *go and do likewise*. Otherwise, the decade of 2000 will likely not show any lessening of the software crisis that has carried over from the 1990's."[3]

The Underlying Reasons Are Complex

The next step is to consider why we have this problem. After all, bridges do stand, they do span rivers, and they do bear traffic. Why can't software do the same? Ah, but we have had several thousand years to learn how to build bridges. Software development dates only from the middle of the twentieth century. And what did it face?

---

[2]*Guidelines for Successful Acquisition and Management of Software-Intensive Systems*, Department of the Air Force, Software Technology Support Center, Version 3.0 (Hill AFB, Utah: 2000), pp. 1–12, 1–13.

[3]Lloyd K. Mosemann II, "Did We Lose Our Religion?" *Crosstalk* (August 2002), pp. 22–25.

- It faced a horrendous rate of change. Programs grew from a few hundred lines of code to many millions. Programming languages went through four or five generations. The hardware advanced at a rate previously unheard of—from processing a few hundred lines of code per second to hundreds of millions. Users multiplied from a handful of experts in glass-enclosed air-conditioned palaces to nearly everybody.
- It faced a massive increase in complexity. Large programs used to run only on very large computers, or even many computers in tandem. Today, personal computers approach the computational capacity of what were supercomputers a couple of decades ago. Scores of programs jostle each other on a single computer, trying to work together.
- It faced a daunting multiplication of relationships. At first, a single program ran on a single computer. Then several computers exchanged simple messages. Modems attached computers to each other, via the telephone network. The Department of Defense financed the DARPANet for a dozen or so research centers. In the 1990's, this network metamorphosed into the Internet, with hundreds of millions of users worldwide.

The sticking point is this: All these programs have to work in harmony with all the other programs. Sometimes they don't—like several times a week—and your system crashes. If your system is doing something critical, a crash may be destructive.

Competition Stirs the Pot

In the Garden of Eden, infinite time stretched before Adam and Eve, at least until Eve ate that fateful apple. Ever since, we have had to achieve reliable products in a short time, at a limited cost in effort. We are currently calling this milieu "the market-based economy." In other words, to narrow it down to software development, it takes a schedule (months) and an amount of effort (person-months) to develop software at some level of reliability (defect rate).

Since the time of Adam and Eve, entrepreneurs have been caught in this economic vise. They have to get to market in *time* to meet customers' needs. They have to hold *effort* (which translates roughly to cost and price) to a level that customers can afford. They have to reduce *defects* to a market-set minimum. It's a great game. The winners enjoy it. The losers clamor for protection.

In the last years of the second millennium, the Internet upped the ante. Its cheering section invented *Internet time*. Everything was to go faster in Internet time, including software development.

Accordingly, a set of shibboleths attained the status of commandments, as if written on slabs of stone and handed down from the highest mountain in the land:

1. Get the initial product out fast.
2. Get dominant market share.
3. Fix the product later.
4. Better yet, sell periodic updates.
5. Become fabulously wealthy.

A few users of this "get it out fast" software have been heard—at least by attentive listeners—to grumble, "It crashes twice a week." But the users soldier on, for the PC is still far, far better than the portable typewriter of sainted memory.

The Limits of the Possible

Thus, software development is in trouble, not for trivial reasons, but for deep-seated ones. An understanding of the role the five core metrics play is the first step in getting out of this trouble. These metrics are related to each other, as we suggest pictorially in Figure 4-1 and as we will develop in more detail in Part II. In the meantime, however, we can draw these general conclusions:

- If we want to get more work product (that is, more functionality, measured by some metric of size), we have to increase the amount of effort, lengthen the development time, or improve productivity. Of course, we could also augment some combination of effort, time, and productivity.
- If we want a product of higher reliability, that, too, takes increased effort, lengthened development time, or improved productivity, or some combination of the three increases.
- Conversely, if we want to reduce effort and/or time, we would have to limit the functionality of the product (reduce its size), accept less reliability, or increase productivity. We note, however, that productivity remains about the same in the short run, such as the time scale of a single project.

- If we improve productivity (over a fairly lengthy time period, of course), we can achieve more functionality or more reliability at the same level of effort and time.
- With improved productivity, we can reduce effort and time and still achieve the functionality or reliability originally intended.
- With substantially improved productivity, we can achieve even higher levels of the other four metrics.

Figure 4-1:   *Each little gnome (or concept) has to possess the strength (measured by a metric) to support the next higher level.*

Unfortunately, better productivity does not come with the snap of executive fingers. Our records of more than six thousand projects over two decades show that productivity gains come slowly, sometimes not at all. The average gain for the business projects in our database was 8 percent per year and for the more complex engineering and real-time systems, several percentage points less. In the final years of the twentieth century, the record shows even less gain.

Productivity gains at these rather low levels are not going to produce the miracles that the devotees of Internet time hope for. However, in comparison with the general level of productivity gain, these software gains stand out. Only in the final years of the twentieth century did the productivity gain of the United States economy as a whole reach 3 or 4 percent; for decades, it had been stuck just above 1 percent. Then, in the early years of the new millennium, it fell back to the 1-percent range again. The software industry, or at least the parts of it reporting their core metrics to us, has done well.

The industry's problem, really, is to find the way in which it can make the "Faster, Better, Cheaper" mantra work. We can divide that problem into three sections:

- We have to accept the reality that the five core metrics are interdependent, as we discussed in Chapter 2. Only productivity gains get us to all three of the "Faster, Better, Cheaper" goals simultaneously.
- We have to actually do the things that bring about those gains. The interdependence of the core metrics does not, by itself, put best practices into effect. It does not manage projects skillfully. It does not inspire developers. It does not work smoothly with stakeholders.
- We have to accept the necessity for metrics—at least the five core metrics and the relationship between them.

  - They make planning and estimating dependable.
  - They provide the basis for management control during project execution—the comparison of actual numbers against the planned numbers.
  - They provide evidence that the organization is actually making the productivity gains for which it is striving. That evidence, then,

encourages management to continue the effort.

At best, however, productivity gains occur over the long run. Management often has to do what it can in the short run. Realizing that getting all three—faster, better, and cheaper—in the short run is impossible, managers can focus on maximizing the one or two metrics they consider urgent in a particular case:

- If you want to get a software product out *faster* (in effect, reducing time), you can increase the number of people (that is, effort) assigned to the project. You can also increase the quality of that effort by assigning better qualified people to such projects. Alternatively, to achieve *faster,* you can sacrifice reliability, that is, spend less time getting the requirements straight or keeping them current, take little time for analysis and design, speed up coding, skip inspection, and reduce testing; in other words, release an inferior product. It is clear that a lot of software projects have gone this route.
- If you want to get a *better* software product, that is, one with more functionality or more reliability, you have to allow more time or effort. With more time, that is, by spreading the same amount of effort over a longer schedule, a smaller staff can do a better job. With more effort, that is, by packing more effort into a shorter schedule, an enlarged staff can build the product in less time. But you can't indefinitely reduce either effort or time—there are limits, as we note in the next section.
- If you want to develop a software product *cheaper,* in effect, with less effort, you can reduce the emphasis on *faster* or *better.* First, you can extend the time: A smaller team over more time will get the job done at less overall cost. Second, you can skimp on *better.* As the wag said, "If you don't set a specification for the product to meet, I can give it to you next week."

Table 4-1 summarizes the relationships among the five core metrics.

Table 4-1:   *The only way you can fulfill the "Faster, Better, Cheaper" mantra—all at one time—is to improve productivity. As the final column indicates, improved productivity (upward arrow) provides gains in all three mantra goals. The other four columns show mixtures of gains and losses. For example, the first column, Time, reports that, to go faster, you have to reduce time. To get better or cheaper, you have to increase time.*

Mantra	Time	Effort	Reliability	Size	Productivity
Faster	↓	↑	↓	↓	↑
Better	↑	↑	↑	↑	↑
Cheaper	↑	↓	↓	↓	↑

There Are Certain Limits

It is a matter of common sense that a software organization cannot increase or decrease the core metrics without limits. Can we ascertain what those limits are?

The metric that above all others is subject to limits is development time. There is always pressure to get a system out faster. Yet if you try to develop a system in too little time, you will fail, sometimes at great cost. It seems reasonable to suppose that there is some *minimum development time*. You can't complete a system in less than this time, as we discuss further in Chapter 5. The length of this minimum time varies with the size of the system, the area of application, the skill of the developers, and the development environment provided by management. So, is there a way to find out for a particular proposal what this time is?

Yes, and it involves keeping the core metrics on each project. This historic data enables you to find out what your minimum development time is on a system for which you have at least a rough size estimate. This minimum time is good to know. If you get pushed into a schedule at less than the minimum development time, you are automatically set up for at least a schedule failure, very likely a product of less reliability than a reasonable schedule would have produced, and possibly an outright project failure.

Regrettably, if you choose to operate your project at the minimum development time (assuming you have the data to make this choice), you are also locking yourself into two negatives. One is that the *effort* needed will be at a maximum. Consequently, the cost will also be at a maximum. The second negative is that *reliability* is proportional to development time, so it too will be at a minimum.

More happily, there is a favorable trade-off between development time and effort. If you can extend the development time beyond the minimum time, you can greatly reduce the effort. Similarly, reliability improves. The amount of this reduction in effort or improvement in reliability is based on the knowledge provided by the basic metrics.

At the other end of the development time scale, there is no fixed *maximum development time*. Of course, organizations seldom worry about setting that end. Still, beyond about 130 percent of the minimum development time, the trade-off between time and effort lessens sharply, as we illustrate in more detail in Chapter 11. There is little economic point to extending development time beyond 130 percent of the minimum development time. A reasonable schedule lies in the middle of this range, longer than the minimum development time, but short of the maximum development time.

Thus, in software development "small is beautiful," meaning fewer developers over a longer time allowance resulting in a more reliable product. Data on 491 projects from the QSM database confirms this belief, as we report in Chapter 11. Briefly, dividing the projects into two categories, small and large, revealed that the small teams took much less effort at each system size than the large teams.

At this early point in the book, we can only state conclusions like these without providing the supporting details. In Part II, though, we establish more fully the five core metrics and the relationships between them. Then, in Part III, we begin to make use of these relationships in planning projects. By Chapter 11, for instance, we will have the background that will enable us to pursue the "power of the trade-off" and the "small is beautiful" themes in depth.

Part II
The Metrics Needed for Effective Control

In this Part, we climb down from the high level of what stakeholders want to the concrete level of the five core metrics that support the intelligence that satisfies these needs:

1. schedule time
2. effort (person-months)
3. functionality (amount of work, often expressed in size)
4. defect rate
5. process productivity

Our first goal is to define each of these five metrics, enabling us to deal with them mathematically. Our second goal is to find the formula that correctly represents the relationship between these core metrics. Once we do that, we can work out the planning problems that software development presents to management:

- Planning: Given size and process productivity, we can estimate project time and effort from the relationship between functionality (size) and process productivity.
- Project control: Given the planning projection of time and effort, management can compare actuals achieved

against what was projected—and can act to harness an out-of-control project.

- Defect tracking: Given a projection of the defect rate, derived from the other core metrics, management can track defects found against those expected.
- Process improvement: Given the process productivity value on a series of completed projects, management can see whether its efforts to increase capability are bearing fruit.

Chapter 5
The Measurement View

I encountered the anti-manager guy in the lounge of the conference hotel, where he was sitting alone at a cocktail table, sprawled out on an overstuffed couch, quietly downing a nightcap. Recognizing him from my seminar audience, I sat down across from him.

"What did you think of my measurement presentation today?" I inquired.

"You missed the point at every step," he replied, putting down his drink.

I was sort of surprised, but he had been sitting in the back of the room. Perhaps he had not heard me clearly. Then I thought a few drinks might have loosened his tongue.

"How so?" I prodded.

"One of the first things you brought up was that tired old saw, KISS. You said it means: 'Keep It Stupefyingly Simple,' or something like that," he replied.

"You're close, but no cigar. It means: 'Keep It Simple, Stupid.' That old psychological rule 'seven, plus or minus two' applies to software projects, as it does to everything else."

"My hoary old rule is: If something can be measured, it ought to be measured," he proclaimed, waving his hand toward his drink on the low table before us. "KISS ought to mean: Keep It Stupendously Strenuous."

He stumbled a bit over all the s sounds and picked up his drink, fortifying himself for his next sally.

"If management has, say, forty-three measures to track, that will keep them busy," he amplified. "They won't bother us so much."

"It would not work out that way," I tried to explain. "Management wouldn't use forty-three metrics. The time and effort spent on collecting them would just go to waste."

"There you go. You said, 'Use metrics.' That's a no-no."

This fellow had me baffled, but I made another try. "People use metrics all the time, to estimate a project's schedule, effort, and cost, then to track actuals against the plan, even to gauge the progress of process-improvement efforts . . ."

"Yeah, some kind of starry-eyed romantics," he interrupted. "When unsentimental managers have a lot of numbers, they can pick out the ones that make them look good. You know the old acronym, CYA. On a screwed-up project, you need a lot of measures to get a few good ones that you can wave in front of the customer."

I realized that his view had been warped by dismal experience on some improperly measured projects. There wasn't much use trying to talk about the merits of effective measurement with him, I thought, but I decided to take one more stab at it.

"The purpose of measurement is to uncover reality," I said. "And you uncover reality in order to do something real about it."

At that, I noticed that his eyes were closed and his head was resting against the back of the couch. He was gently sleeping. Well, it had been a long day. I went up to my room. Tomorrow would be another session.

—L.H.P.

There is a fundamental disconnect in going from the hot human brain to the cold intelligence—if we may call it that—of the digital computer.

That profound difference is part of what makes it difficult for hot humans to program cold computers.

The Profound Difference

The brain contains about a hundred billion neurons. Each neuron makes thousands of connections to other neurons. These connections convey spikes of varying intensity and frequency. The computer, by contrast, contains merely millions of transistors, and these connect in just two states: off and on. So, the difference in complexity between the brain and a computer is somewhere in the range of 10^{15} (brain) to 10^8 (machine).

That difference—seven orders of magnitude—is really *profound*. It happens to be the difference between the mass of the moon (7.36 x 10^{22} kilograms) and the mass of the sun (1.99 x 10^{30} kilograms). The moon is a cold, lifeless satellite that gives out only a faint reflection of the sun's light. The sun, in contrast, is a huge, white-hot star that illuminates and heats up a large volume of space.

Only a precise stream of rather simple instructions can drive a digital computer at the machine level. At this level, there are only a few hundred instructions.

In contrast, the human mind takes in information in words, images, and other forms through many sensory channels. Natural languages contain hundreds of thousands of words, and the possible combinations are essentially infinite. Image combinations add to the mix. Then, within the human being, there are these things called "emotions." These emotions stir up the incoming infinity into an even higher level of infinity! On top of all this, there is not just one human being, there are millions of them. When we stir information into large numbers of people, we seem to get even more unpredictable results.

At any rate, when we mix rapidly advancing technology with people, we can't be sure how they will react. For example, the glow given off by the Internet boom charged up the neurons in the 10^{15} brain-things. Some of this highly charged emotion tried to juice up the 10^8 transistor-things. The brain-things wanted their Internet sites up and running right away, but the transistor-things work only on precisely formulated instructions and produce only corresponding outputs. Emotion doesn't play a role at the 10^8 level. Software has to operate at this level. Software development has to function in this unemotional world.

However, we must admit that those 10^{15} brain-things do play a role in software development. They do try to deliver software in too little time. There is an interface here between the hot, emotional 10^{15} domain and the cold, "just the facts" 10^8 arena in which software drives computers.

One Fact Is Minimum Development Time

In the software trenches, for example, the *minimum development time* is a fact of life. No matter how many stakeholders dance around the creative fire, each project has a development time that can be no shorter than this minimum. That schedule is determined by the application size and type and the organization's existing level of productivity. Adding people to a project team can get you down to this minimum development time, but adding still more people does not get you finished in less than this time. No project among the more than 6,300 on which we have collected core measurements has ever been completed in less than this *minimum development time.*

Of course, thousands of clients, hard-pressed for time, have tried to do so. They have asked the software leaders, "Are you with us or against us?" Those leaders, lacking measurement data, have had little choice but to acquiesce to the client's schedule. Those with data can at least point out the realities of software development. Nevertheless, those forced to accept the client's schedule fail to overcome that powerful constraint: the minimum development time.

Now, it is one thing to say there is a minimum development time. It is another thing to find out what that time is for organizations of different capabilities, working on projects of different sizes, striving to attain different levels of quality and reliability. That sounds like a job for Measurement Man! We return to this issue in Chapter 11.

In this chapter, we take a closer look at the five core metrics.

The Core Measurements Underlie "Getting Work Done"

Work is what we do under economic pressure, in contrast to play, which is what we do on weekends. That economic pressure is quantitative—we work for a profit or to operate within a budget, in the case of government organizations. One of the many responsibilities of management is to translate that economic pressure into day-to-day implementation.

Making that translation is very difficult, perhaps impossible, for activities that by tradition are called "artistic." Early in the software age, when programs amounted to a few score lines of code and programmers dressed like artists, it was easy to regard software development as an art form. As such, it was hardly amenable to the measurements through which managers manage.

Later in the software age—when programs became huge, project teams numbered in the scores, bids and budgets appeared, and clients pined for delivery dates—managers began to try to manage.

To begin to see how software development might respond to that pressure, we start with a nucleus of ideas that have been applied time and again to different kinds of work:

- Sort out the key *concepts* underlying the activity.
- Find *metrics* that quantify these concepts.
- *Measure* a number of samples of the activity.
- Find the *pattern* in these measurements.[1]

The Key Concepts

The idea that effective management rests upon an understanding of certain key concepts is not new. Peter F. Drucker listed measurement as one of the five basic elements in the work of the manager.[2] However, the usefulness of measurement has not yet been appreciated across the entire breadth of the software development field.

"Our foundations are badly off in this area [metrics and measurement], because we keep trying to apply variations of the metrics that worked well for manufacturing to the highly creative design problems of software," said one information systems engineer, contributing to a roundup discussion on influences in software engineering.[3]

That thought smacks of the belief that "highly creative design" is somehow artistic in nature, dependent on inspiration that comes when it will, not when a schedule calls for it. Sometimes that may be true. It may be very hard to schedule a highly creative activity. Sometimes, that activity may verge on research, an activity that, by definition, is not subject to a strict schedule. In such a case, we should treat the activity as research and not attempt to hold it to a firm schedule and a fixed-price bid.

In other cases, where we have some experience with the work to be accomplished, we should be able to plan it. In addition to laying out the work plan, the act of planning embraces the schedule, effort (or cost), and quality of the finished product. The issue at hand is how to

---

[1]Lawrence H. Putnam and Ware Myers, *Industrial Strength Software: Effective Management Using Measurement* (Los Alamitos, Calif.: IEEE Computer Society, 1997), p. 5.
[2]Peter F. Drucker, *Managing in a Time of Great Change* (New York: Dutton/Penguin Group, 1995), p. 400.
[3]Steve McConnell, "The Best Influences on Software Engineering," *IEEE Software* (Jan.-Feb. 2000), p. 16.

create the plan. The answer starts with finding the key concepts that underlie the accomplishment of any kind of *work*. Remember, work is not play. It takes place under economic pressure. Pressure means that we have to accomplish some task in a relatively short time frame, using a limited outlay of effort. At the same time, we are supposed to reach an intended level of quality.

Well, it turns out that in trying to explain what we are talking about, we have just named three of the five key concepts, already introduced in Part I:

1. schedule time
2. effort (cost)
3. quality of the product

The first two concepts cover the technical definition of *work:* manpower over time. At the time we are planning a software project, however, we don't yet know what the schedule and effort will be. We do have some idea of the product, and that idea gives us some glimmer of the *amount of work* developing the product will require. That is the fourth key concept:

4. amount of work represented by the product

In all kinds of work, workers work at some level of productivity. At one extreme, a handful of workers in a highly automated factory turn out large quantities of sophisticated products. They are highly productive. At the other extreme, in a developing nation, a worker labors all day to produce a driblet. He or she is not very productive. Similarly, in software development, some organizations are believed to be more productive than others.

The currently common expression of this difference is expressed in the five capability maturity levels of the Software Engineering Institute of Carnegie Mellon University. At any rate, productivity is the fifth key concept:

5. process productivity

Because this concept applies to a project or the process a project is employing, and not to individuals, we label it *process* productivity.

Now, if these are, indeed, the five concepts that are key to explaining any kind of work relationship in a market-system economy, there must be a relationship between them. There is and we discuss it in Chapter 7.

Expressing the Key Concepts in Metrics

At this point, the next step is to describe the five metric concepts and to find metric units in which to express them.

Time

Time or schedule is typically measured in calendar months. Sometimes, short projects are metered in weeks. In the old days, projects sometimes ran to many years, and the time scale was given in calendar years. Recently, developers have tended to hold projects to shorter schedules, seldom more than two years to the first release. Enhancements are added in subsequent releases, which in turn are held to relatively short schedules.

There may still be problems picking the precise dates on which a schedule begins and terminates. We deal further with those problems in Part III, where we tie metrics to process.

Effort

Effort is measured in person-months or person-hours. The concept is straightforward, but implementing it presents some problems. We are basically interested in getting a count of the person-hours devoted to the project. Time spent on vacation, sick leave, medical and dental appointments, motor vehicle license renewals, training not related to the project, and so on, should be excluded. This excluded time may be paid time. It may even be charged to the contract, but if counted as part of *effort,* it will muddy up the data.

The other big problem in measuring effort is uncompensated overtime. Organizations may keep no formal record of these hours. Yet, for various management purposes, they are hours of effort spent on the project. On the one hand, projects should count them for that purpose. On the other hand, where we hear of 84-hour weeks, even 100-hour weeks, managers should evaluate those extreme hours of effort with caution. Often they include naps at the desk, pizza parties, half-hour jogging expeditions to clear the fog out of the brain, and even activities better suited to a men's magazine than to this rather austere book.

One infrequent but illegal practice is to charge time spent on existing projects to a newly arrived contract that has plenty of hours available. That really screws up the metric data!

Getting an accurate count of effort is straightforward in concept, but it takes some management attention in practice.

Quality

There is no questioning the fact that the ultimate product of software development has to work, in the sense of being able to function. That seems to be the minimal definition of quality. There is, however, considerable uncertainty about what "work" in this sense means in practice. As a practical matter, all software products larger than a few dozen lines of code are delivered with some remaining defects. In fact, the number of defects remaining at delivery is a common metric. These defects are gradually corrected, as users run across them. In the case of large programs, however, it is unlikely that every last defect is ever removed. Nevertheless, despite the remaining defects, programs do accomplish useful work.

Quality has many other aspects and many of them are measurable. For example, the features and performance specified in the requirements are two such aspects. Measuring requirements churn is one indication of the adequacy of the initial requirements. Developers can plan quality criteria, such as features and performance, to be achieved in each process iteration.[4] They can verify the presence of these features and performance as soon as the development process reaches that iteration.

Development risks, such as the failure to reflect all of the key requirements in the architecture or high-level design, can result in software that does not satisfy the customer's needs. Effective management of this and other risks in early phases results in products with the quality that clients need. See also Chapter 9.

These and other quality metrics have important roles in the development process. However, we are looking for a quality metric that we can project in terms of the other four core metrics. That metric is the *defect rate.* It is the most important single measure of whether a software product works. It is the concept we develop further in Chapter 8.

Amount of Work

We have already defined *work* (in one of its meanings) as the product of manpower over time. Expressed in measurement units, work is person-months.

---

[4]The word *iterate* has a dictionary meaning of doing something over again. It has been used in software development to refer to repeating some of the steps within a phase. The originators of the Unified Process selected iteration as the name of a stage within a phase. In this usage, it is a set of activities, meeting at its conclusion prescribed criteria and resulting in a release, usually within the project, but sometimes to customers. See also Chapter 19.

What we need at this early point is some stand-in for *work,* from which we can figure out effort and time. We might express this stand-in as the *functionality* of the product. From some measure of functionality, we could infer time and effort. By coincidence, one of the stand-ins for this functionality was named "function points." The functions—inputs, outputs, master files, inquiries, and interfaces—are assigned points. From a count of these points, one can estimate the time and effort needed to produce work.

The most common stand-in for functionality, however, is the estimated *size* of the eventual software product. Size is usually expressed in source lines of code, largely because that was the measurement that many software organizations had years ago. In addition to source lines of code and function points, other measures, such as the number of requirements "shall" statements and the number of use cases, are also utilized. There is much more to sizing and we take it up again in Chapter 6.

Estimating the *amount of work* has to be preceded by an initial series of steps, discussed further in Part III:

- delimiting the scope of the project
- establishing an initial set of requirements
- designing a tentative architecture
- evaluating the most serious of the pending risks

Process Productivity

Workers accomplish work at some level of productivity. If we are to reduce software development to a measured activity, we need a metric for productivity. Moreover, if we are to rely on this metric, it must be reasonably accurate. The two approaches customarily employed, conventional productivity and judgmental productivity, fall short of the required accuracy.

The conventional measure of productivity is source lines of code per person-month (SLOC/PM), calculated from the software organization's records of past projects. Unfortunately, it suffers from gross inaccuracy, as Figure 5-1 illustrates. This figure plots conventional productivity against project size, employing a logarithmic scale on both axes. Even on this log-log presentation, the data points, each representing a project, are widely scattered. On a *linear* diagram, that is, one with a numerical scale of regular numbers, the dots would appear to be even more widely separated.

At any one size, this figure shows that conventional productivity differs by two orders of magnitude, that is, by a factor of 100. With successive projects of different sizes, the variation in conventional productivity is even greater.

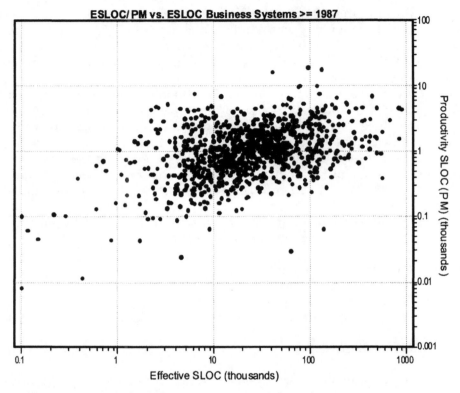

| Figure 5-1: | *Conventional productivity (recorded in effective SLOC per person-month—abbreviated as ESLOC/PM) is a poor gauge of productivity because its value varies widely at any size an estimator is considering—and even more widely from one size to another.* |

Function points measure the functionality of a software product on a different basis than source lines of code does. We can express another version of conventional productivity as function points (FP) per person-month (PM), as shown in Figure 5-2. The dispersion of points is essentially the same as that in the previous figure. It is evident that using function points to measure conventional productivity does not provide an accurate indication of productivity.

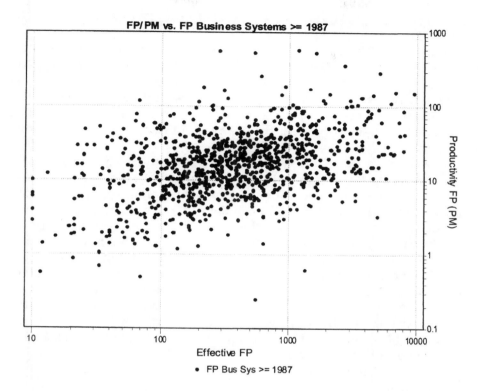

Figure 5-2:   *Expressing conventional productivity in function points per person-month results in the same wide dispersion of productivity values that we saw in Figure 5-1. The use of function points to express conventional productivity is no improvement over the more common SLOC.*

We can only conclude that conventional productivity, however expressed, is not a very precise measure. At any given size, your estimate may be off by a factor of 100 or more. At a different size, your estimate may be wrong by an even larger factor.

Even less accurate is an estimate based on *judgmental productivity,* which refers to a value obtained by some mental gymnastics ultimately founded on judgment. The overaggressive manager who jumps to his feet in the bid/no-bid meeting and harks back to his youth is exercising poor judgment.

"When I first came to this company," he tells all within earshot, "I did a job like this one with four programmers; only one of them had experience on this kind of work. It ended up at 75,000 SLOC, and this one will, too."

That 75,000 SLOC sounds suspiciously like a round number. (Note to managers: Beware of round numbers. There is very little chance that this round number is exactly correct.) The jumping jack manager remembers the four programmers, but he doesn't recollect how many person-months they put in. Let's put him back in his box. We're not going to excavate a reliable productivity value from his fading memory.

Possibly we exaggerate—a bit. Software thinkers long ago tried to pin down judgment by exhaustively defining fifteen or twenty productivity adjustment factors. Then they asked managers, senior designers, and other knowledgeable bystanders to rate each one on a numerical scale. They combined the fifteen or twenty factor ratings into one number and used it as the productivity value. This approach is a great improvement over the jumping jack approach, but it has drawbacks.

The factors are defined in words, and raters often understand something different from what the system devisers intended. The ratings, when reached, have to be reduced to numbers, and the raters may be a few numbers off what would, theoretically, be the correct number. Most importantly, however, there are seldom enough knowledgeable people around to serve as raters. Adding up these difficulties, the net result is that judgment-based evaluations of productivity are off the mark.

We conclude that the software industry needs a more precise approach to productivity and we develop that approach, process productivity, in Chapter 7. But first, in the next chapter, we consider the other core metric—the size of the product-to-be—needed to estimate a project's effort and time.

Chapter 6
Estimating Size as a Measure of Functionality

"He's still scratching his head," said John, looking through the one-way mirror between the observation room and a programmer at work in front of a computer.

"Ho hum," Phil exhaled noisily, "he must have lice up there."

"No, he's thinking. I'm sure of it," John said. "His forehead is all wrinkled up."

"Great, let me know when he pulls his ear."

"He just touched his up-arrow key. That shows some result of his thinking."

"Not really," Phil retorted. "He just killed the screen saver."

We could count the number of times a developer scratches his head or pulls his ear lobe, but such counts would be silly. They would not be a good metric of what his brain is putting out. In contrast, at the output end of the software development process, there is a product that is objectively measurable. It is the bit-stream that feeds the digital machines, as shown in Figure 6-1.

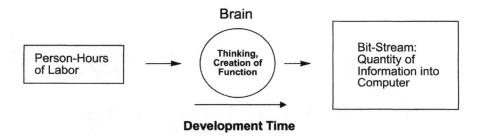

Figure 6-1:   *Person-hours expended over development time in a software development process—a creative activity conducted in the brain—results in functions expressed in source code that transforms into machine instructions, then into a bitstream that drives digital hardware.*

We need a way to measure intellectual work because there is a vast amount of it, and that amount is increasing rapidly. The number of people making a living out of software is variously estimated at between two and three million in the United States and double that worldwide.

The bit-stream at the conclusion of Figure 6-1 is eminently measurable. Unfortunately, at the time we are trying to estimate a software project, the bit-stream is not yet available. It appears at the end of the project. Our challenge is to find a metric that quantifies what is going on in the circle of this diagram, the creation of function by means of thinking. As a start toward solving this challenge, let's think of that circle as standing for a process, such as those introduced in Chapter 3. Then let us think of that process as taking place through a channel. The thinkers do one thing after another in this channel. That brings us close in concept to what Claude Shannon accomplished in the mid-twentieth century at Bell Laboratories. He conceived of communication as taking place through a channel.[1]

Shannon's Path

Shannon's way of thinking can give us some insight into the challenge of measuring the intellectual work of software development. Here is the essence of his mathematical analysis of the communication channel:

---

[1]Claude E. Shannon, "The Mathematical Theory of Communication," *Bell System Technical Journal*, Vol. 27 (1948), pp. 279–423, 623–56. Also, University of Illinois Press, 1949.

1. The channel has a certain capacity, or bandwidth—a transfer rate in bits per second.
2. It has a certain amount of "noise," random electrical signals arising out of the environment that interfere with the transmission of the bits carrying the information.
3. As a result of capacity limitations and noise, some of the bits carrying information are distorted in transmission. The frequency of these distortions, or errors, is known as the "error rate."
4. This error rate may be reduced by improving the channel or by adding error-correction algorithms.

Similarly, we may conceive of software development as taking place through a channel called a process, extending from systems definition and requirements capture to delivery:

1. This process has a certain capacity—mechanically measurable as the number of bits at the input to the digital device that uses the software.
2. It generates a certain amount of "noise," or defects, resulting from deficiencies in the process or errors by the people engaged in the process.
3. As a result of these deficiencies and errors, some of the output bit-stream is incorrect.
4. This defect rate may be reduced by improving the process (for example, instituting reviews) or correcting the product (for example, testing).

Preceding the Shannon-type bit-stream in the software development process are machine instructions. These instructions are transformed into the bit-stream by a mechanistic process. So, its count would be proportionate to that of the bit-stream. Preceding the machine instructions is source code. The mechanistic conversion here is done by a compiler. So, a count of source code is proportional to machine instructions and, hence, to the bit-stream.

At this point, many software people believe that we may take lines of source code as a fairly representative measurement of the work involved in the implementation workflow, or coding, stage. However, they find source code difficult to accept as a measure of their upstream thought process. In their view, coding is only the final manifestation of that thought process, and its output, source code, is not a fair measure of all the upstream work. It is that brain activity—that design creativity, that perseverance, that complex interfacing to other stake-holders—that they would like to characterize in some measurable way.

Actually, there are countable chunks of product functionality prior to source code. For example, requirements "shall" statements and use cases begin to appear as early as the requirements-capture stage. Subsystems, packages, and components show up as architects plan the architecture. Elements such as GUIs, modules, classes, objects, and routines appear during analysis and design. These chunks are especially helpful for metric purposes in that they are available earlier in the development process than actual source code.

For instance, as early as the architectural or high-level design stage, analysts can identify five functions: inputs, outputs, inquiries, logical internal files, and external interface files. From these counts, by a process of weighting for complexity, they obtain a function-point estimate of a program's functionality. All of these counts boil down to indicators of a quantity of functionality. Estimates of functionality such as these are the first step in project planning and estimation.

Critics complain that these counts fail to represent the number of creative thought elements. If the major product of the early phases of software development is little nuggets of "thought stuff," it is true that we don't know how to put a high-technology contraption on the skull and measure thought stuff. We acknowledge the difficulty of looking inside the brain. We merely observe that the entire software develop-ment process is an economic activity, and in a competitive economy, it's a good idea to plan and budget economic activities, if you want to stay in business.

This planning has to begin long before the bit-stream, machine instructions, or source code are available to measure. Therefore, plan-ning has to be based on early surrogates for these late-arriving met-rics. These early surrogates are derived from the chunkings we have been talking about. They are all that is available early in the software development process. Often, it is convenient to express the size of the chunking we are using in source lines of code. That does not mean that, early in the project, we know what the eventual count of source lines of code is actually going to be. It merely means that we estimate, on the basis of some examination of the chunkings, that they will eventually amount to some approximate number of source lines of code.

In this sense, then, early estimates of source lines of code are a metric from which we can derive the amount of work involved in going through all the phases of the development process. For a project of more than toy size, we have to go through all these phases to be assured of getting to the bit-stream. Chances are, if we don't do those phases right, we won't get to the bit-stream. We will end up with a failed project; there will be nothing to count at the point at which we should have source code. In other words, source code used in this way is a metric representing the amount of function we are to develop during the entire software process. That amount of functionality, in turn, is proportional to the work expended during the project.

Representing the Amount of Functionality

Thus, what we are really searching for is not source lines of code as such. It is some way of measuring the amount of functionality a project represents, before we embark upon it. From this measure of functionality, we propose to estimate the amount of work. If we know how much work a project involves, we can plan it—estimate the staff and schedule required.

In addition, there are two further aspects of *work:* It has to be accomplished at some level of quality or reliability to satisfy market requirements, and it has to be performed at a level of productivity that accommodates price constraints. We take up those aspects in later chapters.

We approach the current problem—how to measure the amount of work—from the vantage point of the *functionality* of the product. What is it to do? What are the features it is to contain? All together, the features add up, at least roughly, to its size. If we add a feature, we increase the size. If we delete a feature, we decrease the size. Size appears to be a pretty good stand-in for functionality—just pretty good, not without some deficiencies. For instance, if we figure out some way of rewarding developers for size, they will return the favor by figuring out some way of giving us more size. Of course, more size, as such, is not what we want. We want the functionality that we need, and it may be possible to supply it at a lesser size.

The common way to express size is source lines of code. In Larry Putnam's initial estimating studies, he tried to use the number of files, reports, and screens as the metrics of functionality. These numbers would be good for estimating purposes because they are available early in development. However, he found there was little historical data available in these metrics. The historical data that had been kept was source lines of code. Therefore, he had to analyze past projects in source lines of code.

Later, others extended the count of files, reports, and screens into the function-point methodology for estimating software size. However, it turned out that counts in function points are proportional to counts in source code. For instance, one function point is implemented by about a hundred lines of source code in several of the common programming languages—Basic, COBOL, FORTRAN, C.

Sizing Functionality by Calibration

What is important now in expressing functionality is the availability of a metric recorded on past projects. Past projects supply data in whatever metrics were kept. These size metrics may then be used to estimate the next project. That is what we mean by "sizing functionality by calibration."

That is the approach we used on three large Department of Defense projects involving hundreds of people, multiple years of schedule, a series of releases, and large amounts of commercial off-the-shelf products. In these projects, the primary effort was the integration of existing products at the code level, not the development of new code. Since there was little new code involved, sizing the functionality to be achieved, or the work to be accomplished, in source lines of code or function points would have been rather meaningless.

The question arose: To what is the work to be accomplished on such projects proportional? The general answer is that the amount of work is proportional to something in your own past project experience. In these projects, we used other measures of functionality, such as system development folders, interface definitions, number of development tasks, number of requirements, or number of integration work packages.

An audit-forecast project we performed for a client responsible for system integration provides an example. In an audit forecast, the project is already at least one quarter of the way to completion. To make this forecast, we need an estimate of the remaining work. Ordinarily, we would use an estimate of its size, usually in source lines of code. In this case, however, there could be no estimate of the remaining work in source lines of code because the client was the system integrator, writing little or no application code. The client was hooking together Lotus Notes, a customized version of Microsoft Outlook, and some other commercial systems to make a messaging system. Our assignment was to determine when the current release and the next two releases would be ready to field. That projection, of course, rested in part on the amount of work to be done.

What our client did have was the number of requirements that had been levied for each past release and the number that had been specified for each of the three forthcoming releases. We found that the number of requirements on the past releases correlated well with schedule, defects, test cases, and a crude measure of effort on those releases. So, we used number of requirements as the stand-in for the size metric, that is, as the metric to represent the amount of functionality remaining to be accomplished.

We learned two lessons from this experience:

- As new development practices come into use, new measures of functionality may be needed. One such measure is the number of requirements, as our experience demonstrated. In processes employing use cases to represent the functional requirements, the metric may be the number of use cases.
- Whatever metric we choose to express functionality, that metric must also be available in an adequate selection of past projects. The metrics attached to past projects provide the basis for calibration—and calibration is vital.

Sizing Implications of Reuse

Until recently, projects developed essentially all-new code. Now reuse is growing. Vendor-supplied components are coming on the market. Large companies are establishing reuse organizations to supply their projects with business-specific reusable components. We have to take this development into consideration in sizing functionality.

Sizing the reusable components is not the problem. That would be easy. They exist; their lines of code could be counted. Rather, our task is to estimate the size equivalent of the amount of work that will be devoted to attaching these reusable components to the newly developed software.

We might well expect that reusing components would require less work than building them from scratch. How much less is still open to question. At one extreme, for instance, where interfaces between components have been firmly established and the components themselves are known to be suitable, reliable, and not likely to change, their employment should take little work. Planners could allot just a small portion of the component's actual size to cover the acquisition and integration of the component.

At the other extreme, we face certain drawbacks:

- small components that take work to find and fit together

- interfaces between components that are still loose and require work to match
- component suitability that remains to be established
- reliability that is suspect
- vendors with a history of releasing upgrades every year or so, each requiring more fiddling around

Under such uncertain circumstances, the amount of work required to reuse a component may be as great as that required to build and maintain a new component. It may be even greater. In this situation, software people often choose to develop their own code.

Between the extremes, however, lies a great unknown area. Just where in this continuum is a project manager to place the size equivalent of a particular component? As Oliver Hardy says to Stan Laurel in the old movies, "That's another fine mess you've gotten us into!"

At this writing, one point is clear: Reuse is not entirely free—yet! We hope that components will become larger and easier to find; that they will adapt to the outcome of the analysis of business process more smoothly; that their interfaces will be standard, enabling them to fit together without the "fitting and filing" that machine parts used to undergo in the age before tight tolerances. We devote the entire Chapter 20 to reuse.

Estimate Size

"The future is unknowable," an occasional seer has proclaimed, but most of us keep right on betting on horses, lottery tickets, or stocks, as our fancy dictates. So it is no surprise to find that software development pushes relentlessly into this unknown. However, the future isn't completely "unknown." We know our businesses will need additional software. We know it will be of some size. We know we can get closer to estimating what that size will be if first we can get some idea of what the software is to do. Still, as we enter this jungle, we will not find a size estimate growing like a flower on the nearest bush. We must clear a spot, till the soil, plant a seed, water it daily, fight the weeds, and wait for it to grow. We can reach a size estimate through a series of steps:

- Get the facts.
- Assign knowledgeable people.
- Compare to past metrics.
- Allow time.
- Use a good estimating method.

Get the Facts

First we need the facts about the proposed software product. What is it going to do? In the vision stage, we might hazard a guess that it will be about as big as "Payroll Float," a project we worked on in our youth. Unfortunately, "remembrance of things past" is a weak reed on which to hang an estimate. As we gather requirements, write specifications, and lay out the overall architecture, we accumulate the facts that make a more accurate estimate possible.

Figure 6-2 diagrams the improvement in software size estimation during the development phases. Early in the Feasibility Phase, the spread in the estimate may be as great as several hundred percent of the final size. That spread narrows as the phases proceed and all concerned learn more. It is not until the system is ultimately released, however, that the software organization can pinpoint the exact size. It looks as if we could get a better size estimate if we held off until we had an adequate amount of information about the project. But that is easier said than done, as we explore further in Part III.

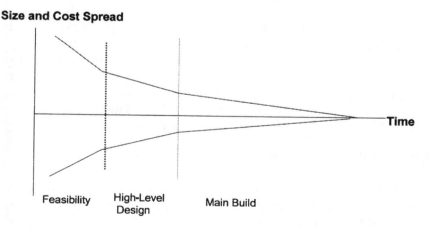

Size and Cost Uncertainty Depending On
Where You Are in the Project

Figure 6-2:   *In the Feasibility Phase, when little is known about the system to be built, estimates of its size necessarily have a wide range. As work proceeds, the ability to estimate size improves.*

Get the People

The second need is for people who are qualified to make a good size estimate. These people need to be familiar with the business or the technical domain, and with the likely architecture of the system. People from the top rungs of the brass ladder have status, but not necessarily this kind of knowledge. It is nice if you have two or three of these talented people. Some will be optimistic and predict a small size; some will be pessimistic and predict a large size. After several days of discussion, their compromise may be about right.

Get the Data

The third need is for metric information. Even gifted people's judgment doesn't spring fully formed from their cultured brows. It rests in part upon knowledge from data recorded on past projects. Your forward-looking estimates are more valid to the extent that you have backward-looking data. Don't bury this data in masses of musty project records. Put it in a computer database that your able estimators can access.

Allow Time

Give these good people time to make a good estimate. Getting acquainted with the proposed project and accessing the historical project data take time. At a minimum, the mechanics of making an estimate from the knowledge at hand may take a few days. At a maximum, gathering the key requirements, considering feasibility, outlining a core architecture, hunting for critical risks, and other such tasks can take as long as you can get from the powers-that-be.

Employ an Estimating Method

The estimating team does more than sit in a room for a few days. It should follow an agreed-upon method. The team can then devote itself to the facts in the case, not to debating how to go about making an estimate. Also, the levels of management above the team can focus on the merits of the particular estimate rather than quarrel with how the team went about its work.

The key feature of a size-estimating method is that it provides a range of sizes, not a single point. "The future is unknowable," and one aspect of it that is especially unknowable is the exact size of the product your project is going to produce 12 or 24 months from now.

- You don't know exactly how you are going to solve all the problems lying ahead of you. You may not even have identified all the serious risks that may materialize.
- You can be sure the requirements are going to grow. They reflect the part of the world the system will deal with, and the world is always changing. Moreover, as the project proceeds, the users and developers learn what the real needs are, forcing requirements growth.

Moral: Don't expect your estimating team to specify 67,167 source lines of code. Ask it instead to indicate a range:

- low
- most likely
- high

Ask the team to set low and high so that the chance of the eventual size lying within that range is 99 percent. (That happens to be the +/- 3 standard-deviation range, handy knowledge to use a little later, in estimating statistical risk.) The most likely size is not necessarily in the exact middle of the low-high range.

The expected value of the size estimate, then, is the low plus the high plus four times the most likely value—all divided by six. This procedure weights the most likely judgment heavily. "Expected" value is what you expect, statistically, the ultimate size to be. The word "expected" carries with it a big implication. It means there is a 50-percent probability that the actual size will be greater than this "expected" value. Or a 50-percent chance that it will be less.

Most things in life follow the *normal* statistical distribution. Software size estimating pretty much does, too. So, we don't wind up with an exact estimate, but we do have some statistical concepts to work with. For example, we can expect that about two thirds of the actual sizes of a series of projects will fall near the center of this statistical distribution. This method does not give us an estimate, precise down to the nearest line of code, but it does reduce the size of the ballpark quite a bit.

Later, for bidding or budgeting purposes, you may have to submit an exact price, but at least you and your immediate superiors know that the size figure (on which you based the bid) is really a range.

It's no secret that risk is an ever-present reality in software development. Getting statistics into the estimating method gives you a means for accommodating the degree of risk. For example, bidding at the expected or 50-percent level, you might win or lose on any one project. Over a series of projects, though, you could expect to break even.

However, you are not limited to bidding at the 50-percent level. There are statistical methods for bidding at any level you choose. If you consistently bid at the 70-percent level, you would expect to make a profit over a series of projects. If you consistently "buy in" at the 30-percent level, you can expect to lose over a series of projects. We are going to take up the problems of software bidding in Part III.

First, though, we must venture into the software productivity jungle for a deeper understanding of what we can promise in our estimates.

Chapter 7
Penetrating the Software Productivity Jungle

It is common knowledge that some software development organizations are more effective than others. They may have attained a higher level on the Capability Maturity Model. They may have a more effective process than other organizations. They may be employing better tools. Their management may be more insightful.

It is also common knowledge that about half of the organizations evaluated rest somewhere in CMM Level One. Study after study has found that many organizations do not even complete some of their projects. Others fail to complete within the planned schedules and budgets. In other words, they are not very effective.

Donald J. Reifer, a veteran consultant since the 1970's, found these negative reports hard to believe. "Most of my consulting clients have had their acts together when it came to software management," he recounted.

Then, members of an on-line discussion group he was participating in contended that he hadn't been living in the "real world." He decided to poll his industry friends to see "where he was living." He got answers from senior managers in twenty software organizations. By an average margin of 73 percent, they agreed with the real-world partisans in answering no to these questions:

- Are your software organizations perceived as well managed? *No!*

- Do they deliver what they promise when they promise it? *No!*
- Do customers and users view your products as high quality? *No!*
- Does your senior management view software organizations as contributing to the bottom line? *No!*[1]

No doubt there are many reasons for this unfortunate state of affairs. Pinning down a correct value for the level of productivity that developers achieve is one of them. That, in turn, rests upon finding the correct representation of the relationship between the five core metrics.

Finding the Right Relationship

In Chapter 2 we noted, non-quantitatively, that the five core metrics were related:

> People, working at some level of *productivity*, produce a quantity of function or a *work product* at a level of *reliability* by the expenditure of *effort* over a *time*.

We restate this observation as an equation in words:

> *Work Product* (at a *Reliability* level) = *Effort* over a *Time* interval at a *Productivity* level

The next step is to restate it in terms that we can measure:

> Size (at Defect Rate) = Effort x Time x Process Productivity

The Relationship of Time to Size

We turn first to the effect of the schedule allowed, or *time*. As the size of a project increases, the schedule time increases, but not in direct proportion to the size increase. Time increases more slowly than size. In other words, the relationship between time and size, plotted on an x-y field, is not a straight line. It is a curved line, concave downward, as diagrammed in Figure 7-1.

---

[1]Donald J. Reifer, "Software Management's Seven Deadly Sins," *IEEE Software* (March-April 2001), pp. 12–15.

Schedule (time)

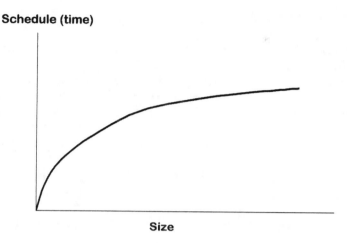

Size

Figure 7-1:　　*This curved line represents the relationship between time (schedule) and size. When such a relationship is represented in algebraic form as a power function, the size term carries an exponent of less than one.*

The Relationship of Effort to Size

We observe the contrary effect in the relation between effort and size. Effort increases slowly with size at small sizes, but more rapidly as the size grows, as diagrammed in Figure 7-2. This time the curve depicting the relationship is concave upward.

Effort

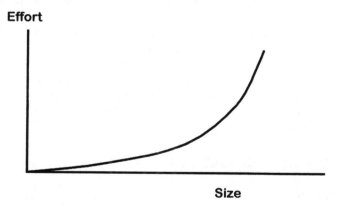

Size

Figure 7-2:　　*This curved line represents the relationship between effort and size. When such a relationship is represented in algebraic form as a power function, the size term carries an exponent greater than one.*

The Software Equation

There is a point to presenting Figures 7-1 and 7-2 and commenting on the algebraic representation of the time relationship to size and the effort relationship to size. The point is that the time and effort terms in the software equation must carry exponents. The relationship, therefore, is of the following form:

$$\text{Size (at Defect Rate)} = \text{Effort}^a \times \text{Time}^b \times \text{Process Productivity}$$

At the time we were formulating this relationship, we had data on several hundred projects. From this data we found these exponents to be

$$\text{Size (at Defect Rate)} = (\text{Effort}/\beta)^{(1/3)} \times \text{Time}^{(4/3)} \times \text{Process Productivity}$$

(Beta, β, is a size-dependent parameter that has the effect of giving greater weight to the effort factor in very small systems.)

That is the software equation. The exponent of the effort term is, indeed, less than one, as predicted by the known relationship between effort and size. The exponent of the time term is greater than one because of the relationship between time and size.

Since first formulating the software equation a quarter-century ago, we have demonstrated its validity in practice in hundreds of companies and thousands of estimates that we followed through to completed projects. Moreover, it has been validated by thousands of systems in the QSM database of completed projects. Many of these projects were done independently by organizations that were not aware that such a formulation even existed. Even so, the numbers they achieved followed this equation quite closely.

It is proper to note, however, that the software equation is not a law of nature, or physics, such as the acceleration due to gravity, 980 centimeters per second per second. Rather, it was derived from data compiled by humans from completed projects and, consequently, subject to some amount of error. In other words, the exponents, 1/3 and 4/3, are close approximations, not physics constants. Nevertheless, they work well in practice.

The Effect on Productivity

In the software world, productivity has conventionally been taken to be lines of source code per person-month. A rule of thumb often invoked is that programmers produce about 10 lines of source code per staff-day, or about 200 lines per person-month. However, programmers are not of equal capability. Their productivity varies by a factor of at least 10. That would mean it might be as low as 40 lines of source code per person-month or as high as 400 SLOC/PM. Thus, a development manager, seeking to estimate the next project, cannot limit his consideration to the single productivity figure, 10 SLOC/staff-day.

Conventional Productivity Varies Widely

When a cobbler, in ancient times, worked longer hours, he produced more shoes. His productivity, shoes per hour, remained the same, and more hours resulted in more shoes. However, when he hired an apprentice with the general intent of making more shoes, production did not double. Because the apprentice was less skilled, the average productivity of the two decreased. The hours added by the apprentice did increase the total output of shoes. Master cobblers concluded that shoes-per-man-hour was a good measure.

Quite naturally, this frame of mind carried over into software development. Software managers adopted source lines of code per person-month as their gauge of productivity. Unfortunately, this conventional measure has two serious deficiencies. It varies widely and it ignores the effect of *schedule time.*

We demonstrated the wide variability of conventional productivity in Figure 5-1. It shows real data from hundreds of completed projects. First, at any one system size an estimator was considering, he would have a wide choice of SLOC/PM values. Second, if a subsequent system were to be of a different size, the range of choice would become still wider. An estimator would have trouble picking a (conventional) productivity value appropriate to the next project from the hundreds of choices this figure provides. For instance, at sizes where there is an abundance of data points, the conventional productivity range extends over more than two decades. One can only conclude that conventional productivity is a very unreliable factor for computing good estimates. At any given size, your estimate might be off by a factor of 100. At a different size, it could be incorrect by an even larger factor.

In Figure 5-2, we plotted conventional productivity expressed in function points per person-month against size. The pattern is essentially the same as that of Figure 5-1—no surprise, since number of function points is proportional to size.

Schedule Is a Factor in Productivity

Is the cobbler's frame of mind the correct one for software development? No, it is not. Does conventional productivity work? No, it does not. To see why this is so, let us go back to the software equation and rearrange it (by algebraic methods):

$$\text{Process Productivity} = \text{Size (at Defect Rate)} / [(\text{Effort}/\beta)^{(1/3)} \times \text{Time}^{(4/3)}]$$

We see that process productivity, unlike conventional productivity, is a function of size, effort, and *time*. Unfortunately (for the sake of progress in software estimating), people have had some difficulty grasping the fact that the schedule planned at the beginning of a project does have an effect on the productivity that the software process can achieve. Let us call on Fred Brooks for assistance on this point. In his justly famed book *The Mythical Man-Month*, he declared, "The number of months of a project depends upon its sequential constraints," that is, one thing has to be done after another necessarily preceding thing.

From that it followed, "The maximum number of men depends upon the number of independent subtasks."

And finally, "From these two quantities one can derive schedules using fewer men and more months."[2]

We are going to pursue Brooks's final thought further in later chapters. For now, however, we turn to nailing down the process productivity relationship more precisely.

How Conventional Productivity Behaves

The software world has found by repeated experience that conventional productivity has not been a good guide to estimating time and effort on future projects. Let us see what the software equation tells us about productivity as conventionally expressed, that is, as size/effort, or SLOC/person-month. By expressing size/effort in terms of the software equation, we can see what really influences conventional productivity. We begin with the software equation expressed in terms of process productivity:

$$\text{Process Productivity} = \text{Size} / [(\text{Effort}/\beta)^{(1/3)} \times \text{Time}^{(4/3)}]$$

We avoid the fractional exponents by cubing both sides:

---

[2]Frederick P. Brooks, Jr., *The Mythical Man-Month: Essays on Software Engineering* (Reading, Mass.: Addison-Wesley, 1975), pp. 25–26.

$$(\text{Process Productivity})^3 = \text{Size}^3 / [(\text{Effort}/\beta) \times \text{Time}^4]$$

Buried in this equation are the terms representing conventional productivity: Size/Effort. Rearranging the equation to pull them out separately yields this:

$$[(\text{Process Productivity})^3 \ (\text{Time})^4 \ \beta] / \text{Size}^2 = \text{Size} / \text{Effort} =$$
$$\text{Conventional Productivity}$$

This relationship shows that conventional productivity varies

- with the third power of the process productivity, that is, the effectiveness of the project organization as a whole
- with the fourth power of the time schedule allotted
- inversely with the square of the size

The presence of power exponents attached to each of these three terms greatly magnifies their effect on conventional productivity:

- If a project enhances its process productivity by a little, the presence of the third power greatly increases the value of the conventional productivity that will be achieved. That would be good. However, the opposite effect, declining process productivity on the project, means that the conventional productivity value used in bidding it was excessive.
- Whatever schedule time management plans, the presence of the fourth power greatly increases time's effect on conventional productivity. If management plans a relatively long schedule or even a reasonable schedule, the fourth power of this large value of time leads to a large value of conventional productivity.
- Let us plow on, fearlessly. If management (or somebody) sets a very tight schedule, the fourth power of this shorter schedule (time) is very much less than the fourth power of the more reasonable schedule, reducing conventional productivity substantially. If the project had been estimated at the value of conventional productivity derived from jobs on more reasonable schedules, the project as estimated on this value of conventional productivity may very well lack the time and effort needed to complete it successfully.

- At the time of estimating, the estimated size of the proposed system may vary from the final size by 10 percent or more. Let us look at the effect of an overestimate and an underestimate of size:

  o Overestimate of size: In this case, according to the equation for conventional productivity stated above, the overestimate is squared, then inverted, actually reducing the value of conventional productivity. Not realizing this effect, however, the estimators would be using a higher value of conventional productivity for planning purposes. In consequence, they would be getting lower estimates of effort and time. The project would likely overrun these low estimates of effort and time.

  o Underestimate of size: This scenario leads to an increase in the value of conventional productivity given by the equation stated above. On the surface, this increase would appear to be favorable. Not knowing this effect, however, the estimators would have used a lower value of conventional productivity for estimating purposes. That would lead to a relatively high bid of effort and time. As a result, the company might not win the bid, though, with an accurate estimate of size, it might have. In either event, an overestimate or underestimate of size, the effect on estimating and planning is adverse.

Clearly, time, raised to the fourth power, has a dominant effect on the value of conventional productivity, according to the equation stated above. Yet schedule time is not even present in the equation of two metrics from which conventional productivity is figured: size/effort. Managers often ignore the effect of schedule, perhaps because it is not explicitly identified in this expression. But it is there implicitly (as we have shown above in relating conventional productivity to the software equation). More powerfully, it is not only there; it is there to the extent of its fourth power.

Expressing conventional productivity in terms of the software equation shows that comparatively slight variations of process productivity, time, and size have very substantial effects on the conventional productivity the estimated project is likely to achieve. Therefore, a value of conventional productivity obtained from past experience is likely to vary widely from the conventional productivity attained on the project under consideration. Conventional productivity, in consequence, is a poor guide to estimating and planning the next project. The project is unlikely to come out the way the planners expected.

How Process Productivity Behaves

In contrast, let us see what effect the employment of the process productivity concept has on the effort and time of a project. We rearrange the software equation to show the metrics that determine effort and time:

$$(Effort/\beta)^{(1/3)} \times Time^{(4/3)} = Size\ (at\ Defect\ Rate)\ /\ Process\ Productivity$$

Two facts jump out at us:

- At the time of estimating, size and process productivity are "known" quantities (or at least specified or estimated values). (Defect rate is not actually a working part of this equation; it is understood, implied, or specified. It appears in another relationship, discussed in Chapter 8.) Therefore, the right-hand side of this relationship is a constant (or at least an "approximate" constant).
- Effort and time are linked by a multiplication operation. If you change one, the other must change accordingly, as Figure 7-3 suggests. The way they change is affected by the Beta parameter, which varies with the size of the software product, and by the exponents attending effort and time.

Figure 7-3:   We visualize time and effort as two gnomes on the opposite ends of a seesaw. When one goes down, the other goes up!

So, if that fellow in the "suit" picks a schedule time to end on his birthday, that selection inescapably establishes the effort that must go with it. Similarly, if the senior manager over a group of projects proclaims that he can make only a certain amount of effort available for the proposed project, that announcement predetermines the time the project will take. The suited fellow cannot arbitrarily set some other time.

Thus, if a management group picks an effort estimate independently of the schedule time with which it should be associated (by just mandating an arbitrary schedule), the result can turn out to be very, very wrong, as Figure 7-4 dramatizes. Sadly, the software industry has been wrong very often by not recognizing this fact and the impact it has on project execution.

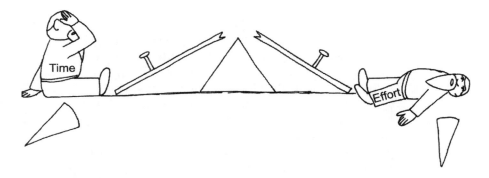

Figure 7-4:   *If you break the true relationship between time and effort, the seesaw doesn't work anymore!*

For a given project, size is pretty much fixed by the requirements of the application. Its process productivity is pretty much fixed, in the time frame of a project, by the environment, the team available, the tools in use, and so on. Only in the schedule time selected is there room for flexibility. Implementing that flexibility rests upon management at the project level, the company level, and the client level. But first, these managers have to understand these principles and be guided by them. These few paragraphs here only introduce the subject, the trade-off between time and effort. We return to it in Chapter 11.

Obtain Process Productivity by Calibration

To use the software equation in project estimating, we need first to obtain the value of process productivity. For this purpose, we rearrange the equation:

$$\text{Process Productivity } = \text{Size} / [(\text{Effort}/\beta)^{(1/3)} \times \text{Time}^{(4/3)}]$$

For completed projects, organizations know the value of size, effort, and time. They can readily calculate the past value of process productivity and employ that value to estimate the next project.

Once again, as we did with Fred Brooks a few paragraphs ago, let us call for assistance. This time the assistance comes from Peter V. Norden. Almost half a century ago, while working at the IBM Development Laboratory in Poughkeepsie, New York, Norden found a relationship between the assignment of people to a research-and-development project and the development time of the work being done. Of that relationship, he wrote,

> . . . the limiting factor is the rate at which ideas or insights can be generated, and that rate is not widely affected, if at all, by the number of men on the job, but rather by some capability level of the group.[3]

In 1975, Fred Brooks put it in what he later called "outrageously oversimplified" terms:

> Adding manpower to a late software project makes it later.[4]

Then, twenty years later, in a keynote address to the International Conference on Software Engineering, he confirmed this insight:

> On balance, I stand by the bald statement as the best zeroth-order approximation to the truth, a rule of thumb to warn managers against blindly making the instinctive fix to a late project.[5]

That is what we have done: translate these insights into numerical terms. Raising the value of schedule time to the four-thirds power magnifies its importance. The greater-than-unity exponent brings the significance of allowing enough time within the numerical grasp of estimators.

---

[3]Peter V. Norden, "Useful Tools for Project Management," Originally published in *Operations Research in Research and Development*, ed. B.V. Dean (New York: John Wiley & Sons, 1963). Reprinted in Lawrence H. Putnam, *Software Cost Estimating and Life-Cycle Control: Getting the Software Numbers* (Los Alamitos, Calif.: IEEE Computer Society, 1980), p. 222.
[4]Brooks, op. cit., p. 25.
[5]Ibid.

In contrast, the effort term is present only to the one-third power. In other words, we have to take the cube root of the effort, greatly reducing its importance in software relationships. Norden anticipated this finding long ago in his insight (quoted above) that the rate of progress in research and development "is not widely affected, if at all, by the number of men on the job."

The software equation, incorporating both time and effort, reduces insights such as these to a mathematical expression that managers can use to carry out six basic functions:

1. estimating time and effort
2. setting dates
3. supplying resources
4. monitoring work progress
5. assuring product quality
6. measuring process improvement

In addition, the software equation focuses on four things that conventional productivity does not:

1. It stands for the productivity of the entire project organization—requirements analysts, architects, designers, testers, and so on—not just the productivity of the code writers. The productivity of a project organization at its current level of process proficiency is what you want when you deal with the six basic control functions.
2. It represents the productivity of the project organization's process during the time period the measurements cover. For estimating the next round, this period is usually recently completed projects. For gauging the rate of process improvement, the period can extend over the entire time for which data has been collected. In addition, the productivity of a project currently in progress can be computed. It must be at least 25-percent completed for the data to be reasonably valid.
3. It takes into consideration in estimating effort the effect on that estimate that the development time (planned or allowed) will have.
4. It allows for the effect of size on the time and effort estimates because it includes a size term.

Don't Do It This Way!

The all-too-common estimating practice runs along these lines. The estimators produce an estimate of size in lines of source code or function points. With this size estimate and conventional productivity (size/effort), they arrive at an effort figure (person-months). Suppose that effort figure is 1,000 person-months. They don't know whether that represents one person working for a thousand months or a thousand people working for one month, to state the two extremes. Of course, these are easily dismissed since no one plans a thousand-month schedule—83 years, or a one-month buildup to a thousand-person staff!

What usually happens is that one of the cigar-wavers says, "We need this program in about two years, but the company's tenth anniversary comes two months before that. Let's set a twenty-two-month schedule."

So the estimators divide 1,000 person-months by 22 calendar months and find they have to assign about 45 people to the project. That sounds logical, but there are serious flaws in the logic.

First, it does not take into account the minimum development time. No one in the conference room has ever heard of such a thing, let alone stops to consider whether 22 months is less than this minimum.

Second, they don't have 45 suitable people available at the start, so they start off with five people. After all, at this point the work isn't ready yet for more than a handful of people. Still, as the work develops, they have trouble finding people with the qualifications suited to the work at hand. The point is, projects often start off with a deficit in their effort application and never come up with the 65 people they might need at the peak of the project effort.

Third, no one ever considers the actual relationship between person-months of effort and calendar months that is set forth in the software equation. The odds are that this project will get into trouble. History shows that a good many projects that begin like this one do get into trouble.

Do It with Process Productivity

With process productivity, you can make better estimates. With better estimates, you can more effectively monitor progress against what the estimate indicates you should expect. With a good indicator of process productivity on current projects, you can see if the organization is doing better than it did on last year's projects. You have a measure of improvement justifying the funds you invested in better equipment, tools, and staff training. Moreover, you can turn that measure of improvement into a return-on-investment figure that enables you to justify continued investment in process improvement.

There is much more to be said on these matters of project and investment control—and we will say it in Part III. First, however, we have carried on too long without getting to that very important attribute, software reliability. It, too, can be measured, controlled, and improved. We turn to it in the next chapter.

Chapter 8
Defect Rate
Measures Reliability

*"What in the world do they mean by that title?" John
asked, looking up from a draft copy of this chapter.*

*"They mean you can count defects," Phil replied.
"You can count the number of defects you find every
week. That is the defect rate. You might like to count
quality, but you can't. There are too many aspects of
quality that are not countable. But reliability is one of
those aspects, and you can count defects to measure it."*

Quality in software is the outcome of meeting the goals, requirements,
and actual needs of the users. It is a positive concept, referring to
such qualities as integrity, interoperability, flexibility, maintainability,
portability, expandability, reusability, resilience, and usability. Qualities such as these cannot, in general, be "counted in"—they must be
"designed in." They are brought in during the early phases of development—requirements capture, analysis, and high-level (architectural)
and low-level design, a subject to which we shall return in Part III.

Obviously, a software product lacks quality if defects overwhelm it.
At a minimum, the code should work, in the sense that it is free of any
major, debilitating defects. Too many defects in a program mean that
it is unreliable, so reliability boils down to the absence of defects or, at
least, to the minimization of the number of defects.

So, quality, for our purposes, is defined as a software program that does what it ought to do—in terms of goals, requirements, and needs. Reliability is defined as a software program that operates without succumbing to defects. Therefore, some indicator of the degree of reliability is the fifth of the core metrics.

The Fifth Core Metric

An *error* is a flaw in something that a human being does. He or she may make an error in capturing requirements, architecting high-level design, detailing low-level design, preparing test plans and cases, or writing code. When the error becomes manifest in documentation or code, we label it a *defect*. Note that if developers commit an error prior to writing source code, it usually turns up in the code, also.

A defect is akin to the bug of hallowed memory, but it is not quite the same thing. Bugs crawl into software of their own accord! In contrast, *you* put in a defect. Supposedly, there is nothing anyone can do about a bug that has free will. It will crawl where it will. There is, however, something you can do about the error you turned into a defect. Namely, you can conceivably avoid committing the error in the first place. You can minimize errors if you are so minded.

We may find it convenient for various purposes to classify defects. One common categorization is by the location in the development process at which the error was committed, such as in requirements capture, analysis, architecture, design, documentation, or coding. Another classification is by location in the program, such as algorithm, interface, or feature.

Perhaps the most common classification is by the severity of the defect. The degree of severity is often based on the time limit within which the defect has to be fixed:

1. *Critical.* The program fails to execute or it leads into a morass no one wants to enter. Fix this before the program is used again.
2. *Serious.* Some results are wrong or performance is substantially degraded, but the user can temporarily make allowances for the deficiencies. Fix soon.
3. *Moderate.* Program executes, but it contains obvious deficiencies. Users can live with them temporarily. Fix in current release.
4. *Cosmetic.* Flaws do not affect program performance or results, such as a misspelled table heading. Fix in next release.

There are at least four versions of the defect metric:

One version is *total defects*. That is the total number of defects accumulated during the development of the software product. Let's say we could project an estimate of this number just before the main build. Then we could count the number of defects detected and fixed during inspections, reviews, unit tests, integration tests, and system test. When that number reached the estimated number, the measured "dimension" would have reached the projected "dimension," and the product would be ready to release.

Another version is *defects remaining at delivery*. There are some residual errors still buried in the software product. That has been the industry's experience as software products go into operation. However, at the time of release, we don't know what the remaining defects are, so we can't count them. The number becomes known only later, as initial users find and report them. So, at the time of release, this number has to be an estimate.

The third version, the most promising one for use in software development, is the *defect rate*. This rate can be projected as defects per week or defects per month over the schedule of the project. Developers can then compare defects found and fixed against those projected, as detailed in Chapter 13.

Mean Time To Defect (MTTD) is simply another way to express the defect rate. It is the average time from the discovery of one defect to the discovery of the next defect during development. MTTD is the reciprocal of the defect rate.

When the project reaches system test or operational status, it reaches the realm of the *failure rate*, the fourth version of the defect metric. That is the number of failures per unit of execution or operation time.

The failure rate, in turn, is the reciprocal of the *Mean Time To Failure (MTTF)*, the average time from one failure to the next during operation (including test operation). For this metric, "time" is system operating time. During development, prior to putting the system together for system test, MTTF is not applicable because there can be no *failures* until the system begins to operate. Of course, *defects* will lead via software faults to failures when the system is put together.

What we are after is reliability—system operation that is free of failures. Of course, inevitably, software of any magnitude will contain at least a few residual faults. Technically speaking, therefore, *reliability* is the probability of failure-free operation for some period of time in the environment for which the software was prepared. For example, a user might expect a system to operate without disruption for five 24-hour days in this environment. That would be good enough to get the week's work done.

Software Development Is in Trouble

"Glitches cost billions of dollars and jeopardize human lives," *Business Week* proclaimed.[1] Software disasters have become so common that the magazine was able to list a big one for almost every month in 1998 and 1999, 21 in all! Robert L. Glass pulled together a whole book on "massive software project failures."[2]

What got us into this mess? In a broad sense, it was the computer age. With the benefits that computers bring, we also get the disasters—or at least the software faults. Why do there seem to be more of them now than there used to be?

- Individual programs have been growing in size. Many are now up in the hundreds of thousands of lines of source code. If we have one defect per thousand lines of code, that adds up to a thousand defects in a million-line program. Even worse, it is not uncommon for business programs to go into operation at five defects per hundred lines of code. That sounds like a lot of trouble.
- Computer memories and disks have also been expanding, providing space for many more programs on each computer. Suppose we have programs coming to fifty-million lines of source code. Help, we're buried in faults! Of course, users seldom get into situations that excite all those defects, but enough of them turn up in the course of a day's work to be highly irritating.
- Most computers are connected to millions of other computers across the world, through intranets or the Internet. The number of faults in all these combinations is boundless. Not only do individual programs contain defects, but the well-nigh-infinite interactions of all these connected programs give rise to still more defects.

Individual programs can be inspected and reviewed to find defects, and can be tested for faults. Unfortunately, inspections and reviews are still not the rule, and many programs are tested only halfheartedly. It is even more difficult to check out combinations of programs, though some efforts to do so are in progress.

---

[1]Neil Gross et al., "Software Hell," *Business Week* (Nov. 6, 1999), p. 104.
[2]Robert L. Glass, *Software Runaways* (Upper Saddle River, N.J.: Prentice Hall, 1998).

The main challenges to reliability are that individual programs contain defects, groups of programs on each computer compound the defects, and connections between computers multiply the number of defects still more. It is evident that avoiding errors and fixing the defects are becoming ever more important activities.

Why Do We Commit Errors?

Software is developed by human beings, and human beings do make errors—about one in every hundred actions, even when they are trying to be careful. We have a rough idea of how the human brain evolved, enough to know that it is not built on the model of a digital computer.

The bare facts running around in the brain might seem to be comparable to data in a computer. In addition, the brain often bathes the facts in emotions. For instance, if the checkbook stubbornly refuses to balance, we get emotional. Then we make even more errors, and so it goes.

As if managing one brain was not enough trouble for each of us, we attempt to produce programs in teams of brains trying to work together. As we know from experience, the results are always error-laden.

So, a human being makes errors, and groups of them make even more errors. We might go one level further: The many different programs on our computers are developed by many different groups. Since the groups do not know clearly how all the programs work together, the result is yet another level of errors. Getting away from errors altogether sounds pretty impossible.

Plan Projects to Minimize Error-Making

Nevertheless, we can diminish error-making. Some development organizations have greatly reduced the number of errors they commit. We can study these organizations, see how they do it, and try to spread their methods to other organizations.

In a broad sense, everything that we do to improve software development reduces the incidence of errors. In that sense, we should say, everyone should adopt the best practices advocated by leaders in the field. Everything helps. However, in light of the emphasis of this book, we describe below the project conditions under which people make fewer errors. What we found was that the other four core metrics—functionality (size), time, effort, and process productivity—play key roles in planning the working conditions under which we humans make fewer errors.

Limit Functionality

The error rate is affected by the size of the project. Large projects are more complicated; there are more interactions between developers and more errors than on small projects.

If the functionality of the proposed system is reduced, its size drops. The number of errors drops accordingly. We are not advocating an arbitrary decline in size. We are suggesting an examination of the system's functionality, to find unnecessary functions. Even if the code for those functions is not called into play (because the functions are not called), the defects they contain may interact with other parts of the system, causing trouble.

Next, search for functions that promise to be little used and consider whether the value of that use offsets the errors they contribute.

The functionality that a project team actually develops may be further reduced, in effect, by employing reusable components. These components have been more carefully developed than system elements developed for a single application. Moreover, they have been employed in other applications. They have been tested in use. As a consequence, you may expect them to have a lower defect ratio than newly developed system elements.

Unfortunately, at the time of this writing, reusable components are less than perfect. As we gain more experience in this area, however, we can expect them to contain fewer and fewer defects. The point is, to reduce defects, we should move toward component-based development.

Allow Sufficient Schedule Time

One fact of life in the software trenches, as we mentioned in Chapter 6, is minimum development time. A software product cannot be developed successfully in less than this minimum time. A corollary of this fact is that the defects introduced are at a maximum at this minimum development time. The number declines as more time is planned. This finding seemed logical: When people are rushed and wrought up, they make more errors. It is also common sense: People working at a comfortable pace commit fewer errors than people forced to rush by a constrained schedule.

The decline is very dramatic, as Figure 8-1 demonstrates. If you can allow more development time (up to about 130 percent of the minimum time), you can reduce defects by up to two thirds. You trade an increase in development time for much less trouble in system test and operation.

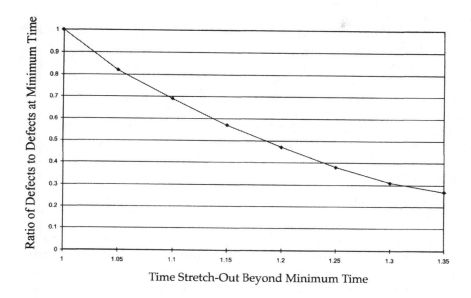

Figure 8-1:   *Lengthening the schedule beyond the minimum development time yields a marked reduction in the number of defects.*

Allow Sufficient Effort

If the effort allowed is insufficient, the number of errors increases. This, too, makes sense: If we don't have the person-hours in which to work carefully and to check our work for errors, we make more errors. If we lack time to participate in inspections and design reviews, we don't look for the errors while their setting is still fresh in our minds. Instead, we sigh, *Maybe we'll catch them in test.* At that late point, finding and fixing takes multiples of the earlier "finding and fixing" hours.

The person-months planned for a project ought to be sufficient to get the work done comfortably. Sufficient numbers of people working at a reasonable pace commit fewer errors than too few people trying to rush. Again, our data confirms this finding, and common sense seconds the motion.

Improve Process Productivity

Competent people employing good methods should commit fewer errors, and that is indeed the case. Our data indicates that errors committed fall as process productivity increases. That is also common sense. We deal at length in Chapter 19 with how to increase process productivity.

Part of establishing a better process is employing software tools in place of human processing whenever possible. Much of software development is tedious detail work. Computers perform that kind of work flawlessly, but humans pile up errors. Take, for example, the figures in this book. Most of them were created with computer tools. The input data could be in error, but at least what the tool does with the data is error-free! To the extent that we can get routine operations out of human hands and into software tools, we can reduce errors. (Of course, tools run on software, and all software has some errors, but established tools are close to error-free.)

Find Defects

Finding defects involves a series of operations—self-checking, inspections, peer reviews, code walkthroughs, unit tests, integration tests, and system test. Each of these operations rests on an extensive body of knowledge. Carrying them out is the real achievement. Still, there are two points on the planning horizon that deserve emphasis:

- Allow time and set aside effort early in the schedule for finding defects.
- Conduct defect-finding operations soon after the times at which errors can occur. The cost of finding and fixing defects increases dramatically the longer these operations are deferred.

It would help us carry out these two points if we could project a curve of the errors we expect to occur. Using the core metrics, we can project such a curve. Further discussion of this curve and its application will be found in Chapter 13, on the Main Build Phase.

Some Defects Remain at Delivery

The defect-rate curve and its counterpart, Mean Time To Defect, extend beyond the delivery date. The sum of the defects under the curve after the delivery date represents the defects remaining at delivery. Similarly, the MTTD at the time of delivery enables users to estimate how long they can expect the software to operate between faults.

After all our wailing in this chapter about the inevitability of errors, we come finally to the good news. Figure B-6, in Appendix B, derived from the QSM database, shows that the MTTD during the first month after delivery has been steadily increasing for the last twelve years. The jump in the last three-year period is especially marked—from about nine days to 12.5 days.

That said, let us once again don our dark-hued glasses. This splendid result has been achieved by the metrics-oriented organizations that report to the QSM database. Metrics-impaired shops can't report, so they are very likely doing worse!

Projecting the defects-remaining curve beyond delivery enables planners to see whether the project is likely to meet the requirement set by the acquiring organization, or jointly agreed to in the bidding process. After all, how could you bid intelligently on a metric such as remaining defects without being able to project something like this curve?

> *"Count defects, indeed," John said, putting down his copy of the chapter. "It gets a little more involved than that."*
>
> *"Of course," Phil replied. "Curvy lines, tracking, thinking ahead—if it were easy, everybody would be doing it."*

Part III
Control at the Project Level

The next seven chapters are devoted to the activities pertinent to planning and controlling a single project. There is much more to a software project of some consequence than coding. At the outset, for instance, several experienced people ought to think hard about whether the concept is feasible, both technically and organizationally. That is Phase One, Feasibility or Inception.

In Phase Two, Functional Design or Elaboration, the team pulls together enough information about the proposed software product to place a size estimate on the functionality to be produced. Size is a crucial metric underlying the estimate of schedule time and effort. Moreover, the time and effort metrics affect each other, as we noted in Chapter 7. They are subject to trade-off, not to separate, independent determination, as we explain further in Chapter 11, devoted to this trade-off.

At best, however, the estimates of functionality, size, and process productivity are uncertain. That means that the estimates of time and effort derived from them are also uncertain to some degree. Clients, however, want single bids. To limit their risk, software organizations can employ statistical methods to select a single bid with higher prospects of accomplishment (Chapter 12).

Following a successful bid, a software organization enters Phase Three, Main Build or Construction, and faces two tasks that employ metrics. One is to forecast the rates of expending effort and of incurring defects over the term of the project. The other is to compare the actual effort and defect rates with the forecasts and to take action if the actuals deviate much from the plan. Prompt action often resolves the cause of the deviation. In extreme cases, the software organization may have to re-plan the project (Chapter 15) and negotiate a new plan with the client (Chapter 21).

Phase Three concludes when the project team believes that the software is capable of operating in the user's environment. The project enters Phase Four, Operation and Maintenance, or Transition in Unified Process terminology. In this phase, the team adapts the system to its new environment.

Chapter 9
Do the Hard Stuff First—
Establish Feasibility

"The software industry continues to tackle problems
that are just beyond our proven capability."

—Alan Davis[1]

"The construction of software is an extremely complex
task—some say it is the most complex task ever under-
taken by human beings."

—Robert L. Glass[2]

Not every project is beyond our capability. Not all are extremely complex. But enough are beyond our reach to make it clear that we need
to take these two statements into account in getting a software project
under way. In other words, the Main Build, or Construction, Phase is
too late for clients and developers to find out that they can't develop
the software. They will have wasted too much time and money by that
point. Even worse, in many cases, the software systems needed to
operate a business profitably will not fall into place within the time
span allowed by competition. Software clients and developers really
ought to begin thinking about what has to be done, way ahead of the
Construction Phase.

---

[1]Alan Davis, in the foreword to Robert L. Glass, *Software Runaways* (Upper Saddle
River, N.J.: Prentice Hall, 1998), p. ix.
[2]Glass, loc. cit., p. 4.

In Part II, we addressed the five core metrics. In this Part, we address their use: estimating and controlling Phase Three. We noted that estimating begins with an estimate of size. To get this estimate, developers must already have a decent notion of what they are going to do. In other words, there is some kind of activity that precedes the Main Build. The size estimate doesn't—or at least, shouldn't—come out of thin air (otherwise known as the space between the ears of those skipping this preliminary activity).

The necessity for engaging in some activity prior to Phase Three has not escaped the more astute among us. The less astute tend to bleat, "Let's get the code rolling—we're not Boy Scouts around here!" That would be a jump to Phase Three. The more astute recognize the need, not only for Inception and Elaboration, the two Unified Process phases we introduced in Chapter 3, but for a "vision" leading to the authorization of Phase One.

The Vision Comes First

Those of us in the trenches (read, Dilbert) tend to be a bit contemptuous of the "big picture" fellows who failed algebra in high school. After all, we smirk, it takes algebra (and all those other hard subjects, such as statistics) to bring the big picture to fruition. True enough, but that is Phase One, which asks, Is the vision feasible? In this preliminary view of what may lay ahead, we want the "big picture."

This vision is our immediate guide to the future we are heading into pell-mell. We may find out in Phase One that the project faces technical, schedule, or cost problems. At this early point, however, the vision provides a glimpse of the path that senior executives (or their advisors) perceive. What they envision may be incomplete or unclear, even to themselves. The vision is, at the very best, a fuzzy snapshot of the never-very-clear future.

The core metrics will later give us an idea of how long the path is (time), how many members we need in our hiking party (effort), and how fast we can hike (process productivity). Without a path, however, we are hacking our way through a trackless jungle, soon to be lost. In those circumstances, the core metrics may be interesting, but we are still lost. Ergo: We have to start with a vision.

Unfortunately, the vision job has become increasingly difficult. Let's look at some of the difficulties.

What to Build

Forty years ago, this issue was fairly clear. We implemented in software a handful of business processes, like payroll, that were heavy on computation. Now, the direction in which to take software is far from obvious.

Should we just implement an existing business process in software? Of course we should, if that makes the process more efficient. Still, we have already done most of that. We've been over that path.

Should we reengineer the business process itself, to focus more on customer needs and less on the several parochial departmental preserves that now share the process? The current state of software development, such as Enterprise Resource Planning, now makes this move possible, though it is still difficult.

Or, should we go one (long) step even further? The fact that elaborate software systems are now feasible feeds back on what the "improved business processes" should be. That feedback, in turn, has an effect on "what to build."

Risk

Doing something that has not yet been fully defined, over months and years into the future, is accompanied by risk. The definition of what to build will evolve; technical risks that were not foreseen may appear; business risks, such as having competition get there first, may materialize. On one hand, it is not the primary concern of the vision people to assess risk. On the other hand, there is little point to laying out a vision that will immediately encounter risks the project can't get around. Good judgment helps a lot.

Economic Constraints

The vision eventually has to be carried out within business limits of cost, effort, and schedule, and it has to meet a quality goal. Again, it is not the immediate business of the visionaries to fine-tune the vision to these economic realities. That is the detailed business of the first two phases. Nevertheless, there is merit to keeping the vision within the ballpark.

An Endless Task

The task of setting forth an enterprise's vision of the future is neverending. As far as we can see, technology will be advancing, world population will be growing, and globalization will be shifting work between countries. This continuous change calls for successive visions as the future unfolds.

One practical idea for those practicing the art of the vision is to keep each successive stage of the unfolding vision within the bounds of the evolving situation. You don't have to extend the vision to the end of time. It will help if the current vision can blend smoothly into the following one. The software architecture should be extendable beyond the termination of the project currently in focus.

Projecting this continuing vision is one of the elements that make modern enterprises increasingly difficult to manage. In fact, some say top management can no longer manage in the detailed sense of past generations. It can no longer bark orders, "Do this, do that, jump this high."

As a result, management is often buffered from the day-to-day reality of the hands-on workers. In *Only the Paranoid Survive,* Intel Corporation Chairman Andrew Grove recalls a staff member who commented on the CEO of a software company: "That guy is always the last to know." [3] From his own experience as a CEO, Grove observes that the software CEO, "like most CEOs, is in the center of a fortified palace and news from the outside has to percolate through layers of people from the periphery where the action is."

If top management, or near-top management, is laying out the vision, Grove would urge those responsible to get out on the periphery and see what is going on, for themselves. Then, in between trips to the outside, they should make it easy for news of change to get through the palace guard.

Grove may have been referring principally to executives in high technology. However, executives in low-technology concerns are also in peril of being blindsided. How about all the local hardware stores that Home Depot and the like have supplanted? The mom-and-pop stationery stores replaced by Staples and Office Max? The department stores out-competed by Wal-Mart? A chief feature of these newcomers has been their ability to apply software systems to old lines of business.

Of one thing we can be reasonably sure: Few organizations will be able to lay out a path that extends very far into the unknown future. It follows, then, that the ability to develop software systems in less than the many years it now takes will be a significant competitive advantage. To achieve this, management must

- figure out successive visions right on the heels of the unfolding future
- craft an overall vision capable of adaptation to the inevitable changes
- allow for make-or-break technical and competitive risks as early as vision time

---

[3] Andrew S. Grove, *Only the Paranoid Survive* (New York: Bantam Doubleday Dell Publishing Group, 1996), p. 22.

The vision statement is often only a few pages long. The next phase, Inception, fleshes it out to the point of establishing the feasibility of the project. The first activity in that phase is to figure out with some specificity the scope of the proposed system. Consider the scope of this classic project:

> In 1516, when King Francis I returned to France from his Italian expedition, the great painter Leonardo da Vinci came with him. Da Vinci is less well known as the engineer to the Duke of Milan and designer of a canal lock of a type still used today. The two considered a canal to link the Atlantic and the Mediterranean across southern France through Toulouse. The canal route would lie between the Massif Central on the north and the Pyrenees Mountains on the south. Here, there is a great natural corridor: the Garonne river flowing to Bordeaux on the Atlantic Ocean and the Aude river flowing to the Mediterranean. Linking the two rivers meant digging a canal over the continental divide between them, at that point only 189 meters above sea level. That could be done by thousands of men with the hand tools of the period.

The Feasibility Question

> Where would the water to operate the several-dozen locks joining the Garonne and Aude rivers come from? The headwaters of these rivers were well below the summit to which the locks led. Steam power and pumps to lift this water were still several hundred years in the future. Sadly, the proposed canal was beyond the sixteenth-century state of the art. The King and Leonardo recognized the infeasibility and abandoned the project.

How We Got into This Leaky Boat

Before the industrial age, man seldom tried to build works that exceeded the technical capabilities of that age. Then, in the unprecedented twentieth century, we experienced a period of remarkable engineering achievements: decentralized electricity, indoor plumbing, the telephone, the automobile, the highway system, the airplane, radio, radar, television, color television, jet aircraft, the atomic bomb, the hydrogen bomb, the atomic-powered submarine, computers, copiers, the Internet—and they all worked. We got in the mode of thinking that scientists and engineers could accomplish anything leaders could envision.

Hence, software people were expected to make anything work, too. In fact, the results of their efforts often did! In the past forty years, software people have implemented billions of lines of software that has revolutionized the worlds of business, industry, and government. But, some of our efforts did not work, and now we have had enough failures to look back on the decision of Francis I and Leonardo with more appreciation.

Perhaps it is time to think again about some of the big failures of the twentieth century—

- front-wheel drive automobiles, which were technically feasible but did not catch on
- the hydrogen-filled dirigible, such as the Hindenburg, which crashed and burned
- atomic power plants, which functioned successfully but had secondary costs that overwhelmed the hoped-for economies, at least under the current price and supply levels of the United States
- atomic-powered aircraft, a concept that didn't work out because the shielding weighed too much
- personal aircraft, which were glorified on magazine covers in mid-century but proved to be impractical because of the finite size of the nearby sky
- supersonic passenger aircraft, such as the Concorde, which was technically successful but a commercial failure

Making the feasibility case means more than having a sweeping vision of a system that would be "nice to have." Many of the foregoing examples illustrate the tendency of visionary leaders to confuse a "nice to have" vision with a *feasible* project. You can check out feasibility, but a vision is more slippery.

The Inception Phase Establishes Feasibility

To move from vision to Phase One and then on to Phase Two, an idea has to pass three checkpoints:

- The especially difficult segments have to be investigated to the point of establishing that accomplishing them is almost a certainty.

- These segments have to be checked against the state of the art to establish that they are doable at this point in time. Not just doable by some ideal organization but doable by the one you have at hand. And doable within the cost framework you can afford and the time limit your circumstances prescribe, such as getting to market as soon as the competition. Moreover, it must be doable at the level of quality the application requirements impose.
- These difficult segments may contain critical risks, that is, risks that if not surmounted will make the system impossible to complete. These critical risks must be reduced to manageable risks.

The steps leading to the feasibility decision are outlined next.

Delimit Scope

The first task of the small group that begins the Inception Phase is to draw a tentative circle around the functionality that appears to be included within the vision statement. In other words, it needs to delimit the scope of the proposed project, as illustrated in Figure 9-1. The group locates the interfaces through which the proposed system will communicate with systems and users beyond this boundary circle.

Obviously, a single project can't do everything. In particular, the group takes a first cut at fitting the amount of functionality to the budget and time scale that are within reach. It may place outside the scope technical risks that appear to be insurmountable in the time the likely schedule provides.

Proposed systems range widely in their readiness to enter development. At one extreme is the totally new or unprecedented system in an unexplored domain. The group exploring such a scope has little background information for reference. Here, a fairly cautious approach may be the wisest course: that is, try a little; see if it works; try a little more; and so on. It may not be reasonable to scope the project firmly with the small amount of knowledge initially available.

At the other extreme, reusable components are available in-house, from component vendors, or both. The group expects that some modifications and some additional modules will be needed, but it foresees no complications. In this case, delimiting the project should be easy.

In between these extremes, groups encounter an endless variety of visions. In general, the time available for translating a noble vision into a delimited scope is short. Use people experienced in the area of interest. Include three or four people, if possible, to get the benefit of a broader experience base and the reconciliation of differing points of view.

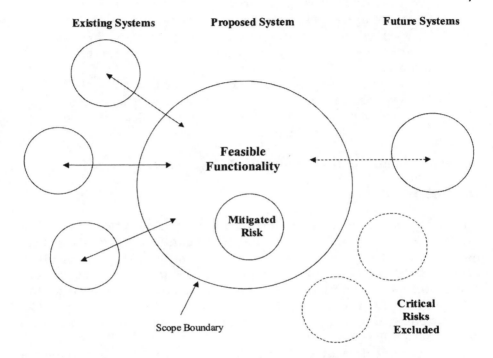

Figure 9-1:   *The Phase One team draws a boundary around the functionality that can be feasibly included within the proposed system. It excludes critical risks for which it foresees no path to resolution.*

Select an Architecture Possibility

In this Inception Phase, or Feasibility study, an organization can normally afford to have only a small number of people work for only a short period. Moreover, this activity calls for highly experienced people, and the number of such people available is always limited. Therefore, this phase should do only the amount of work necessary to reach a few valid conclusions.

One of these activities is to identify sufficiently the core require-ments in order to lay out an architectural possibility. There is no neat definition of just what these core requirements are. However, one thing we know they are not—at this stage—is a thousand pages of details!

Many elements of software architecture are known. Often, it may take the definition of only a few requirements to see that several archi-tectures are feasible. In less familiar areas, you may have to identify additional core requirements before you are satisfied that an architec-ture is feasible. In many parts of the proposed architecture, such as output drivers and devices, architecture may already be well estab-lished. It is not necessary to explore these areas in this phase.

Similarly, many parts of a system are fairly well known, such as monitors, printers, loudspeakers, microprocessors, established soft-ware routines, and so on. When the time comes in a later phase, we will have little difficulty specifying the level of capability that we need in these known areas.

During the Inception Phase, our task is to sort out those system elements that are new, unfamiliar in this application, or stressed beyond their normal limits. Then, for those elements, including soft-ware, we set tentative specifications that are sufficient for the likely needs.

Mitigate Critical Risks

A critical risk is one that, if it materializes, imperils the completion of the project. If the Feasibility team cannot see a way to mitigate such a risk, it should point out to higher management the questionability of financing this project to the bid stage.

Mitigating the risk does not mean solving the problem that arrives when the risk materializes. That may take considerable time and effort, properly deferred to the Construction Phase, when funds are available. Mitigation means seeing a path to the solution of the prob-lem—a path that can be factored into the bid.

A Feasibility Decision, 150 Years Later

We return to our example of Francis I and Leonardo, just as later thinkers returned to the vision of the canal:

> In 1662, Pierre Paul Riquet, the King's tax collector in
> the Toulouse area, saw the outline of the answer to the
> feasibility question. Riquet had the advantage of having

more extensive knowledge of the territory than Francis I and Leonardo. He had been over the territory countless times while collecting taxes; he knew the lay of the land. In addition, he knew what the French called "river men," experts in the flow of every river on the southern flanks of the Massif Central.

In the Montagne Noire, the southern outcropping of the Massif Central, about twenty to thirty kilometers north of the likely canal route, there was water. Moreover, it was high-altitude water, averaging several hundred meters above the high point of the canal system. It could be dammed, and it could flow downhill to the water input at the high point of the canal. This feed-water canal could follow an elevation contour line, falling only a meter or so per kilometer.

Constructing the dams, the feed-water system, and the canal itself would be a difficult engineering accomplishment in this age before power machinery. Nonetheless, Riquet obtained the support of Colbert, the powerful finance minister of Louis XIV. With thousands of men and some women, he built the canal over a period of twenty years, despite many setbacks, financial and technical. But it was feasible. It could be done, and it was done. The Canal du Midi joined the Atlantic and the Mediterranean, facilitating traffic for several hundred years. Of course, technology moved on, and eventually the railroads, and still later the truck highways, took over most of the burden. However, the Canal still operates today, mostly for pleasure cruising.

Make the Business Case

Even if the vision is feasible, is it worth doing? Will the business fundamentals pay off? We have the technical capability to do lots of things that the market will not support. Businesses, large and small, learn this every day. The vision has to satisfy a business case. It has to promise to return more money than it costs.

In general, the Inception Phase cannot make the ultimate business case. Not enough is known. (That knowledge comes in the next phase, Elaboration or Functional Design.) However, at this point, we can make the *initial* business case. More specifically, the Inception Phase makes the first pass at whether or not the project can be done by your organization within the various limits you are up against: time, funds, staff, and capability.

Even if a proposal is technically feasible, though, it may not be appropriate for your organization at this particular time. Your organization may lack certain skills needed for the project, or you may not have the needed funds. Or, the product may not be consonant with your company's business objectives. And so on.

Making the business case means that a small team makes a ballpark estimate of the project's schedule and effort (at a certain defect level), to establish that the project is within the organization's resource constraints. The ballpark estimate is approximate because the study team is in a position to attach only a very rough size to the project—an estimate ranging from 50 percent to 200 percent of the completed size, as previously illustrated in Figure 6-2. Obviously, the cost and time associated with the size range at the beginning of development (left side of the figure) will also be inexact, but those estimates of cost and time may be good enough to assure the sponsoring organization that the project lies within its resource limits. However, these early estimates are not good enough to base a business bid on.

This size-convergence curve depicts the nature of the problem that stakeholders face in planning software development. In the beginning, they would like to have some idea of how long development will take and how much it will cost, but they are stymied by the fact that they know little about the proposed system. Knowing little, they cannot estimate the system size very closely. Yet the system size value is needed for the kind of estimating tools that sophisticated estimators use to calculate effort and development time. In turn, those two core metrics, effort and time, serve as the basis of the cost estimate.

This rough estimate of cost and time is only the first half of the initial business case. The second half is the estimate of the return that will come from employing the software. In the case of a software contractor, that return may not be his immediate concern, but it is the concern of the acquiring organization.

In the case of a vendor developing software for sale or an internal software unit developing software for its own company, the return from the sale or use of the software is a matter of concern. That return has to be estimated, and that value must be greater than the cost of producing the software. Moreover, the software has to get to market or into use in time to meet market or user needs.

Estimating the return and the time to market are not rocket-science procedures. Still, the rough estimate of the return ought to be greater than the rough estimate of the cost. If you don't think about this comparison at all, the eventual outcome may slap you good.

Where Do the Resources Come From?

Ordinarily, the Inception Phase occupies only a few people for a relatively short time. When a significant study of feasibility appears necessary, you may start with two rules of thumb:

- Schedule approximates one quarter of the main-build schedule.
- Effort is about 5-to-10 percent of the main-build effort.

Unfortunately, at the time you begin the Inception Phase, your estimate of the main-build size and the corresponding schedule and effort are more than a bit hazy. At this time, also, there is one more substantial unknown: the nature of the project. Still, these rules of thumb give you a starting point. For instance, if we try to hold projects to a construction schedule of two years or less (by limiting the functionality of each formal release), this phase would take no more than six months.

At the easy end of the project spectrum, the projects are like many we have done before. We know we can do them. We don't need a Feasibility study at all.

Along the middle of the spectrum are all the other projects, likely to take various amounts of time and effort—amounts that are hard to put your finger on.

You can narrow down our rules of thumb and strengthen your own "fact-free" judgment by keeping data on the Feasibility Phases that your organization completes. That data will give you some insight into the type of work your organization commonly does and the approximate time and effort this phase takes.

Difficult as it is to predict the schedule, effort, and cost of this phase, there can be no doubt that resources are employed (except in those well-known areas where feasibility is evident). Who is going to finance the Inception Phase? There are only three choices—the software vendor, the software contractor, or the client organization.

Vendor. The funds come from overhead and are under the control of management. They originate with customers. In other words, the vendor has to set the prices for its current products high enough to cover the cost of establishing the feasibility of developing future products.

Software contractor. These organizations are generally not rife with funds for this purpose. Their funds would have to come from profits on past projects, and those are hard to come by. In consequence, the poorly funded software contractor is tempted to skim over the feasibility phase lightly—and hence gets into more trouble.

Client organization. These organizations may have more funds, but they are not likely, at the current state of the industry, to be in the habit of financing feasibility studies. Still, assuring that the vision is feasible is in their own interest. A project that turns out, during the Construction Phase, not to be feasible will cost many times the resources needed by a feasibility study. Since it is difficult to estimate schedule and effort at the outset of this phase, the financing should be on a research basis.

In any case, the Inception Phase should not be a huge effort. The two or three experienced staff members assigned to it may be overhead people, who do not have to charge their time to a project budget. Fundamentally, you need to determine only that it is worthwhile to proceed to the next phase, Elaboration, or Functional Design, where the problems are explored in more detail. It is not until the end of that phase that you need to commit—in theory, at least—to a firm bid. In other words, the Inception Phase can say, "No, the project is not feasible. Abandon it!" Or it can say, "It's okay to go into the next phase, Elaboration." However, it cannot say, "Yes, go all the way."

The bottom line is that the Inception Phase is aimed at important objectives. Accomplishing these objectives takes time and money. The parties to the phase, in their own interest, should negotiate this time and money.

Furthermore, in addition to whatever funds it contributes, the client must contribute cooperation. Only the client can contribute people knowledgeable about the client's operations, from whom the software organization can elicit the information it needs in this phase. This amount of time, too, is an expense, though it may never be formally posted to the accounting system.

Were Our Ancestors Shrewder?

Today, we abandon many software development projects after several years of effort and sometimes the expenditure of tens of millions of dollars. There are many reasons for these failures, of course, but an important reason is the failure to establish *feasibility* in the first place. Forethought—the consideration of feasibility—seems not yet to have become accepted practice.

Are we less shrewd than Francis I and Leonardo? Possibly, for they were exceptional men.

However, they were heirs to several millennia of civil-engineering experience, even at that point in history. Today, we in software development look back on only a single generation of experience with large systems. But we also have the advantage of great amounts of organized information—in libraries, in our computers, and all over the Internet. Really, we should be doing better.

Chapter 10
Do the Tough Stuff Next—
Functional Design

"We just busted our britches on the hard stuff in Phase One," one reader complained. "Now you seem to be headed into the tough stuff. Have you no mercy?"

Actually, we *are* laden with concern for your well-being—your long-term well-being, that is. If you get the tough stuff nailed down in Phase Two, your project should sail through Phase Three, Construction, the Main Build.

The disjoint between project plans and project performance has puzzled us for years. The gap seems to be much less in building construction, for instance. The performance of that industry suggests that it is possible to make plans, generate estimates, submit bids, and generally live within them. In the software industry, however, the gap seems to be widening. Almost everyone demands ever-tighter schedules.

At the same time, nearly everyone else has been conducting studies for the last two decades, showing that software development is late, over-budget, defect-prone, cancellation-prone, stalled on Capability Maturity Level One (Chaotic), nearly impossible, or in some other way inadequate. These studies are valid! Our own database provides supporting numbers, but we're not going to bore you with more "software crisis" numbers. The issue is what to do about this sad situation.

The first step was Phase One, Inception, when the feasibility team passed four criteria:

- It devised a candidate architecture.
- It mitigated any critical risks.
- It established an initial business case.
- It gained the stakeholders' assent for the next phase.

What to do continues in Phase Two, Elaboration (in the phraseology of the Unified Process) or Functional Design (in terms of one of the principal activities of the phase). The reasoning of the originators of the Unified Process was that the phase "elaborated" the work begun in Phase One. Identifying it with any one activity tended to divert emphasis from the many activities that developers have to mesh together in this phase.[1]

The Tough Stuff

First of the objectives for this phase is extending the requirements to the point necessary to implement the other objectives of the phase. Something on the order of three quarters of all the requirements is generally sufficient. Filling in the detail of requirements for subsystems that are well understood can be deferred to the Construction Phase.

The extended requirements lead to a fairly complete functional design, or high-level design, or architecture. We intend this architecture to provide a sound foundation not only for the work of this phase but also for the Construction Phase.

In Phase Two, we carry the mitigation of critical risks far enough to estimate the time and effort that may be required to resolve them in the Construction Phase. In addition, we seek to identify the significant risks—those that are less than critical but affect schedule, staffing, or cost plans.

In Phase One, Inception, the Feasibility team made the initial business case. In this phase, on the basis of the additional information the Elaboration team gathers, it extends the business case. Namely, the value of the return expected when the system goes into operation continues to outweigh the planned costs of development. Of course, the cost of development cannot be known with precision until development

---

[1]Ivar Jacobson, Grady Booch, and James Rumbaugh, *The Unified Software Development Process* (Reading, Mass.: Addison-Wesley, 1999).

is completed. Similarly, managers can assess the value of the return accurately only after the system operates.

Finally, we emphasize that the attainment of product quality begins in these first two phases, particularly in this second one. The Construction Phase, essentially, can only build the system that was architected in this second phase. It is important, of course, to build it as close to defect-free as we can, but the achievement of quality in a positive sense begins when we match the functional design to the users' needs. Making this match is what builds in the quality attributes. To get quality, we have to know what we are going to do; we have to know that doing it will not run into unanticipated risks; we have to have enough information to plan the project; and we have to schedule and staff the plan to the level it takes to get quality.

For an insight into the place of Phase Two in the four-phase sequence, refer to Figure 10-1.

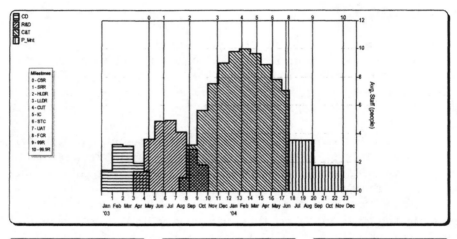

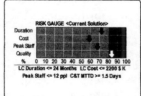
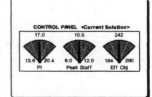

Figure 10-1:   The second phase is the subject of this chapter. The numbered vertical lines refer to milestone (or review) locations. Their exact location and definition vary in different organizations.

Meshing the Activities

This phase is aimed at achieving a functional design (sometimes called high-level design), not only for the sake of technical achievement, but because it enables the software organization to reach the business objectives needed to enter the next phase:

- the business bid
- the business case

We don't mean to suggest that Functional Design is not highly important. Of course, it is. However, the central goal of this phase is to get the project ready to enter the main build. The functional design (the Unified Process calls it the architectural baseline) is a key way station along the route. To reach this functional design, we have to determine the key functional and performance requirements.

Experienced developers also smoke out the *significant* risks during this phase. You recall that the make-or-break *critical* risks were mitigated in Phase One. Significant risks are not of such great magnitude as to condemn the project to futility, but they do raise questions as to how much time and effort mitigating them will take. This time and effort must be factored into the bid.

As we indicated in Part II, the business bid depends in part on the amount of functionality we estimate the product will contain. This functionality is most often expressed, for estimates, in some metric of size, such as source lines of code. To reach that size estimate, we need some grasp of what the product is going to be. This grasp is provided by the key requirements, the functional design, and the evaluation of the significant risks. The further these three elements are carried (in this phase), the more accurate the size estimate—and therefore the bid—will be.

The preceding paragraph may strike you as something of a merry-go-round. Any one of these processes—requirements, functionality, risks, architecture—would be difficult taken by itself. Worse yet, they do not operate in isolation. They are intermeshed. Their interactions multiply the difficulties. Despite efforts to set forth software development processes, solving the actual problems is still very hard work. It does help if there is enough schedule time and staff to do this work.

The *initial* business case, reached in Phase One, found reason to continue into Phase Two. This phase, on the basis of new information, reaches a case for continuing with the much greater expenditure of time, effort, and cost of the Construction and Transition Phases. The final business case, of course, cannot be reached until the product is in use and the benefits of that usage are tabulated.

We carry Phase Two, Elaboration, no further than is necessary to reach these goals. In fact, since financing for this phase is difficult to obtain, software organizations often have to defer Phase Two work to the early part of the Construction Phase, when they obtain the necessary funds. In this eventuality, unfortunately, those funds may be based on little more than intuition. They may not last as long as the project does!

Formulating Requirements Is No Longer Simple

In long-gone days, programmers themselves could draw up a list of requirements for a payroll program. The payroll accountants knew what they did; the programmers could interview them. Development could proceed through the steps of the waterfall model: requirements, analysis, design, coding, testing, operations. For a large program, development might take three or four years. A few very large systems might take more than five years. The waterfall model assumed that requirements stayed fixed, or at least did not change enough to upset the system's functional design. In the new millennium, these circumstances have changed. Nothing stays the same. Development has to survive continuous change.

The mechanics of surviving change varies somewhat in the two basic types of development: for the general market and for a single client. For the market, a vendor has to sample representative users. The vendor's team has to sort the users' many needs into the relative few that can be accommodated at this time; the others will be deferred. Then the vendor has to implement this series of features in periodic releases that are keyed to beat competitors. The vendor has to have within its marketing organization the capability to survey users and to work with its architects and developers on plans to satisfy users' needs.

For single clients, the software organization can define its user focus more narrowly than the market vendor. Still, within the single client organization, users may be scattered through many departments, even different locations. A more serious problem than location, however, is that few users have much grasp of the whole picture. This lack of understanding is exacerbated when the software is planned to implement horizontal processes through a lengthy sequence of vertical department structures. In such cases, only the reengineering analysts understand the new horizontal processes, but they lack the detailed, step-by-step knowledge that workers gain from experience. The pertinent details, of course, have to make their way into the new software.

The situation is complicated enough in a single-client company. To this already complex picture, intranets and the Internet add another layer of complication. The single client may be interfacing to many suppliers or many customers.

The point of all this is that finding just a few people who can specify the requirements is seldom possible anymore. There are simply too many functions, departments, locations, and businesses involved in projects of some size.

Difficulties Fixing Requirements

Requirements don't stay fixed, as we may once have imagined. The environment, technology, business practices, and laws are all continuously changing. Moreover, businesses themselves are continuously reorganizing and merging, necessitating changes in their software.

Even within the framework of a single project, requirements are fluid. During requirements elicitation, as users learn more of what the proposed system can do, their desires increase. As the project proceeds and some code goes into operation, users begin to perceive and list additional features that are not only possible, but are also desirable—even essential.

A problem with the list approach to requirements is that lists get long. It is not easy to visualize from a list of requirements what the system is actually going to do. Users generally have little experience in this art. If they don't see what the system can do, before the time of system test, they won't see before that time the need for system modifications. By then, however, the architecture, design, and even the code are set. Making substantial changes during system test is not practicable, certainly not within the strictures of schedule and resource exhaustion that then afflict the project.

The alternative is to show representative users a mock-up, an algorithm, or a prototype—an example that is meaningful to them—during the Elaboration Phase. At this point, many changes would be cost-free. Even if they carry costs, the Construction Phase plan and estimate are still in preparation.

We are not pretending that we have solved the requirements problem. Requirements evolution is to be expected, more so nowadays than several software generations ago. The need is to cope with requirements changes in such a way that we can get a firm functional design. From this architectural baseline, we can develop a reasonably firm estimate of size, a plan, and a schedule and cost estimate, ensuring that we can do business in a reasonable way.

What We Need to Do

If we accept the reality that requirements will evolve during development, it is common sense to adapt development processes to that fact. The foremost adaptation is to keep projects short, usually under two years. In a seven-year project, the inevitable changes outmode the product when it finally arrives. Software applications, of course, go on and on, generation after generation. That does not mean a particular release lasts for an entire generation, though. A new release generally goes out every year or two, which corresponds to the project duration.

This approach does carry some implications. One is that the functional design carry through a series of releases. Architects have to be mindful not only of the immediate requirements, but of the likely evolution of the system in future releases. The functional design should be flexible enough to permit future releases to add additional features. In most cases, releases should be forward-and-backward compatible. When architects can no longer extend compatibility into the next release, it is time for a new generation, based on a new functional design.

To implement this need, architects and designers have to be able to track requirements over many years, for as long as the functional design lasts. We won't attempt to detail how to do this here. Something like the Unified Modeling Language is needed for that.[2] With it, developers can document the requirements in a widely understandable way that is traceable through the phases of a single release and through many releases.

Key Requirements Lead to Functional Design

Functional design is to software as architecture is to building construction. A frontier youth could construct a woodshed without an architectural blueprint because he had seen many of them. He carried the architecture around in his head. A youth today, however, would encounter difficulty building a mansion for the local millionaire from the architecture in his head. He would need architectural drawings.

Similarly, programmers used to be able to code the small programs of the day without an architectural plan, because they had previously

---

[2]Grady Booch, James Rumbaugh, and Ivar Jacobson, *The Unified Modeling Language User Guide* (Reading, Mass.: Addison-Wesley, 1999).

worked on similar programs. A sizable team of developers on a project of some size needs an architectural blueprint. If the project is novel, they need the blueprint even more.

This phase, however, need not complete the entire functional design. The basic intent is to lay out the architectural baseline. From a business standpoint, this level of detail is sufficient for planning the system. In particular, it is the level at which we can estimate the eventual size of the system, and from that we can estimate time and effort.

This level covers functionality that is architecturally relevant. The architects pay attention to details only to the extent necessary to establish that they are not architecturally relevant. What is relevant, of course, is a matter of fine judgment by experienced people. The features that are important to stakeholders are of primary concern.

This architectural baseline, then, is just a skeleton of the eventual system, particularly those aspects that are novel or difficult. It can be designed, coded, and demonstrated to stakeholders as an executable implementation of the baseline. This baseline may be the result of one or several iterations, whatever the architects need to reach a valid demonstration. That depends upon such factors as the extent of serious risks and the complexity of the apparent solutions. The architects record this baseline in documents that are usable by developers and understandable by stakeholders.

Identify Significant Risks

Significant risks are those that, if they materialize, interfere with planning and estimating the project. They may throw our estimates of schedule, effort, cost, and defect rate well off the mark. They are risks that we are sure we can surmount, but as this phase opens, we are not yet in a position to estimate the time and effort required for overcoming them. We may be unable, for example, to estimate the functionality, that is, the size of the code that will mitigate this risk. We may have to back off to the point of finding or implementing an algorithm to assure that this functionality can be achieved.

In this phase, the intent is not to eliminate risk altogether. It is to understand the risks well enough to assure that we can resolve them within the economic constraints we are establishing for the Construction Phase. In effect, we are identifying significant risks to add to a risk list for full resolution later. We only carry our analysis of significant risks far enough to assure that we can mitigate them within the economic limits of the subsequent phases.

The Business Case at Phase Two

As we indicated in the last chapter, there is little merit in proceeding with a software project if it is not going to pay off. Toward the end of Phase Two, we have gathered more factual information about the two sides of the business case. One side is the cost of the project; the other side is the economic return expected from the employment of the product. The returns should exceed the costs.

Many companies ask for a healthy excess because there are still many unknowns. The construction cost is not certain until the project is completed. The returns are even less certain. In the case of an internal project, the value of employing a software product is difficult to figure. The project can ask the affected departments to estimate the savings they expect, but the margin of error in estimating the potential gains is usually large. However, the exercise at least provides a basis for weighing the gains against the costs.

In the case of a single-client project, the software organization is not formally responsible for the business case. It is responsible only for obtaining the contract at a bid that will cover its own costs. The client is responsible for the other side of the business case. Nevertheless, in the event of an obvious discrepancy between costs and apparent returns, it is professional courtesy to point it out.

In the case of a market-oriented project, markets are notoriously difficult to evaluate. The number of units sold, the price at which the product will sell, and the period over which sales will endure are all matters for marketing to consider and executives to judge.

Still, by the end of the Elaboration Phase, the facts are clearer and the business case is more definite. Sometimes a negative decision is obvious. A decision to go ahead may be less clear, but at least the business case has been considered.

Supporting Phase Two Itself

Architects and developers can accomplish the tasks of this phase more effectively if management is in a position to sponsor the time and effort the phase takes. By the beginning of this phase, the feasibility team will have a better grasp of the product's functionality and size than it had at the beginning of the first phase. Given a size estimate and an estimate of the main-build time and effort, management can apply these rules of thumb:

- Schedule: Phase Two will require about 30 to 35 percent of the estimated main-build schedule.
- Effort: Phase Two will require about 20 percent of the estimated main-build effort.

These estimates are more accurate than the first-phase estimate because we have now narrowed the size estimate. Still, the longer we can delay making this estimate, the more accurate it will be. Alternatively, we can update the phase estimate as the size estimate becomes firmer.

Nearing the Bid Decision

The business objective of Phase Two, you will recall, was to gather and develop enough information about the proposed product to provide an estimate of its functionality or, more specifically, its size. Along with process productivity, size is the major input we need to estimate the time and effort the project will require. Effort, in turn, is the key ingredient of the cost estimate.

Ultimately, the bid will have to cover both schedule and effort. In fact, these two are the key unknowns that we have to estimate. Restating the software relationship for estimating purposes shows that time and effort combined represent a function of size, quality, and process productivity:

$$(\text{Effort}/\beta)^{(1/3)} \times \text{Time}^{(4/3)} = \text{Size (at Quality Level) / Process Productivity}$$

What this means is that time and effort can be traded off, an approach we take up in the next chapter.

Chapter 11
The Power of the Trade-Off

The multiplicative relationship of effort and time in terms of size, quality level, and process productivity, developed in Chapter 7 and cited at the end of Chapter 10, tells us three things:

- For a product of a given (estimated) size, to be built at some quality level by a software organization of a given process productivity, the relationship does not provide a single value of effort or time. Rather, because of the multiplicative relationship between the two, there is a series of values from which estimators must select the time-effort pair to use. The values of time and effort are related so that, for instance, if the estimators increase the time they allow, the relationship reduces the effort (by reducing the staffing required).
- Plotted on a diagram of effort versus time, effort-time pairs lie on a line.
- Since effort and time are exponential in nature, this line is curved.

Figure 11-1 diagrams this line for a project of a given size and process productivity. Thus, for any project for which we have size and process productivity estimates, we can draw such a diagram. Moreover, given the capabilities of computer software, we don't have to go through all the plotting arithmetic ourselves. The computer is happy to oblige! QSM developed programs for this application long ago.

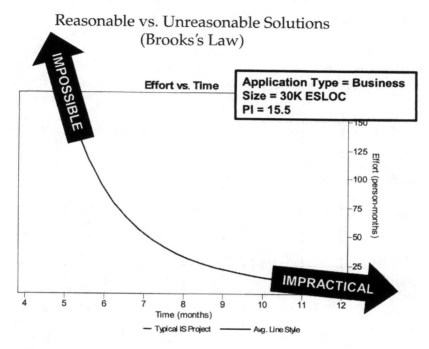

Reasonable vs. Unreasonable Solutions (Brooks's Law)

Figure 11-1: The time-effort pair at which it is practical to operate a software project falls on the curved line between the Impossible and the Impractical regions.

From this diagram, we draw five inferences:

Minimum development time. In the 6,300 projects on which we have collected data, no one has ever completed one in less than what we calculate to be the "minimum development time" for a project of its size, quality, and process productivity. We want to keep the schedule at which we plan to operate out of the Impossible Region in excess of the minimum development time.

Impractical Region. At the other end of the schedule scale is a lengthy development time where it would be possible, but rather ridiculous, to operate. There is no economic reason for going that slowly, since the cost savings would be small and the probability of losing the bid to faster competitors would be high.

Time-effort trade-off. Between the Impossible Region and the Impractical Region, there is a range of time-effort pairs at which we could plan to operate: the Practical Trade-Off Region. At each of these schedule points, there is a different value of effort and, consequently, a different bid price. To decide on an operating plan, we have to select one of these schedule points, with its corresponding effort (cost). This selection is constrained by the business pressures we face on each bid. For instance, marketing may be pressing us to set a very short schedule, but the curve tells us that we can do so only at the cost of much greater effort. The curve is also telling us that it is foolhardy to push the schedule into the Impossible Region.

Time-defects trade-off. There is a similar relation between the schedule and the number of defects to be expected. The number of defects is at a maximum at the minimum development time. The number declines as we plan for more time.

Smaller is better. Our data shows that planning to operate with a smaller staff over a longer period gives better results (in terms of fewer defects) than planning a larger staff and a shorter time.

Avoid the Impossible Region

At a short schedule, shown as five or six months in the particular case diagrammed in Figure 11-1, the curve veers sharply upward. Adding more effort gives us only a negligible schedule gain. If you jam a lot of people on a project, hoping to complete it sooner, you don't. Rather, you head into the Impossible Region. Don't go there. No one has completed a project in such a small amount of schedule time.

So listen up, devotees of impossible schedules! The time-effort curve shows that you can climb up that curve, reducing development time only with much greater effort. But there is a limit to this reduction in a given set of circumstances, and there are only two things you can do to raise that limit:

- Reduce the size of your product. Hold as many features as you can for the next release and/or employ reusable components. Reuse, in effect, reduces the estimated size by eliminating the work encapsulated in the reusable components.
- Increase your process productivity. It's a good idea, but doing so takes time on a scale longer than that of any one release.

Stay Out of the Impractical Region

Competitive pressures being as intense as they are, we have not noticed any unstoppable rush to plan projects in the Impractical Region, that is, on a rather lengthy schedule. Figure 11-1 shows that there is little economic point to over-lengthy schedules. In the Impractical Region, the time-effort curve flattens out. Extending the schedule reduces effort (and hence, project cost) by only tiny amounts.

Trade-Off Time and Effort

Between the Impossible Region and the Impractical Region, we have a considerable range of time-effort points at which we could plan to operate. Before we settle on one, let's take a look at the characteristics of the time-effort curve in this practical region.

- To the left, leading into the Impossible Region, the curve is rising sharply. We are getting a faster schedule at the cost of considerable effort.
- To the right, leading into the Impractical Region, the curve is flattening; it becomes nearly parallel to the time axis. We are reducing effort slowly at the expense of substantially increasing schedule.
- Neither the far left nor the far right of the curve offer promising operating points.

Figure 11-2 puts numbers on these observations. Effort (on the vertical axis) is presented as 1 (or 100 percent) at the minimum development time (to simplify computations). Effort greater than 1 falls in the Impossible Region. Effort less than 1 is within the Practical Trade-Off Region. Planning effort that is less than about 0.4 (or 40 percent) takes us into the Impractical Region.

Time (on the horizontal axis) is also presented as 1 at the minimum development time. Moving to the right, the schedule stretches out. Beyond 130 percent of the minimum schedule, we enter the Impractical Region.

Thus, as a matter of practical selection of the time-effort operating point, we can run effort from its maximum at the minimum development time down to about 40 percent at 130 percent of the minimum schedule. We can cut costs by more than half by planning a schedule that's less than a third longer than the minimum time. In the middle of the Practical Trade-Off Region, we lower costs (effort) by nearly half while adding only 15 percent to the minimum schedule.

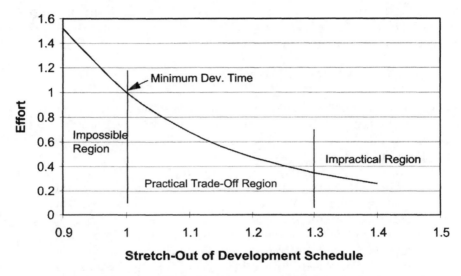

Figure 11-2: *This visualization of the time-effort trade-off law demonstrates the practical range within which estimators can plan software development.*

Trade-Off Time and Defects

The number of errors that developers commit is generally proportional to the amount of effort (in person-hours) they are putting in (assuming that other things, such as process productivity, are constant). It follows, then, that reducing the amount of effort planned for a project by lengthening the schedule reduces the error-committal rate. Therefore, planning a longer schedule (within the limits of the Practical Trade-Off Region) has the additional effect of reducing the defect rate, as diagrammed in Figure 8-1.

Planning three more months on a project with a minimum development time of twelve months, for instance, amounts to a 25 percent increase in schedule. That reduces the defects to less than half of what they would have been at the minimum development time. This trade-off is just common sense. When people are rushed, and that is the case near the minimum development time, they make more errors. That's how we get into tailgating accidents—driving too fast for road conditions.

In many projects, these trade-offs are well worth taking. It is our experience that many stakeholders have little sense of this trade-off of time, effort, and defects. Focused on the pressures of competition, they feel the need to get new software in operation, fast. "Besides," they bluster, "putting a little time pressure on those guys in the tennis shoes can't do any harm." Ah, but it can. We aren't saying the programmers shouldn't be under any pressure, but our analysis indicates that fast schedules do come at the expense of much greater effort and many more defects.

In the constellation of business pressures, time is certainly important, but so are cost and reliability. Sure, you have to get there in time, but you have to get there at a competitive cost with a reliable product. Balancing these three factors—time, cost, and quality—that is the businessman's burden. This analytical method gives him the means to do so. In the next two sections, we support this analysis with data from thousands of projects.

Small Is Beautiful

Small projects, employing less effort over more time, result in products of higher reliability. Could we prove this proposition using the projects in our database? In 1996, we sorted out two sets of projects:

- a set using five or fewer people at the peak
- a set using twenty or more people at the peak

Figure 11-3 shows that the large teams used an average of seven times as much effort as the small teams on projects of the same size. The figure is a log-log diagram with effective source lines of code on the horizontal axis and Construction Phase effort on the vertical axis. The two sloping lines represent the mean value of effort for the two data sets. The upper line (circles) represents the projects with twenty or more people; the lower line (squares) represents the projects with five or fewer.

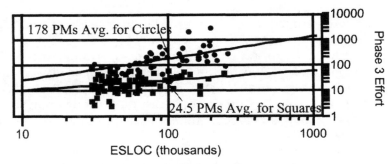

Development Effort vs. Developed SLOC

Circles = Projects that used 20 or more people
Squares = Projects that used 5 or fewer people

Figure 11-3:   *The projects with large staffs, identified by cir-*
cles, required more effort—almost without
exception—than the projects with small staffs
(squares) in the Construction Phase.

Figure 11-4 compares the schedule time of the same two sets of projects during the Construction Phase. The large-staff projects essentially did not get to market any sooner than the small-staff projects. At
first glance, there seems to be just one trend line for the two sets.
Actually, there are two trend lines, but they almost overlap. In the
center of the size range, for example, the large-staff projects completed
in 8.92 months, the small-staff projects, in 9.12 months. The schedule gain was inconsequential.

Figure 11-5 depicts the defects found during system test by the two
sets of projects. Again, the trend lines are far apart. That means that
the large-staff projects (circles) incurred far more defects than the
small-staff projects (squares). We can surmise that the large staffs
may have been less experienced than the small staffs. Staff members
may have gotten in each other's way. They may have been under
greater pressure to perform.

Once More with Emphasis: Small Is Beautiful!

In 1998, we received data from a large corporation, on 491 projects.
This data reaffirms our observation that using small work groups in
software development is a really beautiful idea. The data came from

Development Schedule vs. Developed SLOC

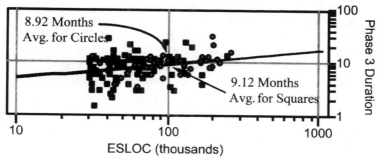

Circles = Projects that used 20 or more people
Squares = Projects that used 5 or fewer people

Figure 11-4:   *Using a staff of twenty or more rather than five or fewer made little difference in schedule. The circles (twenty or more) and the squares (five or fewer) are close together, which one would not expect had staffing made much of a schedule difference.*

Defects Found in System Test vs. Developed SLOC

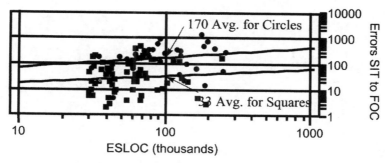

Circles = Projects that used 20 or more people
Squares = Projects that used 5 or fewer people

Figure 11-5:   *Putting a lot of people on a project simply gets you a lot more defects.*

medium-sized projects that contained between 35,000 and 95,000 new or modified source lines of code, not including reusable components that would require little or no new work. All were information systems completed in the previous three years.

We stratified the projects into five groupings according to team size, as shown in Figure 11-6. Note three features of this stratification, in particular:

- The number of projects in each group is substantial.
- The data sets are distributed across the entire size regime.
- The average size of the stratified data sets is 57,412 ESLOC, and the average of each set is within 3,000 ESLOC of this overall average.[1]

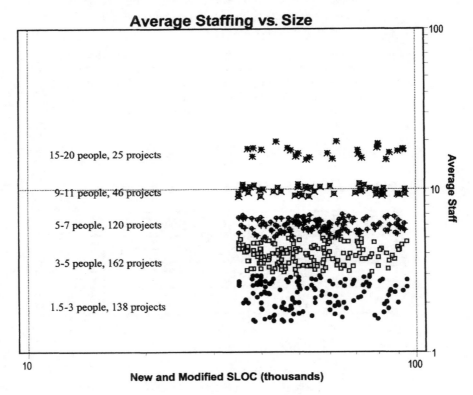

Figure 11-6:   *The projects are stratified in two dimensions: size (horizontally) and staff (vertically). Since both axes are logarithmic, the diagram covers a large range of information.*

---

[1]We are indebted to Douglas Putnam for making this analysis.

Figure 11-7 shows that the three small groupings took less schedule time than the two large groupings. In fact, development time for the three small groupings is about three quarters of the time for the two large groupings.

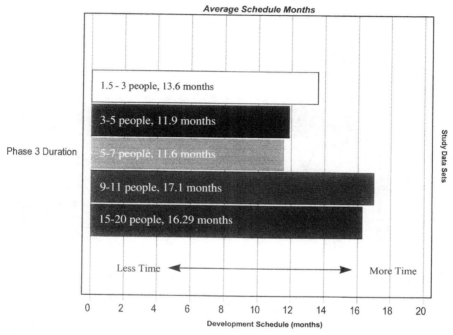

Average Schedule Months

Phase 3 Duration

1.5 - 3 people, 13.6 months

3-5 people, 11.9 months

5-7 people, 11.6 months

9-11 people, 17.1 months

15-20 people, 16.29 months

Less Time ← → More Time

Study Data Sets

Development Schedule (months)

Figure 11-7. *There is a distinct difference in the schedule time required by groups in the one-and-one-half to seven range as compared to the nine-to-twenty range.*

Figure 11-8 shows the pattern for development effort. The difference is much more marked than in the case of schedule. The three small groupings take only about one fourth the effort of the two large ones— even though each grouping is producing about the same amount of system functionality.

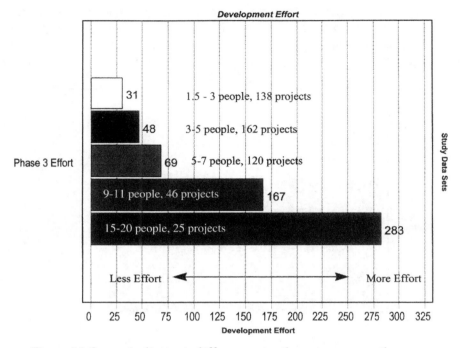

Figure 11-8: *A distinct difference in the person-months needed to do a comparable amount of work begins to show up when group size exceeds eight people.*

In Figure 11-9, we present a different representation of the effort data. Here, the projects completed by teams of two-to-five people are represented (on a log-log field) by squares. The lower of the two trend lines represents their average location. The projects completed by larger teams (nine-to-twenty people) are represented by circles and the upper trend line. The trend lines differ by a factor of four.

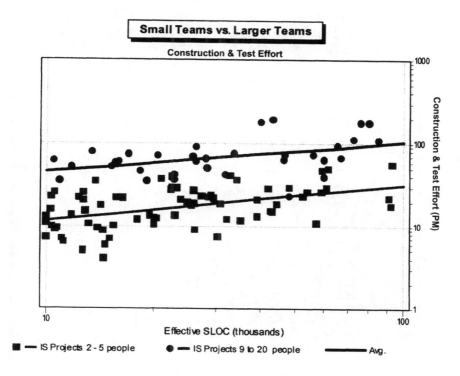

Figure 11-9:   *The larger teams (upper line) take much more*
                 effort than the smaller teams (lower line).

It comes as no surprise that the process productivity of the three small groupings is about double that of the two large groupings, as Figure 11-10 demonstrates. This figure presents process productivity in terms of the Productivity Index, a linear scale ranging from one to forty, though few organizations yet exceed thirty. The productivity indexes of the small groups average 16.28; those of the large groups, 13.38. That is a difference of approximately three index points. Each index point represents a gain of 1.27 times in process productivity over the previous index. A gain of three index points, therefore, doubles the process productivity (1.27^3).

When project size is held constant, process productivity becomes inversely proportional to the schedule and effort terms:

$$\text{Process Productivity} = \text{Constant} / (\text{Effort}/\beta)^{1/3} (\text{Time})^{4/3}$$

Thus, when schedule and effort improve dramatically (that is, when their values are significantly smaller), process productivity improves significantly as well. And indeed, the data shows this is true!

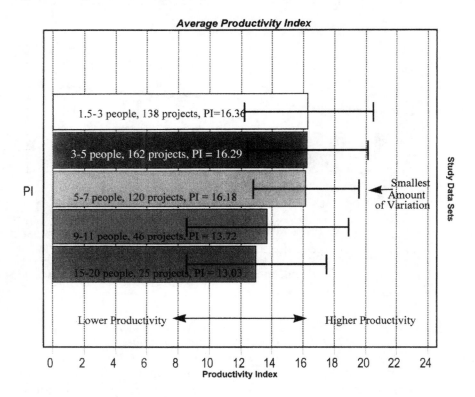

Figure 11-10: The real difference in productivity between the small groupings and the large groupings (a factor of about two times) is somewhat de-emphasized on this diagram because it is drawn in terms of the linear process-productivity index, not the nonlinear process-productivity parameter. The high-low variation bars are set at one standard deviation above and below the mean.

This data verifies our original belief that it is better to develop software in small groups than in large groups. Groups that are larger than seven are shown to pay a severe penalty in time and effort. Most projects seem to be of a size that can benefit from this finding. The average project size reported to us has been declining from about 80 KSLOC in the early 1980's to about 45 KSLOC in the 1990's. Those sizes are well within the range of the present study.

However, between 1997 and 2000, a marked increase in size occurred. The average project size doubled, as detailed in Appendix B. Software was entering new fields—Internet, e-commerce, Web development. There were few reusable components available. Entire systems had to be built from scratch, increasing the size reported to our database. As these new areas settle down, as reusable components become available, and as new tools facilitate the work, we expect that the reduction in size of individual projects will resume.

Still, we occasionally hear about very large projects, usually when they fail. We agree that projects of such magnitude cannot be done by a team of seven. In fact, a project of 50 or 250 people would run right off our diagrams! How do we address these?

Our immediate answer is simple. Huge projects have to be split into little projects that little teams can handle. Doing that, of course, introduces a new problem. How do you make little projects out of a big one? Some stakeholders seem to know how to do it, because some very big jobs have been accomplished. The answer lies in the suggestions we have been making, at first, in Chapter 3:

- Devise an architecture that will last through a series of releases. (Refer also to Chapter 10.)
- Divide a long-duration project into a series of relatively short releases.
- Employ reusable components, thus reducing the effective size of the product. (Chapter 20 is devoted to reuse.)
- Establish solid interfaces between subsystems, making it possible to treat each subsystem as an independent project. (Solid interfaces are one of the essentials for effective reuse; see Chapter 20.)

Selecting the Software Relationship

Thus far, in this book, we have limited ourselves to the software relationships between functionality (size), quality (reliability or defects), time (schedule), effort (cost), and productivity (process), as set forth in the QSM software equation. Let us call this relationship the *first* estimating methodology, since it came first in this book. However, a number of vendors provide estimating methodologies based on these same core metrics. Some of these products are based essentially on a second concept. We will call this concept the *second* estimating methodology. We apply three tests to the software relationship: There must be one; it must be reasonably accurate; and management must use it.

There Must Be a Relationship

The first methodology provides a multiplicative relationship between effort and time, as discussed earlier in this chapter:

$$(\text{Effort}/\beta)^{(1/3)} \times \text{Time}^{(4/3)} = \text{Size (at Quality Level)} / \text{Process Productivity}$$

With this relationship, it is clear that effort and time affect each other. In an estimating situation, the factors on the right-hand side are "given," that is, known or predetermined (though size may not be precisely known at the time of estimating). Therefore, $(\text{Effort}/\beta)^{(1/3)} \times \text{Time}^{(4/3)}$ is equal to a constant. It follows, then, that if estimators seek a faster schedule, that is, less time, they must plan more effort. If they seek to reduce effort and its costs, they must allow a longer schedule, as we detailed in the first part of this chapter.

The second estimating methodology, on the other hand, estimates effort with *one equation* and time with a *second equation*:

$$\text{Effort} = \text{Constant} \times (\text{Size})^{\text{SmallPower} > 1}$$

$$\text{Time} = \text{Constant} \times \text{Cube Root of Effort}$$

The "small power" is usually slightly more than one. This small power allows for the effect of size on the effort required. The outcome of this first equation is the *nominal* effort. Time (in the schedule sense) is then derived from effort by taking its cube root. Taking the cube root greatly reduces the impact that the amount of effort has on the time schedule.

As stated above in its nominal form, the first equation does not take into consideration the differing levels of capability or productivity that software organizations provide—except to the extent that capability or productivity may be subsumed into the constant. Even so, one constant does not fit all cases.

This limitation is overcome by multiplying the nominal effort by *effort multipliers*. The summation of these effort multipliers is assigned a value of 1.0 in the nominal case; in other words, they have no effect at that level. An effort multiplier that is judged to increase the capability of the organization is given a value *less than* 1.0; values less than 1.0 reduce the nominal effort. To reflect a reduced capability, an effort multiplier is set to a value *greater than* 1.0, resulting in increased effort. Managers and experienced software people establish the value of the individual effort multipliers as a matter of judgment.

Note that there is a marked difference in the way the relation between time and effort is handled in the first methodology (both in the same equation) and in the second methodology (each in a separate equation). In the same-equation methodology, the relationship is *multiplicative.* When planners reduce one, the other increases. In the two-equation methodology, the relationship is the opposite. When planners reduce effort (by appropriate selection of effort multipliers), the second equation also reduces time (though by only a small amount—the cube root). Contrariwise, when planners increase effort, time also increases. Thus, it is evident that these two methodologies represent the reality of software development in two different ways. Nevertheless, both methodologies agree on one point: There is a software relationship among these core metrics.

The Relationship Must Be Reasonably Accurate

The software industry needs an accurate estimate and bid for all sorts of business and commercial reasons. It also needs accuracy in order to estimate and obtain project schedules and staffing levels that maintain staff motivation over career-length time periods. It is unlikely that the second methodology—two successive equations—correctly represents the reality of software development for two reasons. First, as a matter of common sense, the application of more effort, within reason, shortens the schedule time, not lengthens it. Second, our examination of the core metrics from thousands of systems, from a broad range of companies, has verified this commonsense observation.

Even though the software relationship itself is reasonably accurate, estimating methodologies operate in the presence of two major sources of inaccuracy:

- The size estimate may vary from what at the time of delivery turns out to be the true size, for the many reasons discussed in Chapter 6.
- The productivity value may be uncertain. The process productivity employed by the first methodology (one equation), being derived from the core metrics of recent projects, is as accurate as the metrics are. The effort multipliers employed by the second methodology (two equations) to reflect organization capability, being based on managerial judgment, are inaccurate to the extent that judgments are flawed.

The software industry may reduce the error in the size estimate by refraining from making it until the proposed product is defined and architected. As we noted in Chapters 9 and 10, that takes understanding on the part of the client. It may mean going so far as to finance this preliminary work on a research basis. It is only common sense to note that, until you know with some precision what you are going to do, you can't know how long it will take or how much effort it will cost.

The industry may improve the accuracy of the organization-capability factor by moving to process productivity, based on the core metrics of completed projects, instead of effort multipliers based on managerial judgment.

Moreover, there is a difference in the way the two estimating methodologies represent the relationship between the core metrics. Figure 11-11 shows the relationship between effort and time in the first methodology, the one in which effort and time are in the same equation. The expected values of the effort and time pairs lie on the solid curved line. Planners select the pair that best meets the circumstances they face, as explained earlier in this chapter. Note that the line curves down to the right. As planners plan more schedule time, effort declines. The dashed lines enclose the range within which the effort-time pairs may fall as a result of the uncertainty of the size and process productivity inputs.

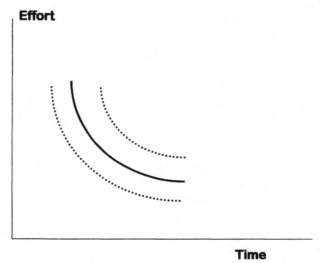

Figure 11-11:   *Two key points underlie the first estimating methodology: (1) the relationship between effort and time is multiplicative; (2) effort-time operating points fall in pairs on the solid curved line (or between the dashed lines if we allow for the uncertain values of the size and process productivity inputs to the methodology).*

In contrast, Figure 11-12 depicts the comparable relationships under the second methodology, the one in which effort appears in the first equation and time in the second equation. The first equation, which finds effort, establishes that effort lies somewhere along line (1), since time has not yet been established. Again, the dashed lines represent the uncertainty band resulting from the uncertain values of size and effort multipliers. Application of the second equation then determines time, represented by the single vertical line. Since there are no uncertain values in the time equation, this vertical line is not banded by dashed lines.

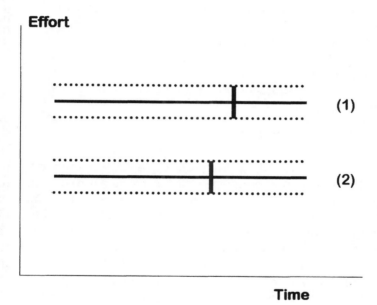

Figure 11-12: *The key result of the second estimating method-ology is that effort and time move in tandem. If planners set less effort, time shortens. If a client allows more effort, schedule time grows, assuming that the planners continue to use the same values for the effort multipliers.*

Now, in the situation represented by line (2), we assume that the client, management, or marketing sets an arbitrarily lower value of the effort estimate of this same project. (The value of line [2] is less than the value of line [1] on the effort axis.) The corresponding value of time moves slightly to the left—slightly because of the effect of the cube root in the second equation of this methodology. As the figure shows, a decline in effort is accompanied by a decline in time. This decrease in both effort and time is the opposite of what occurs using the first methodology. Contrariwise, if someone in a burst of good will increases the effort allowance, the time value moves in the opposite direction, slightly to the right, an increase. Again, this movement of time in relation to effort is the opposite of the one produced by the first estimating methodology.

Of course, there always remains at least a minimum amount of imprecision in any plan or estimate prepared in advance. In a fundamental sense, there are only two ways to cope with this remaining imprecision:

1. The client can set aside a reserve, assuming that the price initially bid is likely to be low and that the price will have to be supplemented out of this reserve, later.
2. The development organization can bid a little high, increasing its probability of successful completion within the bid values of time and effort, as discussed in Chapter 12.

Management Must Use the Relationship

Even with more than a half-century of software development behind us, many software organizations are still not using estimating methodologies. Many are not keeping records of the core metrics that would permit them to use these relationships. The fault for these failures lies not so much in ignorance as in competitive pressures. Software management feels the pressure from its own marketing management or directly from its clients to deliver in an unrealistically short time— unrealistic by the standards of the estimating methodologies, yes, but also unrealistic by the actual experience of projects committed to management's guesses on time and effort.

Time and again, software managers feel forced to commit to time and effort bids that they believe to be inadequate, even though they lack the more precise knowledge provided by formal estimating methods. Then, because the schedule is short or the bid is low, the client grabs it and the job descends on the apprehensive software managers.

There is only one way out for the harried project manager. He or she has to compress time and reduce the cost of effort to what the bid provides. Typically, a project manager tries to compress time by cramming more work hours into the schedule period, as suggested in Figure 11-13. For instance, there are about 2,000 hours in a standard work year of 40-hour weeks. However, there are about 4,000 hours in that same year for people working 80-hour weeks! The project manager can cram two years of effort into one calendar year—and be a hero and get stock options! Moreover, if he or she pays these developers only the 40-hour stipend (plus the cost of an occasional beer bust), the manager holds costs within the parameters of the contract. (That's the standard the accountants use: Salaried employees—in certain categories in the United States—are exempt from the law requiring pay for overtime. Moreover, the overtime hours actually worked are not formally recorded.)

Yes, the 80-hour week is a bit of an exaggeration. On that regime, people would get so tired before the year had closed that the whole plot would collapse. But 50- or 60-hour weeks are physically possible. Nevertheless, in time, these hours erode motivation. That seems to be where the unplanned part of the software industry is today.

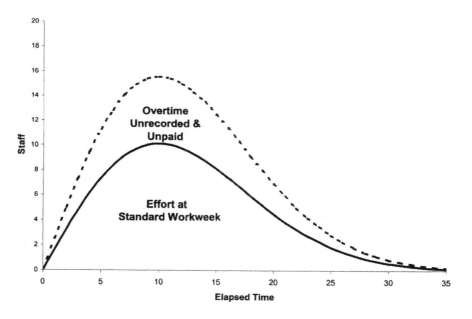

Figure 11-13: *Managers sometimes succeed in packing extra effort into the same time span through the overuse of unpaid overtime, often unrecorded. The practice, carried to excess, may encounter twin dangers. First, staff members get tired and discouraged and drift away, imperiling the later stages of the project. Second, no one really has a metric for the effective hours actually worked on the project, throwing future estimating procedures into disarray.*

The Bid Is Different from the Estimate

As we observed in Part II, software estimating starts with the size (functionality) of the product and the process productivity of the project organization. The organization's productivity is derived, preferably, from experience on past projects. The size estimate comes from what the team learns about the project during the Elaboration Phase. To make a realistic estimate, the team has to pursue the phase to the point where it has a good grasp of the amount of functionality to be implemented in the Construction Phase.

Even at the end of Phase Two, though, this grasp is less than complete. Functionality is not fully known; size will be uncertain until the product is delivered. Moreover, process productivity, though derived from past experience, is still uncertain to some degree. The next project team and the problems it encounters will not be exactly the same as the previous projects from which process productivity was calibrated.

If these two inputs to the estimating formula are uncertain, it follows that the schedule and effort outputs will also be uncertain. That is, the best we can do is say that the estimates of time and effort will fall within a range. They do not come out on a point. We can employ statistical methods that enable software estimators to determine what this range is. Still, even if we can estimate rather handily what this range will be, clients expect the bid to rest on a point. We have to bid a single number.

On top of that expectation, there is one more complication. Clients expect software organizations to bid long before they have enough information and have reduced the risks to known levels. In other words, they expect a bid before the team completes Phase Two. At this stage, the size estimate is still wider than it would be at the end of Phase Two, as Figure 6-2 showed. So, bids are often unrealistic, and clients and software organizations get into trouble in the Construction Phase.

That brings us face-to-face with a new issue. If the inputs are uncertain (as, indeed, they are), then the outputs—the estimated values of time and effort on which the price bid is based—will be uncertain, to a comparable degree. Yet clients want a point bid. How can we buffer our estimating and bidding method to avoid this trap? That is the question we take up in the next chapter.

Chapter 12
Turning Your Range Estimate Into Your Client's Point Bid

At the end of Chapter 10, we had an estimate of functionality expressed in some measure of size. Actually, this estimate was not a single number; it covered a range of possible sizes. We also had an estimate of process productivity. Again, this estimate covered a range. From these two uncertain values, plus all the uncertainties of a development situation in general, clients expect us to bid a single number. In this chapter, we look at the effect these uncertainties have on the business bid:

- The single time-effort curve depicted in Figure 11-1, between the Impossible and Impractical regions, is in reality supplemented by a series of curves parallel to it, as shown by figures later in this chapter.
- The constraints that a business faces usually restrict its bid to a portion of the Practical Trade-Off Region.
- The client's desired single-point time estimate and single-point effort estimate are, in reality, a range of possible time-effort points.
- This range of time-effort points provides a means for managing bidding risk.

These four effects may impress you as being a bit cryptic. Indeed, they are. It will take the rest of this chapter to decrypt them. No one ever promised you that getting to bidding heaven would be easy. Press on!

The Uncertainty Drivers

The input values that drive estimating uncertainty are size and process productivity, as diagrammed in Figure 12-1. The most likely value is the mean line, but the range of values is suggested by the curves. The height of each point on a curve is proportional to the corresponding value's frequency of occurrence.

Uncertainty Drivers

Size   Process Productivity   Staff Buildup Rate

Figure 12-1:   *In addition to size and process productivity, we employ a third input metric, the software organization's historic rate of staff buildup on projects. The degree of uncertainty of each estimating input is symbolized by the curve around the central, mean line. Size is usually the most uncertain of the inputs, since the other two are calibrated from completed project data.*

In addition to these two inputs, there is a third, as shown: staff buildup rate. It, too, is a function of effort and time:

$$\text{Effort/Time}^3 = \text{Staff Buildup Rate}$$

This rate refers to the buildup of staff during the early part of the Construction Phase. It is calibrated from completed projects for which effort and time are known quantities. When estimating a new project, then, staff buildup rate is a known quantity. (The use of this equation is not relevant to the explanations in this chapter. However, it is used in the detailed calculations: Since effort and time are two "unknowns," we need two equations to solve for them.)

The Time-Effort Curve Is Uncertain

Because the size and process productivity estimates that locate the time-effort curve are uncertain, the location of the curve itself is also uncertain, as illustrated in Figure 12-2. The degree of uncertainty is suggested by the dashed lines that run parallel to the curve. Statistically, these lines are set one standard deviation plus and minus the mean line. The normal curve of the statistics discipline straddling the mean line suggests the likely distribution of time-effort curves about the mean curve.

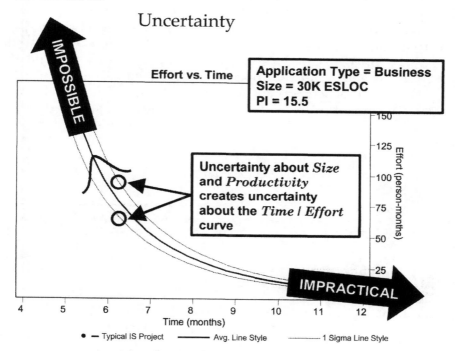

Figure 12-2:   *When an estimator selects a time-effort operating point in the Practical Trade-Off Region, it may actually fall somewhere above or below the solid curve, as suggested by the circles, since the location of this curve is itself uncertain.*

Estimators Face Constraints

The business situation often constrains the freedom of estimators to pick locations in the Practical Trade-Off Region. For example, they may face a target date by which the hardware portion of a real-time system is expected to be ready. They may be asked to have software ready for a conference demonstration date. In space science, the planet conjunctions may determine a lift-off date.

The number of developers expected to be available from other projects may also set a limit on how much effort the estimators can expect to have available for the new project. Difficulties in acquiring developers in a tight personnel market may limit the effort available for the new project.

Figure 12-3 illustrates the effect that these business constraints have on the operating point. In this case, the operating point is restricted to the small stretch of the effort-time curve between the Time Constraint and the Effort Constraint blocks. These constraints are in turn constrained by the location of the Impossible Region and the Impractical Region. Thus, the operating point is initially constrained to fall within the Practical Trade-Off Region between the Impossible and Impractical regions. In this case, it is further constrained to fall between the limits imposed by the business constraints on time and effort.

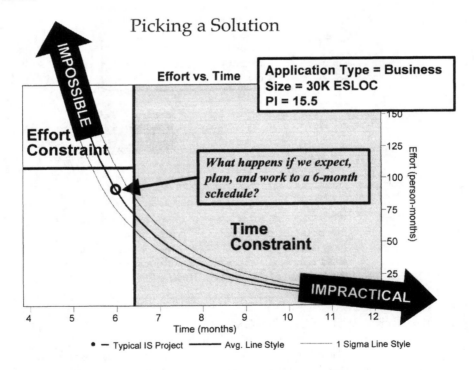

Figure 12-3:   *When the business situation dictates a time or an effort constraint on the selection of the time-effort operating point, estimators face a restricted Practical Trade-Off Region. If the time constraint is rather severe, as in this diagram, effort, and consequently cost, is driven up.*

The estimators picked the six-month operating point on the mean curve, midway between the two business constraints. Because of the uncertainties, however, the actual operating point may deviate from this six-month point within a range represented by the dotted lines. Figure 12-4 projects these two uncertainties to the time and effort axes.

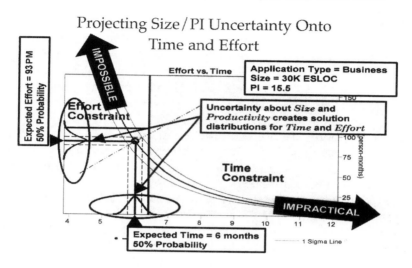

Figure 12-4:   *It is quite likely, statistically speaking, that developers can complete this project within the time and effort constraints imposed upon them.*

There is a 50-percent probability that the schedule, when realized, will meet this six-month target. Then, on the vertical axis, there is a 50-percent probability that the effort will be 93 person-months. However, note that the statistical normal curves do extend slightly into the constraint regions. That means there is a small probability that the project will overrun one of the constraints. In fact, if the statistical curve is a *normal* curve, the probability is 90 percent that the developers will complete the project in less than the 6.4 months set by the time constraint. Similarly, the probability is 80 percent that they will finish within the 110 person-month effort constraint. In the world of software development, there are few certainties, and those are pretty good odds. Chances are, the estimators will go with the six-month schedule.

Manage Estimating Risk

The time-effort trade-off at which we elect to bid is a point, not a range. At this point (on the solid-line time-effort curve), the probability of completing the project within the bid is statistically even—50-50. The uncertainty that we are up against in bidding derives from the inevitable uncertainty of the size and process productivity values with which we begin. We could reduce this bidding uncertainty if we could

- wait until we knew enough to narrow our size estimate or, failing that,
- bid a range of effort and time, or
- bid a single figure, plus and minus a range, or
- reserve the right to re-bid periodically as we refine the size estimate and as we find out from actual measurements what our process productivity on this project is going to be.

Alas, those options are not the practice in business, industry, and government. All want point bids. Moreover, they usually want the bid before we are far enough along in the preliminary phases to have good information on which to base it.

That brings us face-to-face with the issue. If the inputs are uncertain (as indeed they are), then the outputs—the estimated values of time and effort on which the price bid is based—will be uncertain to a comparable degree. Yet clients want a point bid. How can we buffer our estimating and bidding process to avoid this trap? Fortunately, there are statistical mechanisms that enable us to buffer the bid to reduce our risk or to "buy in" the job, as our business situation dictates.

Get Out of the Uncertainty Trap

The methods of probability, statistics, and simulation provide a way out of this trap. The personal computer provides the computational means for applying these methods. All the estimator needs to appreciate is the general idea, which we present next. A software program handles the details.

If we were satisfied that we had three firm, single-point input values (for size, productivity, and staff buildup rate), we could solve for the two unknowns, time and effort, *once* and get *one* set of answers.

Ah, but we don't have single-point inputs. Because of what we've described as the inherent uncertainties in the input values, we have a range of input values distributed in accordance with a frequency curve (such as the statistical normal curves on the foregoing figures). We want to solve the problem in such a way that we take into account these inherent uncertainties in input values and map them through the computations to a good approximation of the uncertainties in the output values we are seeking.

To do this, we apply the technique of Monte Carlo simulation. This technique does not solve the equations just once; it solves them many times. Each solution employs input values sampled from somewhere along the frequency curves over which the input values range; the inputs are taken in proportion to the frequency of their occurrence. That is, many samples are taken from the midpoint of the curves, where the frequency of occurrence is high; few are taken from the outskirts. Computations based on these frequencies produce a range of answers that are themselves distributed as similar frequency curves.

Thus, each of a thousand solutions could be visualized as a dot around an operating point like the one in Figure 12-4. The cloud of black dots would represent the whole range of possible solutions that could occur in practice. The dots would be most dense right around the operating point, indicating a high frequency of occurrence at that point. The dot density thins out toward the periphery of the cloud, as the frequency of occurrence declines.

In turn, the software program projects this cloud of dots downward to the schedule axis and to the left onto the effort axis. In Figure 12-4, the frequency distribution of the dots is represented by the normal curves.

The result is a distribution pattern on the two axes, showing how schedule and effort values are likely to occur. Obtaining this distribution pattern is highly significant. Without this approach, we really have no good feel for the magnitude of the variation of schedule and effort. Now, though, we have a probability distribution centered around the expected values (the peak of the statistical curves) for schedule and effort. We can use these probability distributions to buffer the risks that result from the uncertainties of our size and process productivity estimates.

The most likely values of schedule and effort are located at the center lines of the probability curves shown on the two axes. The probability of achieving this most likely value, called the expected value, is 50 percent. The least likely values are at the extremes of the frequency curves. If we know the nature of the frequency curve, we can predict the probability of any given value's occurrence. The frequency distribution of the normal probability curve, for instance, is well established. The normal curve is representative of the distribution of many human-influenced variables, and we make use of it in these computations.

Work with Uncertainty, Not in Defiance of It

The sad fact of life in development circles is that the uncertainties represented in Figure 12-4 hem in everybody concerned. You have a project of a given size that you are trying to estimate (though you could cut back its requirements and reduce its size). You also have a known productivity level (mostly fixed in the short term, although you can improve it over a period of years).

Though these levels are given or known, they also have an inherent uncertainty. We know at the end of the Functional Design Phase approximately what size the product will be, but we won't know for sure until it is built. Likewise, the process productivity will vary because this project will be different in complexity from prior projects, it will have some different team members, different tools, and so on.

Accordingly, the ranges of effort and schedule you can expect to achieve are symbolized by the bell curves on the figure. They represent the realistic variation built into our answers to the estimating problem. So, how can we intelligently buffer the bidding risk?

The basic idea is to use the probability curves to let us back off from the planned schedule far enough to provide the risk protection we need. Our work plan must always be located on the time-effort trade-off line. It must always be the most likely outcome, at 50-50 odds. However, we may not want to quote these 50-50 values of time and effort to the customer because there is only a 50-percent chance of making them. Rather, we want to quote a longer schedule, based on the probability curve we have generated. That quote gives us the buffer we need to obtain the level of protection desired.

Let's say we want a 90-percent assurance of not exceeding the six-month schedule the customer desires for putting a new system into operation. Our approach is to test possible operating points by figuratively sliding an imaginary bead along the time-effort curve to the right, until we reach the 90-percent point on the schedule probability curve, as shown in Figure 12-5. Now, 90 percent of the schedule probability curve is to the left of the six-month mark on the schedule axis. The six-month point on the schedule has now moved over to this location, labeled Constraint / Desired Probability on the figure. The center line of the normal curve, labeled Expected Outcome / 50% Probability, now is located at 5.5 months.

The next step is to develop a plan to work the job on a 5.5-month schedule. That may call for assigning more people, or other resources, to the project than the six-month plan would have required. However, we have only a 50-percent probability of completing the project in 5.5

months (that is what planning at the 50-percent point means). So, when we get to 5.5 months, we may have completed the project (50-percent chance) or we may not (also 50-percent chance). By planning in this way, however, we still have 0.5 months before we reach the customer's requirement, six months. We continue to work. We have a good chance (90 percent) of completing the project by the customer's date. The risk buffer of 0.5 months guards against the unknown contingencies that can (and to some extent will) occur on the 5.5 month plan. The risk buffer provides a period in which to recover from unexpected problems before the customer's due date.

Figure 12-5:   *The customer wanted a firm commitment to deliver at the constrained value on the schedule axis (in this case, 6.0 months). By planning to operate the project on a 5.5-month schedule, the software organization secured a 90-percent probability of meeting the customer's request.*

On the other hand, a customer may insist on a more rapid delivery, say, 5.0 months. If you accede to this schedule, you are, in effect, agreeing to move your operating point to the left. You are reducing your probability of delivering on time to 20 or 30 percent. Of course, software organizations that lack this analysis framework get themselves into overly short commitments like this one all the time.

Like it or not, a software organization operates under the constraints of this pattern. It can play safe by bidding a little longer time (while still planning to operate at the earlier 50-50 point). Or it can play risky by bidding less than the 50-50 time. Safe or risky—that is a business decision. But marketing or management executives who choose risky need to be mindful that the chance of pulling it off drops to 20 or 30 percent on that schedule.

A quote set to a high probability of success buffers the project against the inherent uncertainties of software development. A quote set to a low probability point—a low bid—may get the job, but it is very likely to run into a schedule overrun, a loss, or both.

Monte Carlo simulation allows us to select the points on the probability curves (on the two axes) that enable us to accomplish two goals. The first is to select the right operating point (always on the solid-line time-effort curve) for the situation we face. The second is to obtain the risk assurance protection we need and to quote the corresponding time, effort, and cost to the customer. However, we have to work to the 50-50 plan (corresponding to the operating point on the time-effort curve) to obtain the level of risk buffering that we want.

If you have followed the pattern of planning described in this chapter, we applaud your persistence. Knowledge work is admittedly complex, and planning it can get pretty hairy. Just remember, risk protection is doable—and a software program can do most of the work. Thinking it through pays dividends.

Chapter 13
The Main Build Leads to Operational Capability

The Main Build Phase produces a software system that's ready for release to the operational environment. The product is intended to satisfy the requirements and to provide quality and reliability appropriate to the application. After the development organization commits to the financial and schedule arrangements by which the phase is to be governed, the phase begins with the assignment of the initial staff.

There is usually a delay between the submission of the bid and the final award of the contract (or the internal go-ahead, in the case of in-house development). That delay, in itself, may introduce some deviations from the plan on which the bid was based. For example, some of the staff that worked on the Functional Design Phase may have become attached to other projects during that interval. Replacement people will have a learning curve to mount, possibly lengthening the planned schedule or increasing the effort.

Ideally, the Main Build does not begin until the Functional Design team has carried that phase to its logical conclusion:

- Identify the requirements needed to define the product.
- Specify the core requirements needed to block out the architecture.
- Prototype an architectural baseline.
- Discover the critical and significant risks and plan ways to mitigate them.

- Block out the functionality to be created, to the degree that supports an estimate of size and, hence, a reasonably accurate estimate of schedule and effort.

If circumstances permit the Functional Design team to carry that phase to this level, the development organization has the ingredients enabling it to set up a Main Build that runs smoothly, stays on schedule, and completes on time and within budget.

Unfortunately, in many situations, the software organization has been forced to bid before getting that far, so the schedule and effort contained in the bid award may be insufficient. In such a case, some of the work assigned to Functional Design has to be carried out, instead, in the early part of the Main Build. The project may not be able to lay out the plans that should control this phase until it completes this preliminary work. Under these circumstances, we expect the Main Build to run less smoothly.

Attempting to write code prematurely is counterproductive. Doing so may be all right on small programs that you can get your arms—and your head—around, but it is not all right on big programs. Here, the ages-long experience of the traditional engineering disciplines tells us there is a process to go through:

- Figure out what the system is to do.
- Analyze what that means in the technical field where the system is to operate.
- Lay out the functional design or architecture.
- Carry this high-level design into detailed design.
- Review or inspect each step along the way.
- Develop the test plan, beginning from an early point.
- And only now, finally, write some serious code.

You will probably need to write some prototype code along the way—to establish that a new algorithm actually works, for instance—but you don't sit down to write the final code until you know what you are supposed to do. Programming, in the sense of writing code, is only 10 or 20 percent of software development. So, just where you begin the Main Build depends on how far you were able to carry the Functional Design Phase.

Next, to control the progress of a project through the Main Build, you must have the ability to chart the progress you expect. First, you need to allocate the total effort over the project's duration. That is the first of the core metrics to control. Second, you project the occurrence rate of two other core metrics, size and defects. Then you compare actual progress on each metric against the planned progress.

Staff Allocation

As a result of our estimating activities in Phase Two, we have an estimate of the schedule length and the total person-months of effort needed. In most cases, we will not at this point have carried staff planning to the level represented by PERT diagrams. Nevertheless, with these overall estimates of time and effort, we now have to spread these person-months over the schedule.

Figure 13-1 illustrates how effort was expended over all four phases of an actual project. The number of staff (represented by the stepwise line) increases during the first part of a project, reaches a peak, and then declines. The area under the stepwise line is equal to the total effort.

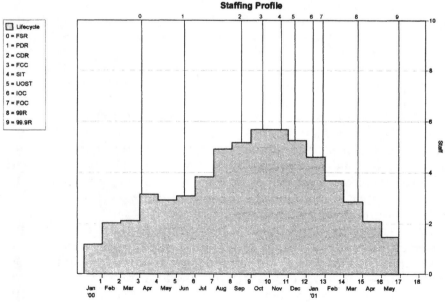

Figure 13-1:   *The up-down pattern of the four phases is characteristic of development projects. The numbered vertical lines represent review points identified by the abbreviations in the left-hand box, which stand for: Feasibility Study Review, Preliminary Design Review, Critical Design Review, First Code Complete, Systems Integration Test, User-Oriented System Test, Initial Operating Capability, Full Operational Capability, 99% Reliability, 99.9% Reliability. Their type and location vary in different organizations.*

"Some *portion* of the needed work on some elements cannot be begun unless some other *portion* of the work on some other element has previously been completed," Peter V. Norden of IBM's Poughkeepsie Development Laboratory wrote after studying several score development projects. "There are regular patterns of manpower buildup and phase-out in complex projects."[1]

"The number of people working in the group at any given time is approximately proportional to the number of problems 'ripe' for solution at that time," he observed.

At first, in Phase One, few problems are "ripe," and few people are usable in this phase. Later, in the Main Build Phase, as the initial work makes still more work available, the expanding work volume effectively utilizes more and more staff members. The number of people reaches a peak. Then, as the project winds down, the staff number declines. The staff "curve" in Figure 13-1, based on an actual project, is a bit uneven. One can readily imagine, however, that when diagrammed, the mean of many staff curves would be smoother. The smooth curve can be represented algebraically by the Rayleigh function, enabling a computer program to calculate the value of points along the curve. The mathematical details behind the curves reviewed in this chapter are available in our earlier book, *Measures for Excellence: Reliable Software on Time, Within Budget.*[2]

For now, the point is that it is possible, using the Rayleigh function, to project a curve of the staff needed by a project. More specifically, at the end of Phase Two, having estimated the overall amount of time and effort needed for Phase Three, we can project the staff curve for this phase, as diagrammed in Figure 13-2. Moreover, since the curve is backed by algebraic equations, a computer can readily calculate the number of staff and the amount of effort represented by each week or month along the time axis.

In recent years, other models have come to the fore under such names as incremental, rapid prototyping, rapid application development, spiral development, iterative design refinement, and frequent builds. These models are characterized by development within successive iterations, as suggested by Figure 13-3. Here, the Main Build embraced three increments before proceeding to completion. In the case on which this diagram is based, completing the requirements and high-level design pertinent to each increment stretched into the Main Build.

---

[1] Peter V. Norden, "Useful Tools for Project Management," *Operations Research in Research and Development* (New York: John Wiley & Sons, 1963), pp. 218, 221.

[2] Lawrence H. Putnam and Ware Myers, *Measures for Excellence: Reliable Software on Time, Within Budget* (Englewood Cliffs, N.J.: Prentice Hall, 1992).

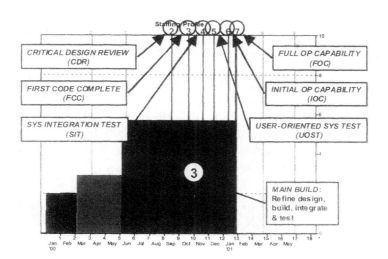

Figure 13-2: The Main Build, or Phase Three, is featured in this diagram, together with the series of reviews employed by many software organizations. This curve is representative of the traditional waterfall model of software development.

Tailoring Example: DoD Incremental

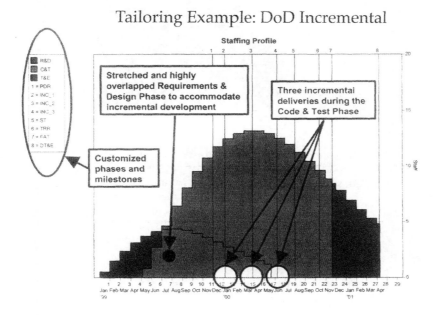

Figure 13-3: New development patterns divide the Main Build into iterations, each resulting in an increment of the product. The completion of each increment provides an occasion for review, indicated by vertical lines 2, 3, and 4.

Figure 13-4 illustrates another phase pattern that promises to become increasingly common as component-based development matures. In applications of this sort, there is little question of feasibility. Phase One is largely devoted to the evaluation of existing packages. Phase Two continues to be high-level design, influenced by the packages available to implement the architecture. Phase Three builds up rapidly because there is little detailed design and coding. However, more staff is planned for integration and system testing, late in the phase. At the current state-of-the-*component*-art, making the reused packages function together successfully still takes considerable effort.

Tailoring Example: Package/COTS

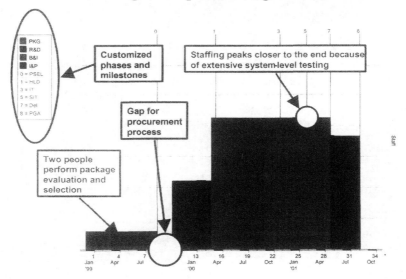

Figure 13-4:   *The phase pattern of a project employing commercial off-the-shelf software packages differs in several respects from traditional patterns: Much of the initial phase is devoted to the selection of packages that are suited to the architecture. The third phase tends to peak late, when the packages first start working together.*

As Norden observed, development projects approximately follow the Rayleigh curve's up-down pattern when staffed to meet the work requirements. However, there are exceptions to this pattern. One is the very small project, employing only two or three people. Management may assign this small staff to the project right away and extend it through all four phases. This pattern is called level loading.

Another exception is a project to which management assigns people in accordance with its own priorities, rather than the needs of the project itself. For example, management may have a surplus of available people (*Will wonders never cease!*), so it plows them into the first handy project, hoping they may do some good there—or at least learn something.

Moreover, as new technological approaches, such as component-based software engineering, come into use, new staffing patterns may become appropriate. Figure 13-4 displays such a new pattern.

As we shall see, later in this chapter, when we check actual measures of what is going on against projected measures, these additional people will show up as staff in excess of the control curve. The excess may do no great harm, but these people may be desperately needed later in the project, at the peak of the Rayleigh curve, when managers no longer have project funds to cover them. They spent too much, early in the project, on people the project did not need at that point.

Projecting Functionality

Forecasting effort is important. After all, effort gets the work done. Still, it is even more important to forecast some indication that the work is getting done. The result of effort being applied is the functionality of the product, as we discussed in Chapter 6. The tangible measure of that functionality is a metric expressing the product's size, such as source lines of code.

The second indicator of progress in achieving functionality is the series of reviews, such as those noted by the numbered vertical lines on the foregoing figures. The progress monitored by these reviews is less subject to counting, as noted in Chapter 8. For a projection of the progress in creating functionality, we turn to size.

Source lines of code is the metric used to project progress in code writing. Its great advantage over other measures of size is that computer programs can count it. Configuration managers can monitor the amount of code that's written and unit-tested during each time period. Function points, requirement statements, the number of use cases that have been coded, or other representations of functionality are more difficult to define and count.

The rate at which code is produced is proportional to the rate at which person-months of effort are spent on writing it. This proportionality rate is dependent on the process productivity of the software organization. Thus, given the projected effort curve and process productivity, a computer program can forecast the rate of source code production.

Different approaches to the development process have given rise to different points on the schedule for the commencement of coding. In the classic approach, represented by the waterfall model, serious coding was not intended to begin until after the critical design review (shown as CDR, line number 2, in Figure 13-2). After this review, design was supposed to be complete. Coding could begin with little fear that the effort would be wasted because the architects or designers would later find that the code did not fit the still-evolving architecture or design.

In iterative development, however, some prototype coding may begin as early as the first two phases. Generally, this early code does not survive unchanged into the Main Build. Planners should exclude it from the code projection.

Then, several iterations may be planned within the Main Build. Developers may write configuration-controlled code during an early iteration, before considering the detailed design of subsystems coming up in a later iteration. This way of working may result in code that becomes available for counting a little earlier than in traditional approaches.

The lines of code that have been unit-tested are the best countable indicator of project progress. However, it is not quite as good an indicator as it used to be, for at least two reasons. First, leading organizations are doing more requirements investigation, architecture development, risk abatement, analysis, and design up front. Completed code is coming later in the process, but it takes less time to produce; the problems have been worked out ahead of time.

Second, since component-based development reuses previously developed building blocks, there is less new code to count. Putting the components together and testing them takes time and effort that does not show up in a simple projection of the new code count, as we implied in Figure 13-4.

From the point of view of projecting a count on which to base project progress, the fact that configuration-controlled code is coming later in the development process means that we have less control early in the process, at least by this means, than we used to have. Developers are spending more time in the early stages. This is as it should be. But it also means that we have to put greater weight on setting up other criteria and considering whether they have been achieved at the review points.

Detecting Defects in Test

Projects often defer the detection of defects in code until integration tests, or even system test, begin, as depicted in Figure 13-5. The staffing projection, labeled People, comes first, with the area under the curve representing the metric, effort. The code-projection curve comes a little later with commission of coding errors taking place at about the same rate. Finally, in the absence of much review or inspection, testers find code defects mostly in integration and system testing, as shown on the figure.

That pattern of defect detection, delayed into the test period, is the result of putting too much emphasis on producing code for the sake of early code counts, even if that code is error-laden. Projection of an error-committal curve, discussed later in this chapter, focuses developer attention on earlier detection.

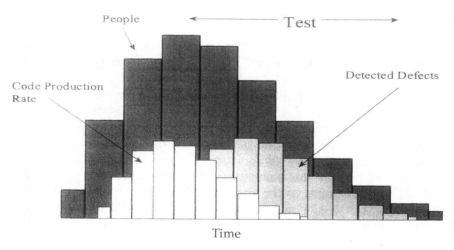

Figure 13-5:   *Greater emphasis on early inspections and reviews, iterative development, periodic builds, and so on can move the Detected Defects curve to earlier points in development (that is, to the left).*

Apply Statistical Control to the Core Metrics

The principle of statistical control of a process has been used in manufacturing since the early twentieth century. For example, a part has to be manufactured to a certain measurement, plus or minus a tolerance, in order to assemble smoothly with other parts into the next higher assembly. The part is satisfactory if it remains within the tolerance limits. If the deviations (within tolerance) are mostly clustered near the nominal dimension, the operator assumes that the process producing that part is operating satisfactorily. However, if the measurements begin to cluster near one of the tolerance limits, though the parts themselves are still usable, the process itself is evidently veering out of control. The operator needs to recheck the machine or the tooling. The tooling, for instance, may be wearing down.

Software development, of course, is far different from the manufacture of machined parts. Still, like manufacturing, it is producing something. That "something" has two measurable aspects. One of these aspects is the count of gross code, that is, the code with defects in it. The other is the count of detected defects, taken from valid trouble reports. Moreover, the defect count is proportional to the code count, for example, 5 percent.

By projecting the rate of code production and the rate of code defect occurrence, we can take the first steps toward statistical control. Those rates are comparable, for control purposes, to the measured dimension in manufacturing. The next step is to find what amount of variation from these rates we can expect. These variations are comparable to the tolerance in manufacturing.

In Chapter 12, we saw that effort and time estimates were uncertain because the size and process productivity values from which they are derived are themselves uncertain. Therefore, the projection of staffing and effort over the time period of the project will also be uncertain. There will be a most likely staffing line, paralleled by less likely staffing bands. Since the quantity of code produced and code defects incurred is proportional to the rate at which effort is applied, both the code rate and the defect rate are also uncertain. In addition, the code production rate and the defect rate are affected by other factors, such as the skill of the developers.

The result is a most likely rate of code production or defect occurrence, marked by the plan line in Figure 13-6. This line of most likely occurrence is paralleled by uncertainty bands, labeled Acceptable Variation on the figure. We set the width of the inner band that surrounds the most likely line so that it contains about two thirds of the actual measurements. Actuals that fall in this band are coming out close to what is expected.

Sample Control Chart

Object Construction Plan vs. Actual

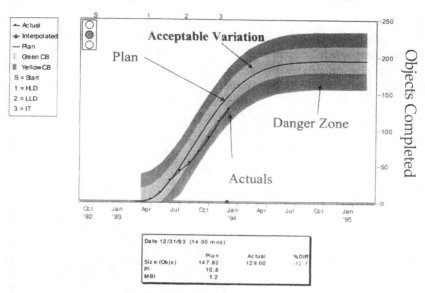

Date 12/31/93 (14.00 mos)			
	Plan	Actual	%Diff
Size (Objs)	147.82	129.00	-12.7
PI	10.8		
MBI	1.2		

Figure 13-6: *The development plan projects the code production rate or the code defect rate over the duration of the project, as shown by the solid line at the center of the two "tolerance" bands paralleling it. If measurements of what actually happens (black dots) lay close to the planned line, the project is in statistical control.*

The outer band is the danger zone. If actuals begin to turn up there (or, even worse, beyond it), the project is not proceeding as planned. Something is wrong. That something may be the plan itself. It may be turning out to be unrealistic. It might also be that the plan is not being followed. For instance, management may be unable to assign staff in the numbers planned. The third possibility is that the staff is running into problems that the plan did not anticipate.

The control chart does not tell you what is wrong, it tells you whether or not operations are proceeding according to plan. Because the actuals get posted every week or every month, the control chart tells you as you go along whether things are going well or badly. You still have the time (and the funding) to respond.

Track System Size

Figure 13-7 illustrates what happens when the early part of the Main Build has to be devoted to nailing down the requirements instead of producing any code. However, after the developers and the client cleared up the requirements, the developers quickly brought the amount of code produced to above the planned level. Thereafter, code production was close to plan. In a case like this one, we suspect that some sly planner built in a little extra time to straighten out those requirements!

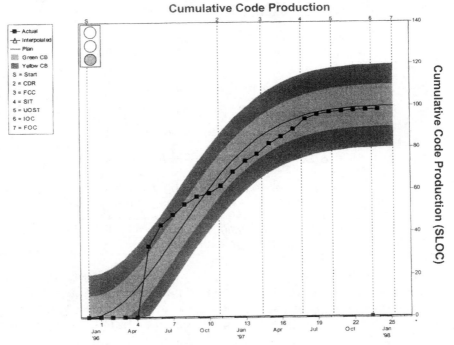

Figure 13-7:   *After some difficulties in the first five months, when no code was produced, the project swung into gear, overproducing code for the next three or four months. Thereafter, the size metric remained within control limits.*

The project diagrammed in Figure 13-8 also encountered serious mis-understandings getting started. It got down to business after the sixth month and proceeded happily for the next four months. A few months later, however, the client insisted on several major new requirements. Then the team discovered that the new requirements substantially reduced the amount of reuse included in its original plan.

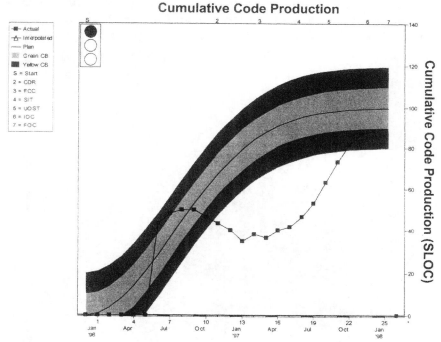

Figure 13-8:   *When a project runs into a lot of trouble, the siz-*
ing control chart may look like this one: trouble
getting started, trouble in the mid-period, and a
premature ending at the client's initiative. This
control chart clearly spells out trouble.

Team members had to replan some of the project and do a lot of it over. They had to throw some of the code away and redo it another way. As the control chart shows, code produced fell way below the old plan. The client actually terminated the project before the planned ending date by taking a scaled-down product—not what he originally wanted.

Unhappily, that was not the end of the story. A few months later, the client requested bids for the next phase of the program. The hap-less team lost that bid.

Track Defects

The defect-control diagram, shown in Figure 13-9, emphasizes that errors happen from the beginning of the project onward. They don't suddenly descend from a clear blue sky when we begin system test. (Of course, we all know that, but the curve keeps rubbing it in.)

Such a curve also shows the approximate number of errors to expect every week or every month as the software process proceeds. It gives us a target number of defects to find.

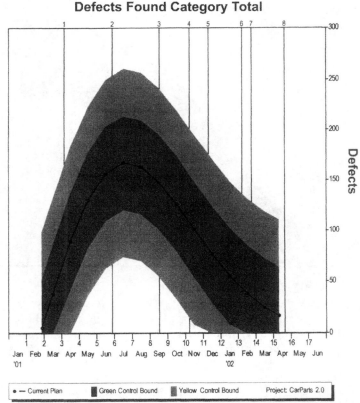

Figure 13-9: *The rate at which developers commit errors, plotted against project time, increases as we apply more staff to the project, reaches a peak when the work is in full swing, and then declines as the staff turns to testing. The solid line is the expected error rate; the parallel bands represent the range within which the counts ought to fall.*

The error-rate curve of Figure 13-9 follows essentially the same path as the staff or effort curves. The rate of committing errors is proportional to the rate of producing code. The smooth curve we depict, of course, is idealized. If managers followed the dictates of the work and built up staff gradually as work became available, both the staff curve and the error-rate curve would resemble the figure. In practice, however, managers have other pressures bearing upon them, such as their sheer inability to find appropriate staff at the time needed, and real staffing curves usually deviate from the idealized one. Consequently, the error-rate curve also departs from the smooth curve we show.

The point of importance, however, is that this curve does go up and down. Many organizations have recorded defect rates, and the fact that the pattern of occurrence follows a curve of this nature is well established. The area under the curve represents the total number of defects.

The particular curve we show is the well-known Rayleigh curve. Its trailing slope is similar to the declining exponential curve many software people have employed to represent the occurrence of faults during the system test period. Here, the Rayleigh curve enables us to plot the occurrence of defects during the earlier stages of software development. Having this curve staring project people in the face encourages them to do something about it.

Given such a figure, or the corresponding table of data, developers can employ the principle of statistical control. They can post the rate at which defects are found, as shown in Figure 13-10. So long as the find rate is within the parallel bands, development is going as expected. We are making the expected number of errors, and we are finding them.

The solid line in these two figures is a projection of the average rate at which errors are committed each week. In practice, of course, we don't actually know this rate. What we do know is the rate at which defects have been found in the past. It is that knowledge on which we base the error projection.

Defects would be found some time after the errors are committed. Hence, we might imagine a second curve a little to the right of the error-projection curve, representing the rate at which defects are discovered by self-checking, inspections, reviews, and tests. As we show in Figure 13-10, this second curve tends not to be smooth, but to zigzag up and down above and below the smooth line because of the way projects carry out the find-and-fix cycle. One month, especially during the test phase, people focus heavily on finding defects; the next month they spend fixing the defects they found and testing the fixes.

In the finding month, the discovery rate is high; in the next month, it is low, producing the up-and-down pattern we frequently see. In effect, the finding "curve" is far from the smooth curve of theory because of the many deviations from the ideal that beset real projects.

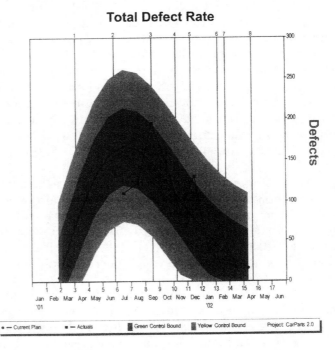

Total Defect Rate

Figure 13-10:   *Projects post to the defect-rate diagram the number of defects discovered each week. As long as the postings stay within the tolerance bands, the project is in "statistical control." The up-down pattern is typical of the find-and-fix cycle.*

Nevertheless, on this project, the developers are discovering defects within the tolerance limits set by the error-projection curve. In fact, all but two or three are within the control limits of the curve. The jagged line marked by little squares is the actual defect-discovery "curve." Managers can feel, quite correctly, that the reliability of the developing product is under statistical control when the actual defects are tracking within the control bounds.

Also, having a projected error rate provides a strong incentive to look for defects along the way. It is having this statistical control process that induces both managers and developers to provide time for inspections, reviews, and tests as they go along. It persuades managers that time spent this way is not wasted. It offsets the natural urge to just turn out more code—filled with defects as it would be without early checks.

Artifacts (including code) that have not been subjected to this kind of defect-correction process actually contain a large number of defects. The defects have not been found because they have not been looked for. Eventually, however, they turn up in system test. There, the failures bite us. The time it takes to find and fix this big pulse of defects at the last minute results in a schedule-killing scramble. Customers drum their fingers impatiently.

All of this sounds pretty good—project the error rate, find defects close to the time the errors are committed, and fix them right away. In fact, it is downright excellent.

The Essential Point: Control

We have to seek control because we are operating with a restricted amount of schedule and staff—because we are in this competitive economy. We have to check progress all through a project so that we can be in a position to take corrective action while we still have staff, time, and finances available.

Companies may find it useful to track additional metrics, but certainly everyone should track these three core ones. Don't overdo the number of metrics. Keeping track of them takes time, and this does take a little energy away from actual development. But the gains from using metrics to get early notice of developing problems will more than offset the cost of using them.

Let us again stress that control charts merely highlight the possibility that a problem lies behind the gap between the plan and the actuals. If there's a problem, the development team has to find it and do something about it. That battle often takes high skill and hard work. Control charts are part of your ammunition.

Chapter 14
The Operation and Maintenance Phase

My interest in planning and budgeting the Operation and Maintenance Phase goes way back to 1972, to my first tour of duty in the Washington headquarters of the Department of the Army.

—L.H.P., Introduction

Just what is the Operation and Maintenance Phase? A generation ago, the budget analysts in the Office of the Secretary of Defense had trouble understanding it. Isn't a software product finished when it reaches full operational capability? Sorry to say, no. A lot of work still remains. Sadly, this work is still poorly understood. "The software maintenance process is poorly characterized in general," a 1999 Department of Defense study concluded.[1]

The Unified Process terms this phase Transition in the sense of transitioning the software product into the user environment. The word Maintenance in the Operation and Maintenance Phase name has now become somewhat outmoded. Software maintenance continues for the life of a software product, but Phase Four ends after a finite time. In this chapter, we will show where the phase starts, what goes on in it, and where it ends. Our intent, however, is to focus on how to

---

[1]Elisabeth K. Bailey Clark et al., "Mission-Critical and Mission-Support Software: A Preliminary Maintenance Characterization," *Crosstalk* (June 1999), p. 17.

estimate the effort and time the phase takes and the degree of reliability it can achieve.

Where Does Phase Four Begin?

The Operation and Maintenance Phase formally begins at full operational capability (line 7), as shown in Figure 14-1. This milestone is reached when a system meets its requirements to the degree that users are willing to employ it in everyday operation, in their own environment.

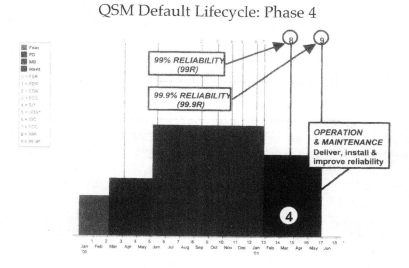

Figure 14-1:   *The Operation and Maintenance Phase (labeled 4) begins when users first employ the product in their own environment. Work in this phase consists of fixing defects found in operation, improving reliability, and making minor modifications to better meet users' needs.*

This willingness does not mean that the system is perfect. It may require tuning to meet some of its performance requirements. Users may find that the system doesn't quite satisfy the needs they experience in trying to operate it. There will still be residual defects. At this point, the code may still contain about 5 defects per 100 SLOC, also expressed as 95-percent reliability. This level of reliability (in the sense of absence of defects) seems to have been adequate for many applications. At least, they are getting along at that level. However, that may be less than some applications need.

Increasing reliability to 99 percent (1 defect per 100 SLOC) requires the commitment of additional time in Phase Four, amounting to about one quarter of the time spent in Phase Three, the Main Build. That point is represented by Milestone 8 on Figure 14-1.

Increasing reliability still further, to 99.9 percent (1 defect per 1,000 SLOC) requires another quarter of the time spent in Phase Three. This point occurs at Milestone 9 on the diagram. Both of these time estimates are rules of thumb derived by experience, subject to some variation in use. Note that we carry defect removal only out to 99.9 percent. Experience reveals that some few defects always remain to be disclosed, perhaps years later, by some very unusual combination of operational circumstances.

Moreover, there are differences between the Main Build developers' environment and the Phase Four users' environment. The computer system on which the software runs may be somewhat different. The staffs operating the system are different. In the latter part of Phase Three, the operating staff has been development people, sometimes with user people looking on. In Phase Four, operating responsibility transfers to user staff, with less depth of system knowledge. In addition, some of the users' established programs may not work quite right on the new system. All of these are problems to be worked out in this phase.

In some instances, Phase Four may begin closer to the previous milestone, Initial Operational Capability. IOC is the milestone at which users begin to use the system, under the control of the developers. It is not yet ready for routine, unsupervised use. Just where along this continuum a particular system enters Phase Four depends upon the understanding between the development organization and the user organization. It varies with how the two organizations define their own lifecycle phases and milestones. In the case of software vendors, Phase Four usually begins with the general release for sale. At that point, the product is not much better than the beta test-versions.

What Goes On in the Phase?

The overall intent of this phase is to bring the system up to the level that meets the users' needs. These needs have to be limited, of course, for business reasons, to what the software people can accomplish in the time and effort made available for this phase. What they can accomplish—what they can plan for—are four kinds of activities:

- finding and fixing defects remaining at the beginning of the phase
- increasing the system's reliability
- adapting the system to the operational environment
- making minor modifications to meet needs that are discovered as users operate the system

In addition, the Phase Four staff may have to spend time considering modifications that turn out to require more time and effort than is available in this phase. Major modifications have to be set up on a separate time and effort budget and are usually held to a later release.

Find and Fix Defects

The inspection and test activities of the Main Build fall short of perfection, of course, and some defects remain undiscovered as a system enters Phase Four. In our experience, business systems or information technology systems often enter this phase with about 5 percent of the total defects still undetected. The more intensive employment of the system that users begin to provide naturally turns up some of the remaining defects. During this phase, the development organization is responsible for fixing them.

Most software vendors initiate beta testing toward the end of Phase Three, at the point labeled Milestone 6, Initial Operational Capability, in Figure 14-1. However, internal development testing continues. Beta users report their findings back to the development organization, and these reports serve as a guide for modifications and defect corrections.

Improve Reliability

Software systems for real-time and engineering applications, in particular, may not serve their intended function satisfactorily at the 95-percent reliability level. Developers may use Phase Four, not only to fix defects that happen to turn up in operation, but to take formal steps to improve reliability. Figure 14-1 shows that reliability improved to 99 percent at line 8 and to 99.9 percent at line 9. The Phase Four staff attains these levels by the conscious application of more intensive testing than the time available permitted in Phase Three. Alternatively, these tests may be carried out by a separate operational test and evaluation organization.

Adapt the System

The host environment in which the new system is to operate may not be identical to the one provided in the developer's facilities. For instance, incoming data may not arrive in the format or at the rate originally specified. Occasional spurts in the rate at which data arrives, not originally specified, may require the program to divert data in excess of what can be immediately processed to holding storage.

Again, we have to assume that the adaptations are minor, meaning that the Phase Four team can accommodate them within the time and effort planned for this phase. If the adaptations turn out to be major, taking time and effort beyond what Phase Four provides, the Phase Four team has to call for a new estimate of time and effort.

Modify the System

In the course of using the new system, users are apt to note features that do not quite implement the business processes as they now exist. It is difficult to specify at the often abstract stage of requirements capture exactly what will best suit real-life users several years later. Development of prototypes of new or unusual features and clearing them with representative users in the early phases can minimize this difficulty. At best, however, we can expect that *minor* modifications will be necessary.

A modification is minor if the Phase Four team can implement it within the existing architecture of the system, if the work involved appears to be no more complicated and time-consuming than fixing a serious defect, and if the team considers it doable within the limits of the time and effort available in this phase.

A generation ago, software people argued over whether maintenance took 50 percent or 70 percent of a system's budget. Many products entered into use before they were ready for day-to-day operation. Some systems were redesigned and rebuilt from the ground up in the name of maintenance! No wonder maintenance was so costly.

Today, no one wants to "bootleg" a substantially new system under the pretense of maintenance. That would be too costly. The Phase Four funds do not finance that much work. In the old days, systems were not the outcome of extensive requirements capture, architecture development, performance analysis, and software design—all of which have now become more common. Most systems begin routine operation in better shape than those developed then.

In the current generation, however, the technical and administrative world in which software systems operate is constantly changing.

Between the time when the requirements are firmed up and when the system enters Phase Four, there will be changes in the world in which the system is to operate. Consequently, there is still a need for system changes, but we have become accustomed to drawing some lines in the sand:

- Minor modifications are permissible in Phase Four. A minor modification is one that can be implemented within the time and effort allowances of this phase.
- Major modifications, proposing significant functional improvement, should be accumulated and accomplished within the framework of a new release, that is, a new estimate of time and effort. A modification, as the word is used here, reflects a change that fits within the existing system architecture. There may be cases, however, in which both parties want to accomplish a major modification right away, that is, within the time frame of Phase Four. In that case, they need to agree upon the time and effort budget required to support the work in that phase.
- Beyond modifications, we come to changes so extensive as to require a new architecture, a new generation of the product, and, of course, a new estimate.

When Does the Phase End?

Phase Four ends when the rate of finding defects declines to a low level, when reliability reaches a level appropriate to the application, and when the minor modifications have been completed. In practical terms, the phase ends when the software supplier, by agreement with the client, ends its commitment to the phase.

The point is that it does end. It does not stretch on endlessly, as it did in the old days. That is not to imply that the product is perfect and requires no further maintenance. It is to say that it has reached a level of adequacy at which the deep understanding of the development organization is no longer needed on a day-to-day basis.

There may well continue to be problems with the software. For instance, no software program of some size is ever wholly defect-free. To cope with these continuing problems, Phase Four may be succeeded by other arrangements:

- The development organization may agree to continue support service under a new arrangement.

- The user may embrace the system within its own software support organization.
- The user may contract with a third-party organization for support.
- The user may simply endure occasional further defects, as we all do with personal computer software, simply waiting for the next release to correct these defects.

In effect, by agreement between the software organization and the user organization, the phase ends. Further work involves a new agreement.

The development organization's "deep understanding" of the system often resides in the minds of the senior developers, who seldom carry over to these later arrangements. New people pick up the responsibility. They can work more effectively if the architecture and design of the system have been kept current in standardized artifacts or models that the support team can understand.

How to Estimate the Phase

At the end of Phase Two, we had an estimate of the size of the eventual system and a value for our own process productivity, based on our past projects. From these two figures, we estimated the time and effort for Phase Three and projected expectations over time for three of the core metrics: size, effort, and defects. As Figure 14-1 shows, these estimates can be extended to Phase Four.

The effort reached in this way declines during Phase Four, matching the drop in the workload as we expect to complete the remaining tasks. At this point, we want to avoid manning this phase at a constant level of effort. That approach can be wasteful. The excess people may do little. More likely, they will be utilized on major extensions of the system. Such extensions tend to escape the normal management controls that accompany the scoping and planning of a new project. "Bootlegging" extensions applies effort to needs felt at the project level that may be less urgent than those elsewhere in the larger organization.

Late in Phase Three, we know with greater precision both the system size and the process productivity being achieved on this project. We are in a position to make a more precise estimate of the time and effort Phase Four will take. Of course, many uncertainties are still present as a project begins Phase Four. One is the extent to which the tasks of Phase Three have actually been accomplished. The following questions are typical at the start of Phase Four:

- Have 95 percent of the defects actually been found and fixed?
- Is 95-percent reliability high enough for the circumstances this system faces?
- Does the product in its current state meet the users' needs, as we now understand them, or have we done a poor job of eliciting requirements or building the product to accommodate those we did specify?
- Will the product meet the performance levels the user actually needs in this operation, as opposed to performance requirements that may have been set forth in the earlier requirements without a clear knowledge of the actual needs?

Moreover, as projects enter Phase Four, they differ in terms of meeting performance and reliability requirements. Theoretically, system test at the end of Phase Three establishes that the system meets users' requirements, but system tests are not perfect. Systems may pass this test and still wind up with different amounts of work yet to be accomplished. To bring their applications to a higher state of reliability, the Department of Defense, the Federal Aviation Administration, the National Aeronautics and Space Administration, and other organizations turn to specialized Operational Test and Evaluation organizations.

These differences are influenced, to some extent, by the process productivity achieved on the project and by the pressures that an insufficient time allowance engenders. As we have seen, low levels of process productivity and schedules that are too short increase people's propensity to error. As we approach Phase Four, we have that information for this system. The latest versions of this information can influence the forecast that we make for Phase Four.

One of the objectives during the Operation and Maintenance Phase is to control the rate of expenditure of time and effort on the project. There is a temptation on the part of those directly at work on the phase to recognize a substantial need and to go about satisfying it immediately. Unfortunately, if what's needed to satisfy that need exceeds the resources planned for this phase, the software organization is caught in a dilemma. On the one hand, it may be unable to complete the agreed-upon work of the phase as planned. On the other hand, it may exceed the expenditures planned for the phase and run into a loss.

Let us reemphasize our conclusion: We confine Phase Four to defect correction, reliability enhancement, adaptation to the operational environment (as contrasted to the development environment), and response to very minor requirements changes resulting from users' operational experience. We estimate as a new project an enhancement of any magnitude, subjecting it to the controls that surround new projects.

Chapter 15
Replan Projects in Trouble

"All too often our software is predictable—predictably late, predictably too costly, and predictably rigid."
—Emmett Paige, Jr.
former Assistant Secretary of Defense for
Command, Control, Communications, and Intelligence[1]

That is a striking sentence, but usually the participants don't know their project is in this predictable trouble until late in the Main Build. At that point, we must ask, What can we do about it? Can the project be retrieved? Can it be replanned?

Before we consider these questions, however, let us look at how we got into this trouble. In Phase One, if we overlooked the critical risks, they will nip at us in the Main Build. In Phase Two, if we never bothered to find a workable architecture, we shouldn't be surprised that the components don't go together in the Main Build.

If we obtained a reasonable grip on the system's functionality and then turned that into a fair estimate of its size, we can make a decent estimate of the Main Build. If we turn that estimate into a low-risk bid, we can have the business underpinnings of a successful Main

---

[1]Emmett Paige, Jr., "Predictable Software: Order Out of Chaos," *Crosstalk* (June 1994), p. 2.

Build. But there is one more step: Our organization has to negotiate a price and schedule with the client.

Negotiate an award—this phrase suggests some to-and-fro exchanges. And to-and-fro-ing takes time. It is not unusual for several months to pass between the submission of a bid and the award of the contract or other go-ahead document. What are the members of the Feasibility and Functional Design team doing during this sometimes lengthy interval? They are being scattered among projects that desperately need their services. It is usually difficult to reassemble them when the start date looms. The fresh people then available to start the project face a steep learning curve. They get a slow start. The outcome is that the process productivity on which the original team based its estimate is not quite achieved.

To-and-fro-ing also results in a few (or many) changes between the bid and the award. The client probably insists on a new schedule— always shorter. It may even have good reasons for this schedule. Clients also feel the pressure of cost. In software development, that means: Try to do the job with fewer staff members, less effort. Unfortunately, clients are allergic to the idea that less functionality is the natural outcome of applying less effort over a shorter time.

Our negotiators, usually marketing and executive management, feel their own competitive pressures. They have to keep business coming into our organization. Besides, most of them have optimistic natures. "Maybe the software people can pull this chestnut out of the fire," they tell each other hopefully.

Schedule-driven projects result from these pressures. "A show of hands at a recent meeting indicated that only three of the seventy attendees were working with schedules on which they had some input," two consultants found.[2]

The Award Differs from the Original Estimate

As an outcome of these business pressures, our project may be in trouble when the award arrives, before we even begin the Main Build. Suppose our negotiators agreed to a tighter schedule at a lower price than we had urged upon them. Suppose they had not cut back on the system functionality. In project terms, we are supposed to do just as much work with fewer people in less time. (Doesn't sound too shrewd when it's put so bluntly.)

The first step we can take is to rethink the project plan. That rethinking can be more effective if we base it on sound theory. Sound theory says that we can trade off time and effort, as we outlined in

[2]Donna L. Johnson and Judith G. Brodman, "Applying CMM Project Planning Practices to Diverse Environments," *IEEE Software* (July/August 2000), p. 45.

Chapter 11. But theory also says we can't reduce both at the same time unless we reduce the size of the product or increase the process productivity of the project organization. Unfortunately, our negotiators did not reduce the functionality to be delivered, so the size remains the same. And we have been trying to improve process productivity all along, but it goes slowly.

Nevertheless, let's take a second look at process productivity. There is not much chance of greatly improving our methodology in the short span of a single project, but we can try some other angles:

- The people who worked on the first two phases, the second phase in particular, have a head start on the intricacies of the project. If you can get them back, or at least the best of them, you will be in slightly better shape. Of course, you'll need to pry them away from their current managers. You can argue that you are working on a very important project with an extremely short schedule, for a very demanding client whose satisfaction is critical to the company's future. The project managers where these experienced people now work won't be impressed, but the executives who walked you into this impasse can make them see how sensible a transfer is.

- While you are on the staff trail, you should use your little black book of people who have helped you out of jams before. Accession of these people would give you an immediate jump in your process productivity. Again, the executives—who are now beginning to worry a little—can help you pry these people loose.

- Some of the best people are freelancers and some of them work for subcontractors. Some of them specialize in the very areas in which your in-house people are weak. You hadn't been planning to use them, because they are expensive and usually over-scheduled, but maybe you should reconsider that now. It's true your award doesn't carry a lot of money with it, but maybe the importance of getting something done in time to meet the client's real needs offsets the money angle. What do your senior executives think?

- You did not factor much reuse into your original plan, because in the haste of getting the bid out, you did not have time to explore what components were available.

Now that you have the award, you have the time and staff you need to look around. You've heard that more components are now available. Even if you have to do some tinkering with them to make them fit the proposed system, that might be faster than building them from scratch. Some of those freelancers and subcontractors might have some leads here.

- You've been trying to use software tools all your professional life. You are convinced that, in theory, good tools save time and effort, and that is exactly what you need right now. But tools cost money. They take time and effort to learn how to use effectively. Moreover, they ought to be applied more widely in the company than on your single project. You probably can't expect much in the short run from better tools, but what the heck! You're in for the long run, too. You've got a little lever in this project from hell to move the executives with.

Now let's take another look at the other core metric, size. So far as the award goes, we are still stuck with the original functionality and the corresponding size. We are pretty sure we are not going to improve our process productivity enough to deliver the whole system on the new date. But is there an essential set of features that we could deliver? Could the client carry out its critical functions with that set? Sometimes, horror of horrors, there are bells and whistles that *pointy-haired* executives threw in.[3] They may not even be employed by the client any longer. (They may have gone back to their comic strip!)

There is a whole host of development methodologies that are focused on doing first things first: evolutionary, iterative, incremental, spiral, and frequent builds. The underlying concept is first to build a little bit that works, then add to it, always keeping it workable. The theories behind these methodologies may help us set the order in which to build this system. When the delivery date arrives, we won't have it all, but we will have something that works.

The client might even be happy to have a starter system, with the rest following later. Of course, in preparing the starter system, we may use up all of the effort (and the corresponding funds) provided by the award. The question lingers: Who is going to pay for the rest of the

---

[3]The reference to the pointy-haired executive may escape readers who live beyond the reach of the comic strip *Dilbert*, which runs in the business section of several hundred newspapers. This clueless boss sets up some impossible requirements for the software engineer, Dilbert, to struggle with. Real-life bosses sometimes set up requirements that fall short of impossible, but are unrealistic.

system? Maybe our negotiators will absorb it as a loss to our company. After all, they committed to deliver the system for an inadequate amount of money. Fortunately, clients often recognize by this point that they have pushed too hard and now graciously assent to pay for more time and effort. In fact, some sophisticated clients make it a routine practice to hold back a portion of the funds available for the system. Years of sad experience with software development have taught them they will need these backup funds.

The Award Reflects the Estimate

In the opposite situation, our negotiators understand that the bid originates in an estimate that is itself the outcome of a valid methodology. They understand that the work to be done, the functionality to be achieved, has passed the tests of feasibility, risk analysis, and functional design (or architecture). They negotiate an award under which we enter the Main Build in good shape.

Nevertheless, building the system is still going to be arduous. The development of software is perhaps the most difficult activity the human race has ever encountered. It automates almost every other activity and therefore embraces all their complexities. It is, itself, an ethereal entity that is hard to comprehend. Given these entanglements, we may not carry out the tasks of the first two phases perfectly. Our errors or omissions return to plague us in the Main Build.

That's why it is a good idea to track the building process—the rate of employing staff and effort, the rate of developing code, and the defect rate—as we discussed in Chapter 13. If actuals deviate significantly from these projections, we are encountering trouble. Effort, code rate, and defect rate are trackable metrics, but there are also many more criteria of concern. To monitor them, we set up, at the time of planning the Main Build, a series of review points, each with a listing of the criteria that we expect to achieve at that point. If we fail a criterion at a review point, we know we have encountered more trouble.

The aim of control projections and criteria reviews is to discover trouble early, while there is still time and effort available to overcome it. There isn't much time and effort left if we wait until system test to see if the parts go together and work in harmony. Moreover, a deficiency left uncorrected early in development multiplies itself as it impacts more and more design and code. If the project has been carefully considered and planned, it can carry out within its schedule and effort plan the fairly routine course corrections that turn up. The project would not have to be replanned.

Replan Troubled Projects

Some time in the Main Build, whether by means of control charts, periodic reviews, or just overwhelming trouble, it dawns on us that our project cannot succeed within the schedule and effort originally planned. It is one of the troubled fraction that must be replanned.

The original estimates of schedule, effort, and defect rate rested upon two other core metrics: size and process productivity. The values of these two metrics were themselves uncertain at earlier points in the lifecycle. Perhaps we are now in trouble on this project, not because the work itself is going poorly, but because the original estimate was inadequate. Since we are farther along the time line of the project, we are in a position to make more precise estimates of the size and the process productivity being achieved. Moreover, some of the risks that were merely hypothetical in the early phases have now materialized. We have done more work on them and are better able to plan their resolution.

A more precise estimate of size basically depends on the more extensive knowledge of the functionality of the system that we now possess.

We can calculate a more precise estimate of process productivity from the improved knowledge of functionality (size) and the actual amount of time and effort expended up to the point of replanning. The value of process productivity we used in the original estimate was calibrated against values of size, effort, and time obtained from past projects. That value reflected the process productivity achieved in the past, which may well have been somewhat different from the process productivity being achieved on the current project. For instance, the earlier projects may have been in easier application areas; the mix of staff may have been different; staff members may have had fewer tools and used them less skillfully, and so on.

To be in a position to make this more precise estimate of process productivity, we have to be far enough along to have some source code (or some other size metric) to count. For this count to be significant, we usually have to be at least one quarter of the way through the Main Build.

With new estimates of size and process productivity, we have the basic data from which we can project a revised plan of effort and schedule. However, revised values of what the remaining time and effort ought to be do not appear by magic. We must still work through the trade-off of time and effort. Suppose we originally planned time and effort on the basis of a 70-percent probability of completing the system on plan. Now, since we are admittedly in trouble, we are probably going to find that we cannot find a combination of time and effort that will enable us to complete the project at the 70-percent probability level. The best combination we can find may have a probability of success of much less, say 30 percent. That may be worth going ahead with, but our chance of completing the project as planned has dropped significantly.

Let's take a more extreme outcome. The replanning shows that the probability of successful completion within the original estimate of time and effort has declined to 5 percent. In other words, there is almost no chance of completing on the original terms. To complete the project, you would have to extend the schedule and/or add more staff, requiring more funds. As many have learned, though, simply pouring on more flesh to achieve the original schedule is a dubious proposition. There are two more possible outcomes: You (and the management-client structure) can reduce the scope of the product to what the project team can complete in the remaining schedule, or you can close down the project.

Replan Periodically

"The final and most challenging step in planning is for you to constantly re-implement the planning process throughout the life of your program," the Department of Defense advises its acquisition officers.[4]

Except for the simplest and most repetitive systems, software development, as illustrated in Figure 15-1, is fraught with uncertainty. At the beginning of the lifecycle, it is almost impossible to pin down exactly what users want, let alone what they actually need. The various intermediaries between the actual users and the development organization exacerbate this difficulty.

Then, based on this incomplete knowledge of what is needed, the development organization tries to figure out the functionality of the eventual system and from that estimate its size. From this uncertain beginning, the development organization's estimators try to project a range of effort and schedule levels. Management turns this range estimate into a point bid at a "probability of success" point, such as 70 percent. In the course of negotiating the final award, it is often forced to agree to still another price figure, multiplying the uncertainty.

Consequently, the project gets started on what often amounts to a plan that's far divorced from the reality of what follows. That reality compounds the uncertainties inherent in the planning. Then, software

---

[4]*Guidelines for Successful Acquisition and Management of Software-Intensive Systems*, Department of the Air Force, Software Technology Support Center, Version 3.0 (Hill AFB, Utah: 2000), p. 275.

development itself is very difficult, introducing still another batch of uncertainties.

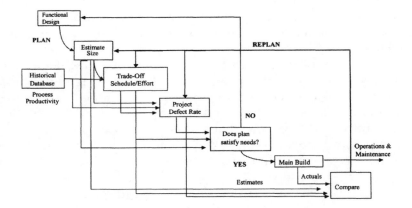

Figure 15-1:   *Based on the information coming out of the Functional Design Phase and the historical database, the development organization estimates size and process productivity, trades off schedule and effort, and projects the defect rate. If this plan is satisfactory, the project goes into the Main Build. If the plan seems to be lacking or, later, if actuals fail to match estimates, the project goes into replanning.*

Even at this comparatively early point, before the Main Build begins, it is wise, as the figure shows, to ask, "Does the current plan satisfy the needs of the stakeholders?"

A frank answer may compel the participants to go around the planning circle once again.

If the project gets past this question, the Main Build commences. Actual data on staffing, source code production, and defect rate become available to compare with the planned rates. Because planning is imperfect and development is difficult, the actuals may not fall within the limits set by the "noise" of the software process.

If actual rates fall close to projected rates, the Main Build continues as planned. If they deviate a little, it is a cause for investigation. If the deviation is significant, it sets off replanning. Even if the project appears to be proceeding smoothly, with actuals falling close to the planned rates and criteria being met at reviews, we ought to run through a replanning exercise periodically, if only to see that we are likely to complete as originally planned, bid, or awarded.

Part IV
Control at the
Organization Level

Life is lived so intensely by hard-pressed staff members inside the cocoon of a faltering software project that they easily forget the realm beyond the project. But we must not forget. The software world is huge and much of it reflects back on the progress of the individual project. To examine that world in this concluding Part, we follow the practice of Elizabeth Barrett Browning, wife of the English nineteenth-century poet Robert Browning, who once said, though in a lovelier setting, "Let us count the ways."

1. An organization acquiring software under contract from suppliers can evaluate contractor capability, validate bids against the core metrics, and even encourage contractors by measuring their improvement. (Chapter 16)
2. An organization contemplating outsourcing can compare the core metrics of the contenders. During the relationship, the client can monitor the outsourcing contractor's metrics. (Chapter 17)
3. A senior manager overseeing a number of software projects can plan the transfer of resources, particularly of staff, from projects that are winding down to projects that are gearing up. (Chapter 18)

4. Project managers and senior managers, watching the increase in process productivity, are encouraged to continue their efforts. The hierarchy above them feels satisfied to continue its financial support. (Chapter 19)
5. As component-based development becomes more prevalent, responsibility for architecture, interfaces, and the components themselves shifts to organizations outside the project—even as far as standards bodies or component suppliers. Control through metrics has to shift as well. (Chapter 20)
6. Basing estimating, bidding, and award bargaining on objective criteria enables management to harmonize project-level negotiations with the best interests of the overall organization. (Chapter 21)
7. Wise use of metrics-based methods builds a superior organization over career-length time out of once "average" new hires. (Chapter 22)

In addition to the people directly involved in software development, other interests benefit from the metrics approach:

1. Purchasing agents, acquisition managers, and high-level managers who are responsible for selecting and monitoring the progress of development contractors or outsourcing organizations.
2. Management and staff, above the project, who monitor estimates and bids, progress on the project, replanning, resource allocations, and so forth.
3. Executives and staff in corporate headquarters who allocate projects and compare performance in scattered divisions.

Thus, we see that software development is increasingly involved in relationships that extend beyond the projects themselves. The challenge facing the industry is to replace the hunches of old with the facts needed for effective management. These facts rest on the core metrics. With metrics—and an understanding of their application—responsible managers can make better decisions.

Chapter 16
A Telecommunications Company Evaluates Its Software Suppliers

A few years ago, a college in Southern California planned to build a new theater arts building with funds donated primarily by a single benefactor. The architectural firm hired for the job, from Oregon, submitted with the detailed plans its estimate of what the construction costs should be. When the contractors' bids were opened, however, all of them were substantially in excess of the architect's figure. They were close together, too—within a few hundred thousand dollars of each other.

The relative proximity of the bids implied that the contractors knew what they were doing. The college's building committee felt that the contractors' range of figures was probably realistic. In fact, the committee soon found out from the architect that his estimate had been based on his experience in Oregon, where the costs of construction were lower than in Southern California.

Unfortunately, the funds available for the project fell short of the bids. The building committee's first response was to reduce the features of the building to lower the cost to what had been donated. The benefactor sat through these sessions, not actively participating but becoming visibly and increasingly agitated. Finally, he exclaimed that the building was losing the very features that made it specially suited for teaching theater arts.

"Hold off the downsizing," he said. "Let me see if I can raise some more money."

He did find some more money and the building was constructed as planned.

Lessons from Construction

The management of building construction is different from what's required for software development. First of all, the building field has a few hundred years more experience in planning and carrying out projects. We in the software field can learn the following from this experience:

- The architect's estimate of what a building should cost can be wrong. *(Early efforts to estimate software development costs can be way off.)*
- When actual bids from established builders fall in a range, that range is likely to be the reality. *(When a bid from one software contractor is well below the range of bids from other contractors, that firm has probably missed a beat somewhere.)*
- The project can either drop features or add money. *(Software has the same choice.)*
- That decision is the client's, not the contractor's. *(Software clients have the final say, too.)*

In the case of building construction, a building committee has two sets of facts to guide it: the architect's detailed architectural drawings and the architect's estimate of building costs. In most cases, the architect develops the plans in the first place to fit within the client's budget. In software construction, we need the kind of facts that architects' plans and estimates provide to building committees.

Lack of Facts Leads to Pain

In 1995, the county welfare department of a major city solicited bids for a system to track the county's hundreds of thousands of welfare cases. The lowest bid—from a large, well-known company—was $86 million.

The second-lowest bid, from another corporate giant, was $147 million. Was either bid realistic? Was one company "buying in"? Was the other company "gold-plating"? Because of the amount of money involved, the selection decision went up to the Board of Supervisors— five elected politicians, all of long experience. They were troubled by the vast difference between the two lowest bids.

"The difference was so substantial, it looked bizarre," one of the county supervisors recalled, three years later. But the company had assured the Board it could bring the project in on budget. Besides, the Board felt that state and federal standards required it to accept the lowest bid.

By 1998, the low-bidding company wanted more time and $52 million more, bringing the cost up into the range of the next higher bidder. Of course, the county still needed the system. By then, it was apparent that the higher bid had been the realistic one. The supervisors reluctantly granted the additional funds and more time. However, they did not escape entirely unchastened. An editorial in the city's daily paper condemned the Board's adherence to the low-bid practice, citing several "best practice" state standards intended to avoid poorly qualified low bids.

Aye, but there's the rub. There are thousands of pages of standards intended to guide acquisition officials at every level. Applying them in specific situations is not easy. For a software vendor, the temptation to "buy in" is high. When a contractor succeeds in getting in by this route, his next goal is to get well, that is, to recover in some way from a bad deal (discussed further in Chapter 21). The role of a government, or a corporation for that matter, is to resist the effort of a contractor to buy in at an unrealistically low price. That leads to an adversarial relationship during the execution of the work, as the Department of Defense points out.

"In light of the fact that a congenial relationship is almost indispensable to the successful completion of the project, it is in the government's interest to avoid awarding to an offeror who is buying-in if it is at all possible," the Department of Defense advises its acquisition officers.[1] (The DoD operates under laws and regulations that sometimes make it difficult to avoid the acceptance of buy-in bids.)

It is in everyone's interest for seller and buyer to match at a congenial bid, one that is neither too high nor too low. In the real world, however, many software contractors are still at Level One of the Capability Maturity Model, that is, they lack the ability to repeat their software process the next time around. If you can't repeat your process,

---

[1]Jerome S. Gabig, Jr., "Software Source Selection," Appendix S, *Guidelines for Successful Acquisition and Management of Software-Intensive Systems,* Department of the Air Force, Software Technology Support Center, Version 3.0 (Hill AFB, Utah: 2000), p. 893.

you have little solid basis for estimating how long the next project will take or how many dollars to bid. Contractors at this level do not keep very good records of "last time" any way. And organizations acquiring software seldom have much factual knowledge of the extent to which the circle of bidding organizations with which they deal base their bids on accumulated data.

Lower Tier, the Same

The lower tier of software developers is much the same the world over. When PTT Telecom BV (now KPN Telecom BV), providing telephone service to the Netherlands, began to consider its software acquisition options back in the early 1990's, it found a study covering 597 Dutch companies. The researchers reported the following:

- More than half (57 percent) did not have data on previous projects in an accessible form.
- More than one third (35 percent) did not draw up an estimate of their projects; they flew blind, so far as knowing the status of time and effort in relation to a plan was concerned.
- Among those who did make estimates, 62 percent were based on nothing more than intuition; only 16 percent used an estimating model.
- Then, among those who had some kind of an estimate, only half (50 percent) compared progress against the estimate.[2]

In this sorry state of managerial oversight, what was the outcome of the projects?

- Nearly all (80 percent) overran whatever budget or schedule they were operating under.
- These overruns averaged 50 percent of whatever budget or schedule had been set.

PTT Telecom BV's own experience with its vendors paralleled this study:

- It had little data on vendors' previous experience.

---

[2]Heemstra, F.J., W.J.A. Siskens, and H. van der Stelt, "Kostenbeheersing Bij Automatiseringsprojecten: Een Empirisch Onderzoek," *Informatie*, Vol. 31, No. 1 (1989).

- Projects were often late and cost more than expected.
- After delivery, reliability was uncertain.
- System maintenance costs often seemed excessive.

PTT Telecom BV Gets Real

The PTT's software buyers had become aware that systems tended to expand during development. Requirements were added as developers and users learned more about the application. This expansion could not be stopped. In fact, much of it was desirable, but it also added to schedules and cost. It was evident that it ought to be put under tighter control.

The purchasing staff began to realize that software suppliers were primarily focused on technical issues. They seemed to be little aware of management practices that were well established in other types of suppliers:

- projecting the course of key variables (plan) at the beginning of the project
- measuring the variables periodically as work proceeds
- comparing actual measurements with the plan
- investigating deviations and correcting them accordingly

The purchasing organization began to recognize that it was not without fault. It was issuing contracts for software development with little understanding of the magnitude of the work or the project-management capabilities of the vendors. It had no organized way to spot unrealistic planning by bidders.

Purchasing had long been aware of the painful stress that erupted between vendors and the PTT when planned deliveries began to slip. It realized that other managers within the PTT often had to recast their plans because the software was not ready. Yet Purchasing heard little but vague mumbles from its vendors. Often, this mumbling seemed to reduce to weak complaints that the amount of work had increased. But Purchasing had seen no purchase-order changes pass through. The PTT's official practice, of course, was to confirm additional work with a change order, specifying what it was and the additional funds to cover it.

From the standpoint of the purchasing organization, the PTT had specified what it wanted. Purchasing felt that it had a right to expect contractors to build to specification within the budget and schedule to which the purchase order committed them, or else to request pur-chase-order changes. It was clear that something was wrong. That something appeared to be primarily in the management, not technical, sphere. That was an area that Purchasing could work on.

The PTT Faces Competition

In 1989, PTT Telecom BV was privatized and began to feel the pressure of competition and its effect on its income. The purchasing depart-ment realized that its own contribution to the overall efficiency of the new organization, KPN Telecom BV, was a reflection of the competitive power of its suppliers. If the suppliers performed badly—and most of the software suppliers did—the Telecom itself would be hindered in moving from the shelter of the state into the arena of competition.

Within the Telecom, plans already called for less money, less staff, and fewer suppliers. In the software area, though, the technical devel-opments in progress pointed to more and more software. There could be only one conclusion: The surviving suppliers should be the best performers. Not only that, they should perform better than they were then.

The Telecom Considers What to Do

The purchasing organization started by analyzing the purchasing func-tion itself, asking, What good management practices should we imple-ment?

1. Before inviting vendors to bid, the department should identify the most productive suppliers, develop ongoing relations with them, and encourage them to be among the bidders.
2. When proposals come in, the department should have the ability to identify the unrealistic ones.
3. Only then should it select the best among the surviving proposals.
4. In the course of issuing the purchase contract, the department should, in consultation with the vendor, set the baseline—schedule, price, and quality level (such as Mean Time To Defect at delivery).
5. At the same time, the department should reach agree-ment with the vendor that a change request will be processed for any change that affects schedule, cost, or quality.

6. Furthermore, the periodic submission of data on project progress is to be mandatory.
7. Then, as the project proceeds, the department should compare reported data against the baseline and detect any variance from the plan.
8. The department is to notify the parties in the Telecom that are affected by any variance and, in conjunction with the vendor, correct the variance before it gets out of hand. (Early correction often costs little time or effort; late correction is much more expensive.)

At this point in its planning, the purchasing department had no organized knowledge of how projects were getting along, aside from an occasional comment from a Telecom engineer just back from trying to solve a technical problem with a vendor. Vendors themselves seemed to have little organized control of their work, and Purchasing had no formal knowledge of what the Telecom unit ordering the software was doing in its technical contacts with the vendor. Despite the failure of both vendors and Telecom-using units to keep Purchasing informed, no one doubted that technical discussions affecting cost, schedule, or quality ought to be reflected in the formal purchase documentation.

How to Do It?

That was the question. One point was clear—the purchasing organization, as well as its suppliers, needed to work from objective measurements, such as the five core metrics. Purchasing knew that many of its contractors already had measures of size, time, effort, and defects, though not always in a readily available form. It believed that the rest could be persuaded to keep data this simple.

Process productivity could serve as a single-figure indication of contractor capability. It was solidly based on the contractor's own past work, not on the results of an expensive field survey. This figure would enable Purchasing to identify the most productive suppliers. Purchasing could cultivate relations with them and make sure they received requests to propose.

When bids were received, Purchasing could use the process productivity figure, computed from data on earlier projects, to identify estimates of size, effort, and schedule that were unrealistic (as we have explained in earlier chapters). In some instances, unrealistic bids could simply be set aside. In others, the data could serve as the basis for a frank discussion with the vendor. A low bid, for instance, would be counterproductive for the Telecom if it presaged a late delivery, a cost overrun, or an inadequate product.

The same analysis, of course, also identified the realistic proposals—the ones likely to be delivered on schedule, within the price bid, meeting the Mean Time To Defect requirement. From those, Purchasing could make a selection on the basis of the other factors procurement weighs.

A vendor can achieve a realistic plan only if the inescapable changes are incorporated into revisions of that plan. Purchasing would make clear to its vendors that the PTT expected them to process change requests. It would also make clear *within* the PTT that growth in requirements, while probably desirable in many instances, also affected the management numbers: size, time, effort, and reliability. These numbers underlie the project plan, which in turn underlies the purchase contract. Software changes of any magnitude always affect the plan and consequently the contract.

After a vendor commences work, it would be committed to a continuing relationship with Purchasing:

- to report monthly source code completed and person-months expended
- to report the date on which milestones (established by the plan and contract) were achieved
- to submit change requests

With this continuing data flow, Purchasing could compare progress with the baseline plan as originally set (and perhaps later modified). A deviation of actuals from the realistic plan would be a signal to investigate and possibly to act. From data submitted periodically by the vendor, Purchasing would compute the process productivity actually being achieved on the project. A value less than that on which the "realistic" plan had been based would be a signal to investigate further.

Purchasing Alerts Management

In the Telecom case, the purchasing function had taken the initiative to set up this pattern of project control. Of course, the purchasing function is not intended to possess the capability to plan or revise software projects. It can recognize a deviation of actuals from plan as a signal of some kind of trouble. It can refer the deviation to the responsible functions in the Telecom and the vendor for investigation and resolution. Purchasing's role is then to reflect that resolution in a purchase-order change.

Perhaps most importantly, the deviations are found soon after the problem causing them appears. There is still time and effort in the schedule to correct them. The stresses that otherwise beset the system test period are greatly reduced.

The Telecom had scores of software projects under way. To call the troubled projects to the attention of higher management, Purchasing devised the *metric traffic light,* as illustrated in Figure 16-1. It placed one of these figures—with the red, amber, or green active—opposite each project on periodic reports to upper management.

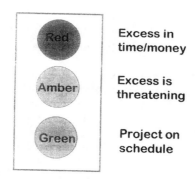

Red — Excess in time/money

Amber — Excess is threatening

Green — Project on schedule

Figure 16-1: *The metric traffic light highlights the status of each project for upper management with a color scheme.*

The color scheme devised by Purchasing is detailed below:

- Green: on schedule, no cause for management concern
- Amber: a little behind on schedule, cost overrun threatening, management should monitor what the supplier, the telecom user, and the purchasing organization are doing about it
- Red: excess in budgeted time and money, calls for management involvement

The Telecom Gets Results

The control staff of the purchasing function began to bring projects under this plan at the beginning of 1993, as shown in Figure 16-2. "The chart substantiates what we have always known," the control staff manager, Geerhard W. Kempff, told us. "Software development is not easy! Getting it under control takes time. Metrics gives us a means of knowing when it is in control."

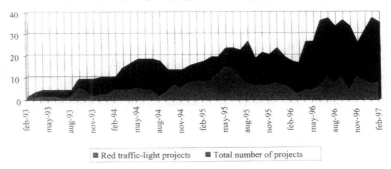

Overview of Red Projects Against Total Number of Projects

Figure 16-2:   *The number of projects brought under the control plan steadily increased during the first years (upper line). As indicated by the lower line, the number of projects in the red zone, calling for immediate management attention, has always been substantial. The relative number has been dropping in recent years, however, as all concerned became better able to cope with the difficulties uncovered by the plan.*

During the period represented in Figure 16-2, the control staff tracked 49 projects and obtained these results:

- More than one third (36 percent) were delivered on time, bettering the industry average of 20 percent.
- Baselines were revised an average of two times per project, with an infrequent maximum of six times.
- Completed size averaged 125 percent of initial estimates, implying a comparable expansion of the requirements.
- Process productivity increases, attributable to using more productive suppliers, reduced cost by 30 percent.
- By resisting the temptation to accept the most optimistic schedule, often at the highest cost quote, and by instead relaxing the schedule to a more practical level, the PTT obtained up to 25-percent cost reduction.

In addition, the control staff learned several nonnumerical lessons:

- Do not push details of methodology on the suppliers. As independent businesses, they have the right to run projects in their own way. "We just ask for the data we need," Kempff said. "It is their business to figure out how to supply it. If they cannot structure their process to provide it, very well. It is then our business to move to another supplier."
- Do not track "chaos," meaning by that a supplier with so little "process" that it does not know where it is aiming or what it is doing. Again, just look elsewhere.
- Do not be taken in by hype; instead, look for management capability to work with the available resources.
- Do not insist on precise data. "Good enough" is close enough for control purposes. Especially in the early stages of a project, some level of uncertainty is nothing to be ashamed of.
- Do not place much confidence in assumptions. Poorly thought-out assumptions pave the road to failure.
- Do not depend on the miraculous arrival of whiz kids to pull a project out of the fire. Often they fail to arrive. Even when they do, they are usually more kid than whiz.

Results on Sample Projects

Project A. The contractor proposed what analysis by the control staff found to be a very tight schedule for this system, initially estimated at 76,000 source lines of code. As the software control staff suspected, the size eventually grew to 200,000, but the baseline plan was not expanded accordingly. Instead, a stabilization phase of six months was added after delivery. The contractor had based its original bid on an estimate of process productivity that was more than one standard deviation above average. Control staff members found it hard to calculate from the constantly changing data just what productivity the project was reaching, but they thought it wise to plan the stabilization phase at only an average process-productivity level.[3]

Project B. Tracking this small modification project in the Functional Design Phase indicated that the level of effort being achieved was less than planned. At the same time, defect tracking showed that

---

[3]For these vignettes of the purchasing experience, we credit Geerhard W. Kempff, software control manager, Logistics and Purchasing Department, KPN Telecom (formerly PTT Telecom) BV Netherlands.

errors were relatively high. It appeared that the previous release contained more defects than the modification plan had expected. Anticipating that these two deviations would impact the Main Build, the control staff suggested that the contractor allow more time and effort in that phase. Of course, he was perfectly happy to do so. While at first glance it may appear that a suggestion of this nature is contrary to the acquisition organization's own economic interest, that was not the case. Its interest was to get a valid product, not to save a little time and effort on the way to an unsuccessful product.

Project C. Analysis based on the core metrics of a major pending project enabled the control manager to explain to the KPN Telecom Board of Directors that stretching the delivery time of the first part of the project by one month would achieve the following:

- decrease cost by almost 25 percent
- boost reliability by almost 300 percent

The board then had the facts it needed to weigh schedule time against costs and defect reduction.

Project D. Not every customer likes to bet his company on a vendor's overly tight schedule. KPN Telecom used its ability to analyze the core metrics of software development within a hardware project to tell its customer that the functionality he desired could not be fully operational by the deadline he set. The analysis was convincing. The customer chose to use existing KPN Telecom equipment until the new system became available according to plan. This individual appreciated being taken seriously. He did not like to play schedule games.

In these examples and on scores of other projects, KPN Telecom had a software control staff to analyze what its vendors were trying to do. Its analysis often put a vendor on a development path that was more sound. Sadly, the county with the underbid welfare system has not been as well served.

As these examples demonstrate, the core metrics added focus to KPN Telecom's discussions with suppliers. They kept negotiations more on point, with outcomes that were more successful. Overall, software development, difficult as it often is, became eminently predictable.

Chapter 17
Evaluate Bids on the Facts

There is a tendency among those who regard the making of software as a kind of manufacturing activity to think of coding as the essence of that activity. They declare, "Just get coding under way and all will be well!" That, of course, is far from reality.

The Reality Is Research and Development

Software development is actually a research and development activity, close to research in its early phases and development in the later phases. It is never *manufacturing* in the sense of turning out some number of pieces a week, regardless of the development schedule allowed. The intellectual content of what the project staff does takes amounts of schedule time that do not become indefinitely compressible by adding staff. In consequence, the amount of time the schedule provides for these incompressible activities is a crucial component of the project plan.

During the early phases (Feasibility and Functional Design), the amount of functionality and the nature of the architecture depend on the extent of the project scope and the detail of the requirements that these phases explore. Moreover, a large part of the responsibility for delimiting scope and expressing requirements rests with the acquiring organization (or, from the software organization's point of view, the customer). Of course, the software organization can contribute its technical and operational experience to the mix. In particular, a software organization may be more conscious of the substantial technical risks that some of the requirements bring with them.

Until these uncertainties can be largely resolved, the two parties cannot settle with much precision on the system's functionality or architecture. Until the functionality is sufficiently described, the size required to implement it remains in doubt. In other words, in these early phases, the size estimate is best expressed as a range, not a point.

From a business-management point of view, however, size is the first fact on which estimators rely to forecast time and effort. It is this estimate of time and effort that undergirds the contractual relationship between the organization purchasing the software and the organization proposing to develop it. Consequently, without some reasonable estimate of size, formulating a money-based relationship in which cooperation can flourish becomes difficult.

In this tangle, the two parties need to work closely together. The arms-length relationship implied by the concept of purchase order fails to solve the innumerable joint problems that arise during research and development. Remember, the two parties are, in effect, engaged in a common intellectual pursuit. The acquiring party is not purchasing a fully specified product, such as nuts and bolts.

Getting to the Facts

The first seeds of this relationship are sown long before the purchase contract is signed. The organization that needs software seeks to find out what it can about the development organizations to which it might send requests for proposal or invitations to tender. As soon as the possibility of a purchase relationship becomes evident, the acquiring organization has a motive to seek factual data on the developer's qualifications. Moreover, the development organization, if it grasps the underlying reason for gathering this information, is motivated to supply the information. That underlying reason is to establish a relationship in which the needed cooperation can flourish.

What, then, are these basic facts? It will come as no surprise, at this point in the book, that they are the five core metrics. Some development organizations may be reluctant to provide this core data. The acquiring organization should make clear that the information would be employed only in its ongoing relationship with the developer. Especially, it will not reach competitive development groups. Sharing these facts lays the groundwork for a cooperative business relationship advantageous to both parties.

For instance, on the development organization's side, winning a contract at too low a price and too short a schedule makes it difficult—often impossible, judging from the percentage of projects that fail—to deliver a system with the capabilities the acquirer has to have. Moreover, the less-than-satisfactory system that the developer eventually delivers under such circumstances is likely to have reliability measures, such as Mean Time To Failure, that are less than the application needs.

On the acquiring organization's side, imposing a contract at an unrealistically low price may gain a congratulatory lunch for the hard-bargaining buyer. Similarly, forcing a short schedule on a developer (with so little grasp of its own reality that it accepts the inadequate schedule) may be good for another lunch. It is *not* good, however, for the using organization, for which the late-arriving system is just one cog in a larger, time-sensitive program.

More importantly, the discrepancies between what is needed and what is possible on short rations results in deteriorating relationships. The decline in cooperation amplifies the difficulties of working together. The statistics, regrettably, report that many projects fail. Behind these failures lurks the inability to cooperate. Behind that inability often lurks a deteriorating business relationship, originating in a lack of agreed-upon metrics.

Some prospective bidders may refuse to provide these metrics. Well, that stance is uncooperative. This refusal is good to know about up front. Other bidders may not have any metrics to provide. That should raise the question in the acquiring organization's mind, How can this organization make a valid bid without data on its own experience?

The Bidder Cooperates

The acquiring organization wants to answer two questions:

- Is the bidder's performance reasonable?
- Is the new bid in line with this performance?

The Evaluators Consider Schedule

On the one hand, if the bidder's performance on schedule lies within one of the ellipses depicted In Figure 17-1, it is in line with the performance reported on more than 5,000 projects on which this figure is based. On the other hand, if it falls within the Impossible Zone, completion on that *impossible* schedule is most unlikely!

Stratifying the Database

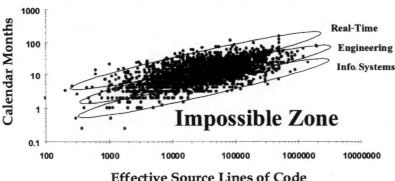

Figure 17-1: *The bidder's historic projects and his bid ought to be within the ballpark of the application under consideration.*

The bidder's bid, its "x," should fall within the ellipse corresponding to the type of application being bid. Just where along the vertical dimension the *x* falls depends on two factors. One is the bidder's process productivity—the better this figure, the shorter the schedule can be. The second is the trade-off between time and effort at which the bidder chooses to operate. (Bidders unfamiliar with the time-effort trade-off are still bidding at some time-effort point.)

A diagram such as Figure 17-2 enables evaluators to locate the schedule bid more precisely in relation to a database. On this figure, the database covers all types of applications, industry-wide. Selected applications or industries could be diagrammed. The center line is the mean of the schedules represented in the database. The upper and lower lines are each one standard deviation from the mean. The heavy concentration of dots between these lines shows that development organizations completed most of their projects in this center range. If the value of the schedule under consideration shows up in this same range, it is in the ballpark. It is realistic.

Fitting Trendlines to Data

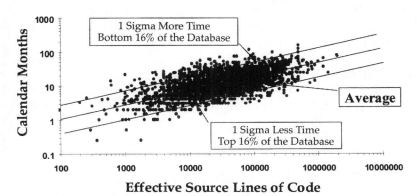

Figure 17-2:   *The bid evaluators might use a diagram like this one to examine on a finer scale just where a schedule bid falls. Here, about two thirds of the projects fall within the upper and lower (one standard deviation) lines.*

The next diagram, Figure 17-3, shows the vendor's current schedule bid in relation to its own past experience.

Positioning Projects vs.
Industry Trends: An Example

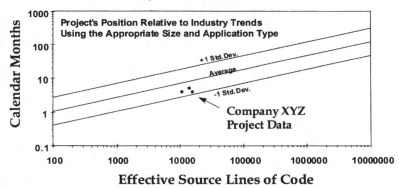

Figure 17-3:   *The bidder's data is better than average on schedule length, permitting the evaluators to conclude that this aspect of the bid is reasonable.*

In Figure 17-3, a couple of the little circles represent the bidding organization's historic schedule data. These two schedules were shorter than the mean (but well out of the Impossible Zone). The third circle is the current bid. It shows the same level of schedule performance as the historic projects. The evaluators conclude that the vendor is bidding realistically in terms of its own capabilities.

The Evaluators Consider Effort

Figure 17-4 provides a slightly different version of the bid comparison.

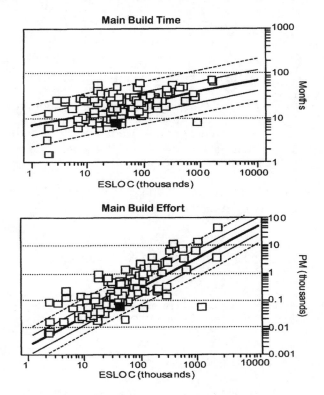

Figure 17-4:   *The white squares show the distribution of the historic projects on the log-log fields of Main Build (MB) time and effort versus size. The two black squares locate the project under consideration. On both diagrams, the black square is on the first line below the mean. The vendor appears to be operating in the top 16 percent of the organizations represented in this diagram.*

In Figure 17-4, these graphs provide two standard deviation lines above and below the mean. The project under consideration (plotted as a black square) is estimated to have a schedule that is approximately one standard deviation shorter than average. The second half of the figure indicates that the effort (in person-months) is also less than average. The evaluators find this pattern encouraging.

The Evaluators Consider Reliability

The occurrence of defects, shown in Figure 17-5, follows the same pattern as time and effort. The bidder's estimated defect rate should fall within the pattern of this figure (or one like it, for the application area the vendor is pursuing).

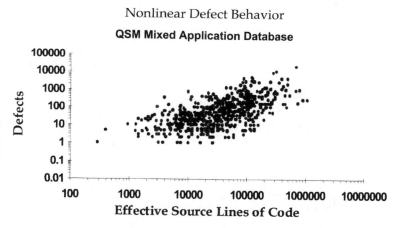

Nonlinear Defect Behavior

QSM Mixed Application Database

Figure 17-5:   *The occurrence of defects follows a pattern similar to the patterns of time and effort. The number of defects grows with the size of the system, but at any one size, there is a great deal of variation.*

The World of Wild Bidding

The marketing folk are sorely tempted to embroider the language of a proposal with elegant words. That is nice. Acquiring organizations expect the folk to believe in their mission. But diagrams such as those we've seen in this chapter, or the data on which the diagrams are based, add a bouquet of factual reality to a proposal. A project that starts out based on facts is more likely to end up happily for all concerned.

In the world of wild bidding, however, the bidder may set the x lower than it should, hoping to impress the bid evaluators. However, with knowledge of the bidder's process productivity on past projects and the schedule/effort/defects it is forecasting on this one, the evaluators can locate fairly precisely where the x should be. Resolving the situation may call for a little of the "cooperation" of which we are so fond!

Unhappily for some marketing folk, the bare facts may reveal that their software people are none too productive. When facts such as these are visible to the acquiring organization, it places its work elsewhere. Well, that is the competitive economic system at work. In our enthusiastic embrace of the glories of competition, we forget that there are losers, as well as winners.

If a not-adequately-productive vendor gets a contract by showering flowery words on its customer, it is merely postponing the sad day on which the project will run into trouble. It is still a loser—just a little later. Its customer is also a loser. It is better for both parties to look the facts squarely in the face before embarking on their joint cruise.

The Vendor Tries to Buy In

The evaluators expect bids to fall near the vendor's historic data points. Suppose, however, that the x's are in much more favorable locations. Why would a bidder do this? It may be trying to buy its way in by submitting a bid that is low on cost, effort, or schedule (and rather carefree about reliability). This low bid may be good for the client if the bidder can afford it—an unlikely prospect, since few bidders can. More likely, the low bid leads to trouble later on—the kind faced by the county welfare system described in Chapter 16.

Another likely pattern is that the bidder is overestimating the process productivity it will achieve in the coming period. The software industry is replete with exciting buzzwords implying greatly improved productivity. Moreover, most of them have a basis in reality—they do improve productivity when skillfully applied. But the promise of improvement as soon as the next project is also a red flag. Our experience in measuring process productivity for more than twenty years is that it improves slowly. Significant improvement, even when it is worked at assiduously, takes several years. The current buzz—whatever it is—is unlikely to speed up the improvement of process productivity in any given vendor very much, very soon.

Still a third possibility is that the bidder has underestimated the amount of functionality the project will involve. That translates into a smaller estimate of size, which in turn, leads to a lower bid. As soon as the evaluators note that size estimate, their relationship with the vendor should slide into the *cooperation* mode.

The Vendor Gold Plates

Suppose the evaluators find the bid data in a location much less favorable to them. It appears that the bidder has *gold-plated* the project, that is, has deliberately bid high. One reason may be that the vendor's schedule is so crowded that it doesn't much want the job. It bids high to cover the costs of expansion.

Another possible explanation is that the vendor has overestimated the amount of functionality. Its size estimate would then be greater than that of the acquiring organization. It is a good idea to bring these conflicting points of view into harmony sooner rather than later.

A remote possibility is that the bidder expects its process productivity to decline. In the real world, that sometimes happens. In fact, there is some evidence that software development productivity did drop in the final years of the last millennium, possibly due to staff shortages or complexity getting ahead of staff capability. However, vendors, naturally optimistic, seldom think along those lines.

Other reasons for high or low bids may turn up, but using the facts provided by the five core metrics, the bid evaluators can examine them in relation to the bidder's recent history. They can see where the bid lies in relation to the background data provided by a large database of such data. The bidder and the evaluators are then immersed in reality, not fine language. The bid-evaluation team can smoke out the games that vendors play with the proposal process.

At this point, the evaluators can put aside the unrealistic bids and compare the realistic ones. They look for the lowest cost (effort), the fastest schedule, the highest reliability, or the most advantageous combination of these elements best suiting the client's situation. With the facts, they are able to assess what each vendor can do in the light of what it has been able to deliver in the past.

Experience Supports the Factual Approach

The authors and their associates have established the value of factual bid evaluation during more than ten years. In addition to KPN Telecom BV in the Netherlands (Chapter 16), here are some of the others:

- Civil Aviation Authority (Jim Greene, an associate in London)

- a procurement run by the Naval Research Laboratory
- the Navy Stand-off Land Attack Missile
- the Navy E2C radar command and control aircraft
- the Joint Mission Planning System (Navy and Air Force mission planning software)
- Railtrack (Anthony Hemens, an associate in London)

Who Needs the Facts?

In addition to acquisition managers, people in several other lines of work can profit from employing this factual approach:

1. estimators or managers at the project level, responsible for initialing or signing estimates or bids
2. project managers or higher-level managers, responsible for evaluating subcontractors
3. levels of management above the project manager, evaluating estimates or bids coming up to them for approval
4. corporate management, comparing software organizations at different locations or in different countries
5. corporate chief information officers, evaluating the performance of outsourcers

All of these executives and their staffs can profit from the ability to get at the facts of software development. With the facts, they can cut through to the reality of what is going on. They can make better decisions.

What we want to urge, above all, is this: Get facts into the relationship between software development buyer and seller. Let historic reality replace unsupported fiction in the proposals. The acquiring organization (as well as various levels of higher management), with its control of "the money button," occupies the commanding heights! It can take a long step toward unwinding the software crisis.

Chapter 18
Managing a Portfolio of Projects

Senior managers "need to know how to juggle a portfolio of projects." They need to "make sure to allocate resources carefully across projects to minimize the constraints on the shared resources. . . . Too often, projects fall short of resources or lose direction because of a lack of agreement among senior business and functional managers. . . . The progress of any individual project is limited by factors outside an individual manager's control."[1]

One of those shared resources is staff. Estimating methodology enables an organization to project staff needs over project time (Chapter 13). If the projection turns out to be incorrect, the organization can replan the project (Chapter 15) and project new staffing for the rest of the project.

Given these staff projections, the senior manager in charge of a number of projects can allocate people in the quantities and at the times the projections dictate. That manager acts with the concurrence of the responsible functional manager, such as the test manager.

---

[1]Jeffrey Elton and Justin Roe, "Bringing Discipline to Project Management," *Harvard Business Review* (March-April 1998), pp. 156–57.

If the senior manager has a holding pool of qualified people, he can make assignments at the times the projections forecast. However, there are seldom enough qualified people. The result is that some projects get short shrift. As a result, they fall behind schedule and their problems multiply. They have reached the all-too-typical state of all-too-many software organizations.

A Senior Manager Can Master-Plan

Making the best allocation of resources such as these is a key task in "managing a portfolio of projects." One of the aids to this management is a master plan. The plan for a single project projects a staff-effort curve over development time. The master plan simply adds up the staff-effort curves of the individual projects under the senior manager's direction, as illustrated in Figures 18-1 and 18-2.

Of course, the master curve shown in Figure 18-2 is not the *solution* to the staffing problem. It is a *presentation* early enough to give the senior manager time to attack the problems it presents. It provides the means by which senior managers can visualize how much staff their organization has, where it is currently assigned, and when projects nearing completion will make staff members available for new assignments.

Single Product Line, Five Releases

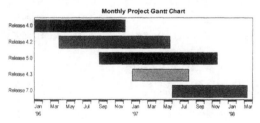

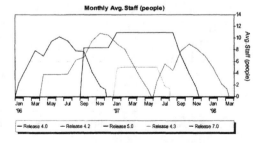

Figure 18-1:   *Five individual releases of a project, overlaid along the time line.*

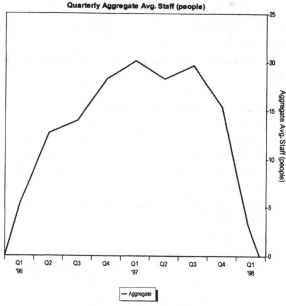

Aggregate Staffing of Five Releases

Figure 18-2:   *A software tool adds up the staff-effort curves*
for the individual projects (already available in
the organization's computer system) to produce
the master curve or master plan.

With the advance notice that the master plan provides, senior managers can build up their staff resources to meet coming needs, perhaps by stepping up hiring or seeking subcontractors. Or, in reverse, if the master plan forecasts a lull six months hence, they can slow down hiring or advance "nice to have" projects to a higher position on the priority list. They have time to think, a luxury sometimes lost in the rush of modern times.

Good Project Plans Underlie a Good Master Plan

The master staff curve is, in effect, an arithmetic addition of the project staff curves. It cannot come into being magically. It depends, essentially, on two fundamentals:

- consistent metric practices
- a software tool to collect, add, and present the information

(A spreadsheet model could perform these functions, but a tool connected to the rest of the metrics adds dynamic updating capability.)

If an organization has no metrics, inconsistent metrics, or no organized record of its metrics, there is nothing for the software tool to work with. By inconsistent metrics, we mean that each project manager uses hip-pocket metrics that he considers well suited to the "unique" needs of his "unique" project. Even if these unique metrics make it into the computer system, they cannot be added successfully to other project managers' unique metrics.

In consequence, a senior manager needs to enforce consistent metric practices throughout his jurisdiction. If several senior managers in a geographic division are to master-plan jointly, the division has to employ consistent metric practices. And so on up the hierarchy of a large, geographically dispersed corporation. As the advantages of uniform software practices become manifest, master-planning will become more widely advantageous.

The next requisite is that the project staff curves be fairly realistic. If they are some kind of dreams, the senior manager will not be able to count on staff becoming available in accordance with them. Nor can he or she safely assume that assigning staff in accordance with a project curve will keep that project on track.

There are three steps toward realism. The first is a sound estimating methodology, as we have been setting forth in Parts II and III. The second is using the staff curves supplied by the estimating methodology—even if higher management has later played games with the numbers to reach the ultimate bid. The original staff curves in such a situation represent the best estimate of what will actually ensue. They form a realistic base for staff planning. Staff plans derived from unrealistic bids will not accurately project staff needs.

The third step toward realism deals with the fact that there are many uncertainties involved in software development. When it becomes evident that a project not going according to plan must be replanned, the new staff curve must be substituted for the outdated one.

The point is to keep the master plan as close to realism as possible. Of course, that realism may spell trouble and it is human nature to avoid trouble. Nevertheless, putting up an unrealistic master plan just postpones trouble; it doesn't avoid it. Putting up a realistic one, even if it represents the current situation unfavorably, alerts managers to the need to do something about the approaching trouble. If a project manager replans the wayward project ahead of the actual disaster, the master plan also changes. The senior manager then has time to modify the overall plan in a disciplined way.

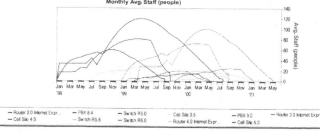

Figure 18-3:   *A portfolio of projects shown overlaid along the time line.*

When these projects' staffing profiles, shown in Figure 18-3, are added up at each time point, we get the aggregate master plan, shown in Figure 18-4.

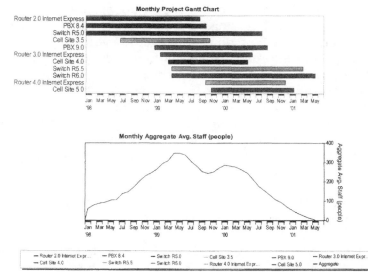

Figure 18-4:   *The master plan's aggregate view of the portfolio of projects, showing the overall staffing profile of the organization.*

What a Master Plan Does

Basically, a master plan plots the staff needs of the projects under a senior manager as far into the future as the projects have estimated their staff needs. In the ordinary course, the master curve should show available staff fully occupied for some time into the future, perhaps a few months. Thereafter, the staff curve might gradually decline as projects wind down. At other times, as the senior manager expects to begin new projects or to replan existing ones, the master curve may show an increase. Sometimes, there will be a "bump" in the near future when several projects contend for people.

The Master Curve Shows Declining Staff

Qualified software staff is scarce. Staff qualified in your particular process, tools, and work content is still more scarce. So, we assume that the farthest thing from your mind is a layoff. The alternative is to find more work for the staff coming off projects or to schedule some long-delayed training.

The work situation varies with the type of software organization:

- Vendor: A software organization marketing products generally has a backlog of planned releases or new products. The senior manager can search among them for one whose beginning date can be moved up to absorb the staff coming free.
- In-house: These organizations often have a backlog that is years in duration. The senior manager can select one to occupy the staff to be available.
- Contractor: An organization of this type is more at the mercy of its clients. The senior manager can try to speed up the beginning date of a project on the way in. Failing this approach, he or she can look among the ongoing projects for those that can effectively utilize a few people until new projects begin.

Another alternative is to find something else to do with the staff coming off completed projects:

- There may be cosmetic or other minor defects in products currently in progress or recently released, to which surplus staff could turn its attention.

- There may be extensions to current products that have had little priority, but could now be added.
- There may be frequently used components that could be turned into reusable components. Making a component reusable beyond its original application involves some additional time and effort.
- Finally, there is always need for training.

A software organization is in a continual process of estimating and bidding. The staff curve gives estimators the means to see if and when they are likely to have staff available. It may influence their judgments as to whether to bid a little low or a little high.

The Master Curve Shows Increasing Staff

In a time of expanding business, the master plan may show more projects with staff needs than the number coming off completing projects. That can be a signal to

- borrow people within the company
- line up contract people
- step up hiring
- survey subcontractors
- defer training and vacations
- stretch out some projects

In some cases, the increase in staff is just a bump. A bump of a couple of weeks may justify the use of overtime. A stretch of overtime running into months is counterproductive.

Control of Project Backlog

In the opposite situation, the staff level is relatively fixed. The senior manager can start or continue projects only within the limits set by the staff level prescribed. He or she can maintain this constant level only by feeding in projects from a backlog. Thus, the backlog has to be controlled. The nature of this control varies in the three categories of software organizations:

In-house. Management assigns priorities to the backlogged projects, subject to the realities of matching projects against staff capabilities. Whether to increase development budgets in order to whittle down the backlog more rapidly is a top-management responsibility dictated by such factors as the pressure to keep up competitively and the state of the balance sheet.

Software product vendor. There is no close-in limit to the number of software products to which a vendor might aspire. A senior manager, however, would normally have a budget that sets the staff level. Within this level, he or she has to meter projects on a priority scale influenced by marketing considerations.

Software contractor. This type of software organization has less influence on its backlog. It may, inescapably, have to increase or decrease staff (or resort to subcontractors) to match its backlog pressures. It can try, however, to maintain a cooperative relationship with its clients, one that allows it to adjust schedules to match staff capacity. It can also adjust its bids, higher or lower.

Coping with Powerful Project Managers

Sometimes, the senior manager is relatively weak, organizationally. One of the project managers, however, may be strong. He has an excellent record of bringing in products of good quality within time and budget. He owes this record to an effective team, a strong architect, and some good designers and testers. His status as a winner may give him the organizational clout to hold his team together even during low spots in his need for staff.

To counter this tendency to hoard staff, the senior manager needs the overall picture provided by the master curve. Buttressed by this curve, the senior manager becomes better able to force the issue of reassigning some of the project manager's people to projects that need them.

Now, decisions of this sort are not easy to bring off. On the one hand, no one wants to break up an effective team. On the other hand, no one wants to see some other project go down the tubes for lack of resources. Getting the most effective use of critical staff and maintaining the capability and morale of existing project teams—the trade-off is wrenching. The staff curve does not solve this kind of problem. What it does is provide project managers and senior managers with a macro level of facts to work with.

Planning Staff at the Enterprise Level

So far, we have been describing how to master-plan the work of a single software organization at a single location. More and more, however, we are seeing very large enterprises with software organizations in many divisions at many locations. It is possible to plan software development at a level higher than a single division.

Each location can forward its master plan electronically to a central planning staff. That staff can summarize the plans. The responsible executive can balance staff and workload over many divisions. This effort rests upon common metric practices among the participating locations. Beyond this minimum, the employment of common methodologies, processes, tools, and reusable components will facilitate the reassignment of staff and the redistribution of workloads.

"Process standardization can increase organizational flexibility," Michael Hammer and Steven Stanton observed. "When all business units are performing a process the same way, a company can easily reassign people from one unit to another to respond to shifts in demand. Its organizational structure becomes much more plastic."[2]

The contrary view is that divisions are little businesses of their own. They are supposed to have the responsibility to satisfy customers and make profits in their own way. Carried to the extreme, this view makes it difficult to balance workloads, even though the enterprise-level staff curve reveals opportunities.

"While corporate executives should be prepared for this reaction, they should not give in to it," advise Hammer and Stanton. "The rewards of standardized processes are great, and they're worth fighting for."

Hammer and Stanton were writing of the conflict between horizontal processes providing products to the customer and the vertical fiefdoms of traditional organization, not of software development. Nevertheless, we believe their conclusion is just as applicable to the processes of software development. The ultimate goal is to standardize the processes, methodologies, and tools of software development, corporation-wide.

---

[2]Michael Hammer and Steven Stanton, "How Process Enterprises Really Work," *Harvard Business Review* (Nov.-Dec. 1999), p. 115.

Chapter 19
Improving the
Software Development
Process

We made the point in the earlier chapters that there are, at a fundamental level, only two ways to do a better job of software development. More specifically, there are only two ways to improve three of the key metrics—time, effort, and reliability.

The first is to do a better job of development. That is the subject of this chapter.[1] The second is to reduce the amount of work a software product involves, by reusing components. That is the theme of the next chapter.

There is little doubt that everyone wants to improve software development. An exception may be those who put getting to market ahead of every other consideration—they are, in effect, indifferent to process improvement. For most, however, the issue at hand is how best to go about process improvement.

In our previous books, we dealt mainly with the nuts and bolts of process improvement. Here we take a broader look. For instance, there is reason to believe that the effectiveness of software development has actually been declining in many companies in recent years. At

---

[1]The use of measurement to monitor process improvement is not a new subject for us. Our first book, *Measures for Excellence: Reliable Software on Time, Within Budget*, devoted two chapters to it. *Industrial Strength Software: Effective Management Using Metrics* assigned ten chapters to it. The third book, *Executive Briefing: Controlling Software Development*, intended for busy executives, made do with one chapter.

least, process productivity of the projects reported to the QSM database fell during the last three years of the twentieth century, as Figure B-5 shows (see Appendix B).

It has also become evident that effectiveness is greatly affected by decisions taken before the Main Build Phase even gets under way. The understanding brought to the game by clients affects those decisions. By client, we refer to the customer acquiring a large software system, not the buyer of personal computer software.

From the client's point of view, a better process in the Main Build is nice. It should enable a development organization to turn out what the client needs a little sooner, at a little less cost. The client's main focus, however, is on what it needs to do its own business better. It wants *performance* that meets its needs.

Performance Comes from the Entire Process

What is this software development process that we are trying to improve? It is almost like the age-old story of the blind men trying to describe an elephant. You know, feeling the trunk, the first blind man says, "It is like a big snake." Feeling one of the tusks, the second blind man says, "It is like a huge tooth." And so on.

Accordingly, in Figure 19-1, we crammed in every aspect of software development that we could think of. Then the first person we showed the drawing to inquired archly, "What about the care and feeding of the people?"

"Darn," we replied, thinking quickly. "That is all over the chart, of course."

Even without a separate line to underscore the importance of the people who do the work, the diagram is complicated. We are going to take a stab at explaining it—briefly. Our main objective, however, is to emphasize the complexity of the software development process. Improving it, in consequence, is going to get a little hairy.

At the top of Figure 19-1 are the four phases, each of which terminates in a major milestone. Within each phase, the work may be divided into several iterations, each terminating in preset criteria constituting a minor milestone. Each phase, or each iteration within a phase, may progress through the workflows shown in the second set of boxes. In parallel with the phases and workflows are twelve activities listed vertically: business case, risk management, architecture, models, tools, reviews, testing, configuration management, metrics, replanning, project management, and client coordination, most of them leading into a string of activities listed horizontally. The vertical line on the left, through the little circles, implies that project management has to manage all of it. This line also suggests that it all has to be coordinated with the client. This complicated diagram, which at best can only suggest the even more complex process lying behind it, is the process that we are tasked to improve.

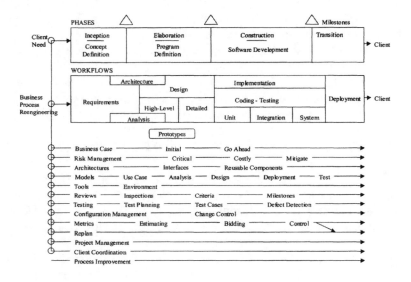

Figure 19-1: The software development process consists of four phases within which software people carry out the workflows guided by the many activities shown on the lower half of the diagram.

Pre-Phase: Needs

Could an existing business process be made more efficient by converting part of it to software operation, or by supporting it with software? That is what happened to payroll preparation long ago. In the beginning of the software age, clients could say, "Let's just turn this business process, say, payroll, over to software as it is."

Today, a client organization has to think through what it needs to operate its own business more effectively. In the age of the Internet, for example, that usually means conducting more of its business in cyberspace—relations with suppliers, relations with customers. It means managing its internal affairs horizontally, with the focus on the customer—not vertically, with the outdated emphasis on the stovepipe departments.

At this stage of the software age, it is more fitting to reengineer the process first. The client establishes the need for software to operate a reengineered business process. That need begins to imply some degree of definition of what the software is to accomplish and what level of performance it has to reach.

The pre-phase covers everything that goes on before responsible executives decide to establish a project and go into the first phase.

Inception Phase (or Feasibility)

This phase delimits what is to be done, takes a first stab at the system architecture, evaluates critical risks, and makes the initial business case. The senior graybeards operating this phase also need to consider the following questions:

- Is the proposed software realistically related to the business processes it is to implement? If the business process has not been sufficiently worked out, the software to implement it cannot be specified with much precision.
- Can the proposed software be organized into a series of releases, so that only what is known about the proposed business process is implemented in the initial release?

In addition, the client has to permit someone—in-house, a consultant, or the software development organization—to take the time this phase needs. In addition to the schedule time needed to do this work, people working incur costs. In one way or another, this cost gets back to the client—often through the overhead tacked onto later contracts.

What does this phase have to do with process improvement? If the criteria properly belonging to this phase are not addressed adequately, the project eventually fails: The process underlying the later phases fails to produce a product. Alternatively, if the project's feasibility is marginal, the developers have to struggle to a not-very-satisfactory conclusion. Again, the effectiveness with which they execute the later phases is reduced. Measures of that effectiveness would show reduced productivity, in other words, the opposite of process improvement.

Our point is that the decisions the client makes as to how to handle this phase influence the effectiveness with which the development organization can later carry out the balance of the process. In other words, not only do development organizations have to work on process, clients need to appreciate that their decisions on handling this first phase have an effect on the level of operation that the software organization can achieve.

Elaboration Phase (or Functional Design)

The point of this phase is to get far enough along in the understanding of what is to be done to permit a software organization to prepare a realistic estimate for the next phase, Construction (or Main Build). "Far enough" implies a sufficiently precise gauge of the functionality and, hence, the size of the proposed system to support this estimate of time, effort, and reliability. The tasks of this phase are to further refine, or elaborate, the requirements, the architecture, and the risks to the point of supporting a bid.

Again, it is evident that the client needs to be deeply involved. Software organizations can carry out the detailed work of this phase, but the performance the software is to provide is surely the province of the client—subject to feedback from the software people as to what is possible in the price and time frame.

Even before this phase gets under way, however, the client has to consider source selection. What organizations will it invite to bid? Surely, they should be qualified. The client has the duty of assessing that qualification in some manner. At the least, the prospective bidders should know how to develop software. To phrase that thought in "process" language, bidders should have a software development process and they should have a record of operating that process effectively. They should at a minimum be able to repeat it. The most unequivocal evidence of that qualification is the core metrics on recent projects. If a prospective bidder can't produce the core metrics, well, that tells you something.

Then, when the bids come in, they can communicate volumes to the client who is disposed to ponder their significance. The key indicator here is realism. Does the bid provide an allowance of time and effort sufficient to carry the project to a product of the performance and reliability needed? Again, an analysis of the core metrics can answer this question more solidly than the voluble promises of a silver-tongued marketeer. All too often, the low bidder is in that position only because it lacks the metrics to locate its bid at a realistic level. To be crystal clear, the award should go to the lowest *responsible* bidder. That is the lowest bidder with a realistic project plan solidly based on a repeatable process.

Construction Phase (or Main Build)

The actual conduct of this phase is the responsibility of the software organization. It is during this phase that what people typically think of as the software process takes place. In reality, as we have been emphasizing, process involves the whole trail, from needs to performance in operation.

The software organization should track its progress on measurable elements such as effort expended, work units completed (source lines of code or function points), and defects discovered. It should apply statistical control to the running results, as outlined in Chapter 13. It should also exert progress control at milestone points.

It is the client's responsibility, then, to track the software organization's tracking control. Sometimes, projects do not go according to plan. At the least, they have to be replanned. In the worst case, they may have to be cancelled. In either case, the client is involved.

Transition (or Operation and Maintenance)

The fourth phase covers the period during which the product moves into the operating environment, either one operating site, in the case of a specialized system, or to many operating sites, in the case of a large deployment. Since these sites may differ to some degree from the in-house system on which the software organization conducted the system test, the system operators have to be trained. Defects encountered in practical operation have to be corrected.

Commercial vendors generally arrange with selected customers to conduct beta testing during the latter part of the Construction Phase. After that, general sale begins. Correction of remaining defects or further improvements await the next release of the product.

Phases Are Implemented by Workflows

Each iteration in a phase is carried out by workflows, as characterized by the second horizontal lineup in Figure 19-1. The principal elements are the familiar requirements capture, design, implementation, and deployment. An iteration employs some selection of the workflows, depending upon where along the phase route it is located and what is to be done in it. Preceding requirements elicitation is the establishment of client need, sometimes by some kind of business process reengineering.

As shown on the diagram, architecture determination takes place during requirements capture and the first part of the design workflow. At about the same time, the analysis function refines and structures the requirements. Architecture determination veers into high-level design. At times, designers may find it advantageous to prepare prototypes of a poorly understood feature to establish that they can, indeed, build it within the constraints of the project. If the feature interfaces to users, the designers may demonstrate the prototype and obtain feedback from users. Detailed designs are then coded and subject to several levels of testing, completed by system testing and field deployment.

In the meantime, the phases and workflows are being worked on, in keeping with the string of activities suggested by the lower part of Figure 19-1. Note that metrics support estimating and bidding. Later, during design and implementation, metrics are basic to progress control. Failure to progress can lead to replanning of the project and revision of the metrics. Project management and client coordination base much of their oversight on the insights provided by metrics. Moreover, as we shall develop more fully later in this chapter, metrics provide the means for measuring process improvement.

This brief description of the software development process hits only the high points. For further information on the Unified Process, refer to *The Unified Software Development Process,* by Ivar Jacobson, Grady Booch, and James Rumbaugh, the process's three principal developers.[2] For entry into the documentary world of the Department of Defense, refer to its acquisition guidelines.[3]

Process Improvement Comes Hard

Some have tried to sugarcoat the human effort involved in software process improvement: You are assured that like the little train that could, you too can go faster and climb that hill. That's true in the sense that a few have done it before you. But many have tried and few have succeeded. For example, let's look at the record of the contributors to the QSM database.

---

[2]Ivar Jacobson, Grady Booch, and James Rumbaugh, *The Unified Software Development Process* (Reading, Mass.: Addison-Wesley, 1999).
[3]*Guidelines for Successful Acquisition and Management of Software-Intensive Systems,* Department of the Air Force, Software Technology Support Center, Version 3.0 (Hill AFB, Utah: 2000).

Process Productivity Rises Slowly

In Appendix B, Figure B-5 charts the average value of the process productivity index of the information technology systems reported to QSM from 1983 to 2000. Its value improved from 13.8 to 17.3, or about 0.23 index points per year. During the three-year period, 1997 to 2000, however, the index dropped to 16.6, about -0.23 per year. (We discuss that decline further in Appendix B.) Thus, it takes about four years for the database average to gain or lose a whole point on this scale.

A whole point every four years amounts to a long time between psychic rewards. During the six years from 1985 through 1990, for instance, average productivity was essentially flat. However, by viewing the process productivity index in tenths of a point, managers can see a tenth of a point of progress (or decline) about twice a year, on the averages cited in the previous paragraph. Of course, if they make a concerted effort to get better, they can see more frequent evidence of progress.

During the eighteen years charted in Figure B-5, the reporting companies were developing larger, more complex systems, and interfacing to larger numbers of other systems than used to be the case. They did well to hold their own and even improve. The overall lesson the data provides, however, is this: Process improvement comes hard.

The QSM database, though it now contains more than 6,300 projects, is a very small slice of the entire software world. How the rest of that world is progressing, this database does not tell us. Moreover, organizations report voluntarily. The mix of reporting organizations is not the same each year. The database does not necessarily track the progress of the same organizations from year to year, though some have been reporting for many years. So, what the database tells us is interesting, but not conclusive. In the case of any single organization, of course, it can reliably track its own process productivity from project to project and from year to year.

Process Productivity Extends Over a Great Range

In Chapter 1, Figure 1-3 displays the distribution of the process productivity metric, expressed in terms of the productivity index. This figure brings out the very great range of productivity found even in the software organizations that are far enough advanced metrically to be keeping track of their process productivity.

From the great range this figure displays, we can draw the lesson that an organization toward the lower end of the scale can do much better if it succeeds in improving its productivity. In fact, each successive productivity-index number multiplies process productivity by a factor of 1.27 over the previous index number. An organization that can move up three index numbers *doubles* its process productivity and reaps the attendant benefits. It cuts the cost of software development a lot!

The figure implies that wherever your organization currently rests on this scale, many organizations are at least three index numbers higher than you! It demonstrates that improvement of that magnitude is possible. Other organizations have already accomplished it. Moreover, some of them may be competing with you.

How about all those software organizations not represented in the QSM database? Most of them don't keep much in the way of metrics. If they did, we would probably find that they rest at the lower end of the scale. We are convinced that if organizations keep the core metrics and apply themselves to improving their process, they can move up the scale.

Why Has Process Improvement Been Hard?

QSM's metric records indicate that some process improvement is taking place. The record indicates that it is possible. Yet these measurements show that many of the software organizations measured fall far short of what is possible. Moreover, the vast majority of software organizations that keep few metrics are very likely doing poorly. The long string of disasters befalling software projects confirms this belief.

We have been in the trenches with this issue—asking why process improvement is so hard—for more than a quarter of a century. We perceive three underlying reasons:

- Software managers are trapped in immediate economic pressures.
- Clients are generally uninformed on the problems of development.
- Development is just plain hard—complicated, involved, complex, as Figure 19-1 suggests, and beyond that, ever changing.

In the following sections, we discuss each of these impediments to process improvement.

Trapped in the Economy

As we discussed in Chapter 2, the resources available to get something done are limited, whether you are in the private sector, trying to compete for customers' money, or in the public sector, competing for the limited budget that some remote legislative body has provided.

This competitive reality has an effect on line managers. It focuses them on the job at hand, on getting it done within the current budget to meet a delivery date that is always too close. They have little time for process improvement. They have no funds to support a wide-ranging effort.

The implication of this shortsighted focus is that these managers might be willing to finance a little improvement that is directly related to the needs of their project. They are not much interested in supporting the broad range of improvement activities that Figure 19-1 implies. That would cost a lot of money, which they do not have. It would divert their meager staff from the project at hand, which they are committed to deliver right soon.

In addition, line managers are up against another obstacle. Process improvement implies a change in their organizational practices. The dilemma is that the existing organization works, at least after a fashion. It will get the software system out. At least, it is working on it. Reorganization would disrupt current project efforts. Eventually, the reorganized organization might be better, but during the reorganizational interval, day-to-day management has the daily work to get out.

For reasons such as these, working management tends to hang back. The result: Attempts to get line managers interested in improvements of this scope seem to have been a losing battle—except for the handful of organizations on the upper end of the productivity scale.

Need for Client Participation

At point after point in the four phases of the software process, the client plays an important role. For example, it is largely the responsibility of the client to decide what the product is to be and what performance it is to attain. It is the client who must allow the time and expense of working through the first two phases. The client must accede to the schedule that provides enough time to complete the Main Build successfully. If time pressure is acute, the client must help sort out the set of functions to be included in the first release. At the same time, however, it is largely the responsibility of the development organization to improve its process in the Main Build Phase. The catch is, unless the client plays its part effectively, the development organization's improvement efforts are seriously obstructed.

Unfortunately, thus far in the software age, many clients have had little understanding of their responsibilities in the overall software process or of how their discharge of these responsibilities affects process improvement. Reaching them is a key challenge. They have many other responsibilities. They don't have the time to master software process in detail. Like a banker, though, who lacks the time to master, say, steel production, but does take the time to look at the steel company's balance sheet, clients could find the time to look at the software equivalent of a balance sheet.

On the banker's balance sheet, the capital budget reflects a client company's commitment to upgrade its plants and machinery for the years ahead. In software development, the gain in process productivity reflects a company's commitment to software tools, methods, process, and other development knowledge. The process productivity numbers reflect the fact that investments in process improvement are reducing cost, schedule, and staffing, and are improving quality and reliability. Thus, the process productivity index is roughly equivalent, for this purpose, to the capital budgeting term on the balance sheet with which executives are already familiar. Process productivity on software development's "balance sheet" provides clients at a glance with insight into the development organization's future prospects.

Software Development Is Difficult

Bridges collapse at rare intervals. Aircraft crash a little more frequently. The tires on sport utility vehicles blow out even more often. Just keeping our own house and its technical contents functioning requires the services of a plumber, an electrician, an air-conditioning technician, and a score or so of other specialized experts, all on call. Software development is the queen of all the technologies. In one software organization or another, it embraces all the other technologies. And much of it is *intrinsically* hard, according to Fred Brooks's analysis.

Brooks divides its difficulties into those that are "*essence*—the difficulties that are inherent in the nature of the software—and *accidents*—those difficulties that today attend its production but that are not inherent."[4]

---

[4]Frederick P. Brooks, Jr., *The Mythical Man-Month: Essays on Software Engineering, Anniversary Edition* (Reading, Mass.: Addison-Wesley, 1995), p. 182.

What is this "essence" that makes software development so difficult? One aspect of this difficulty is software's *complexity.* One of the reasons for this complexity is that software must *conform* to the endless convolutions of the activities it is implementing. On top of that, these activities are *changeable.* The society that software serves is continuously changing. Then, software itself in the form of source code is sort of *invisible* to process participants other than programmers. Standardized drawings (or artifacts) of process steps preceding code, such as architecture, functional design, detailed design, and test plans, are beginning to alleviate interpretation difficulties.

The "accidental" difficulties can be diminished by better artifacts, programming languages, development environments, tools, and the like. Much has been accomplished along these lines and more still remains, as the dozen or more process-productivity index levels above most software organizations attest. But enhancing process productivity is "No Silver Bullet," as Fred Brooks titled a chapter in the book just cited. It is the result of hard, intelligent work. (Brooks did not expect the software field to find a magic, "silver bullet" solution.)

Some might think of the shrink-wrapped products that we buy as silver bullets since we don't have to develop them at all. A more elegant version of shrink-wrap is the big systems that companies such as SAP and Oracle provide. Reusable components may come close to being silver bullets, but that bullet has a ways to go yet. Unfortunately, these potential bullets share a feature: While they spare you, the user, the task of software development, they do force you to shoehorn them into your existing ways of operating. You change—not them! That immerses you in another set of problems.

However, some organizations must develop the shrink-wrap software, the big systems for hire, and the reusable components in the first place. Those organizations and the user companies developing their own software still find software complex and its development difficult.

Some Organizations Are Improving Their Process

The Capability Maturity Model levels of the software organizations monitored by the SEI have risen since the model's introduction in 1987, as diagrammed in Figure 19-2.[5] The report in which the diagram originally appeared covered 6,168 projects in 1,166 organizations. There were 1,512 assessments, of which 283 were reassess-

---

[5]*Process Maturity Profile of the Software Community 2000 Year-End Update,* Software Engineering Institute, Carnegie Mellon University (Pittsburgh: 2000), p. 18.

ments. During these 13 years (1987-2000), the number of organizations assessed at Level One, Initial, has declined from 80 percent of the
total to slightly less than 50 percent, while the number in Levels Two
and Three (Repeatable and Defined) has risen. Few organizations have
yet reached Levels Four and Five (Managed and Optimizing).

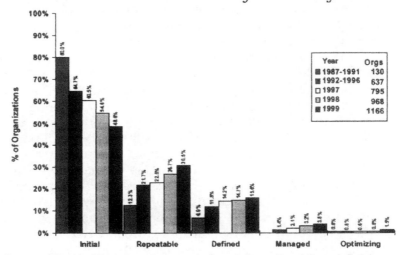

Figure 19-2:   *This diagram, from an SEI report, shows that*
the software organizations assessed since
1989 have been moving up the scale.

Moving up one level (One to Two, or Two to Three) took more than
three years at first, prior to 1992. Since then, moving up one level has
taken an average of two years. With the benefit of experience, organizations are learning how to improve more rapidly. However, getting
from Three to Four is still a challenge; it has been averaging three
years.

Moving up even one level is a considerable achievement, relative to
a process-productivity index point, as the comparison on Figure 1-3
shows. It appears that the effort that the organizations included in
Figure 19-2 have devoted to process improvement is paying off. It is
concerted effort that improves the software process.

The Capability Maturity Model was one of the first steps in that direction, beginning in the mid-1980's. Its principal developer was Watts S. Humphrey, working at the SEI. He described his approach in his book *Managing the Software Process*, in 1989.[6]

During the next few years, as the model came into use, Humphrey observed that it was not the complete answer to process improvement. "The CMM is an organization-focused process improvement framework," he wrote in *IEEE Software*. "While the CMM enables and facilitates good work, it does not guarantee it. The engineers must also use effective personal practices."[7] Humphrey described these personal software practices at length in 1995, in his book *A Discipline for Software Engineering*.[8] His intent was to train developers in what they needed to know to develop effective software. Remember, the CMM functions at the organization level. The Personal Software Process (PSP) applies at the level of the individual developer. During the next few years, he ran a number of individuals through this program and they seemed to profit from it, as individuals. By 2000, Humphrey was able to cite a number of studies to the effect that "even modest use of the PSP methods can be beneficial."[9]

He found, however, that introduction of the Personal Software Process at the organization level was not easy. A broader framework was indicated and that became the Team Software Process (TSP).[10] Instead of sending a solitary PSP-trained engineer back to his organization where his new methods were overwhelmed by the weight of the old methods already in use, Humphrey trained a team and sent it back. The new methods had a better chance of surviving.

The general conclusion is inescapable. Substantial process improvement takes concerted action on three levels: the individual developer, the team, and the organization. Action on this scale is beyond the financial scope of individual project managers. It requires the informed support of the entire executive structure of the company. It also requires understanding and perhaps even some financial forbearance from client organizations. The cost of PSP training, for example, is not inconsiderable—two weeks, full-time (interrupted by a three-

---

[6]Watts S. Humphrey, *Managing the Software Process* (Reading, Mass.: Addison-Wesley, 1989).

[7]Humphrey, "Using a Defined and Measured Personal Software Process," *IEEE Software* (May 1996), p. 79.

[8]Humphrey, *A Discipline for Software Engineering* (Reading, Mass.: Addison-Wesley, 1995).

[9]Humphrey, "The Personal Software Process: Status and Trends," *IEEE Software* (Nov.–Dec. 2000), p. 74.

[10]Humphrey, *Introduction to the Team Software Process* (Reading, Mass.: Addison-Wesley, 2000).

week intermission), at about $1,000 per week per engineer, plus salary and expenses. Moreover, it is advisable to train at least a team. An individual trainee tends to revert to the company norm when he or she gets back.

That kind of cost requires a second look in most companies, so it is not surprising that it has taken Humphrey's three initiatives more than a decade to get into some use. Large-scale improvement such as the CMM and PSP evaluations are now reporting seems to require this larger approach. PSP improves the individual; TSP improves the small team; CMM improves the organization. All three have to work together to get the kind of improvement that is possible.

The Place to Start Is Where You Are

Most software organizations are still down in the rubble of process improvement. They are there, not because they enjoy life in the lower ranks of process productivity, but because they are busy getting the day's work done. Only a few have the depth of understanding that it takes to mount a broad-gauged process improvement effort. We can say, "They should." In real life, they haven't. They aren't likely to, under the cutthroat circumstances that prevail in most of the industry.

Over time, the forces of competition will wash out those lowest on the productivity scales. What can keep you from being one of them, or even one of the middling ones that hang on by the skin of their teeth? Well, measurement seems to be the first requisite. Your organization needs a means of measuring where it now stands in the process improvement marathon. Conventional productivity is not reliable, as we pointed out in Chapter 7. CMM assessments require a get-ready investment and, worst of all, are infrequent.

Process productivity comes from measurements of size, time, and effort at the project level. It is available at the conclusion of each project—or even during the latter part of each project, when the metrics become available. It is inexpensive because it comes from metrics that you need anyway for estimating, bidding, and project-control purposes.

Process productivity can measure whether improvement is taking place, but measurement as such does not improve process. Something else is needed to achieve improvement.

The management sequence is something like this. As knowledge of your standing spreads through the organization and as executives learn where software development stands in relation to competitors, an atmosphere for doing something about it develops. Doing something is going to take time and cost money, but the alternative, drifting, begins to appear even worse. You're ready to take off!

Chapter 20
Managing
Reusable Components

Why do we have a chapter on software reuse in a book devoted to the use of a few core metrics to manage software development? We have this chapter because reuse carries the promise of reducing the *effective* size of the software product. As you have seen in the earlier chapters, reduced size leads to decreased schedule time and effort. It leads to lower cost of development. In the highly competitive economy that the whole world now inhabits, these are critically important objectives. Therefore, a premium on reuse is emerging. As with other economic activities, software reuse has to be managed. And management of reuse implies the presence of metrics for that purpose.

"You are making a big deal out of the obvious," cynical readers might complain. Not so, we insist. If the values of reuse are so obvious, why has it taken so long to get here? Why are we still so far from widespread reuse? There are two answers: Reuse itself has turned out to be very difficult. Managing it, in the sense of controlling the time and effort involved, has turned out to be equally difficult.

The term "reuse" implies a single concept, but we may examine it as a series of five historical stages. The first four of these stages did not work out too well—in the sense that reuse did not spread very widely. We may hope, however, that the fifth stage will be more successful. One of the keys to that success, of course, will be the application of metrics to managing that fifth stage.

The Five Stages of Reuse

Before there was any thought of reusing existing software, projects consisted of completely new work. Projects had a clearly defined size, namely, all the code that they were to write. That size, commonly expressed in source lines of code, was the basic input to estimating the time and effort the work would take. Of course, figuring out the size ahead of time was not easy. At least, trying to estimate the time and effort that *reuse* would take did not distract managers and estimators. Even today, most projects are still in that happy state. And in the less happy state of not reaping the benefits of reuse!

Hip-Pocket Reuse

Before long, of course, some early developers wrote some code that they thought was pretty good. So they put it in their figurative hip pockets, pulled it out on the next project, twisted it to fit the different requirements of that project, and stuck it in. Their personal productivity went up a bit. The programmer on the next desk saw that going on, borrowed the piece of code, and adapted it to another part of the project.

Team leaders, managers, and estimators had some grasp of the fact that experienced programmers were using some *hip-pocket code.* They knew that experienced programmers were more productive than novices were. However, they generally had no numbers telling them the degree of this hip-pocket reuse. Survivors of the olden days estimate that it might have been about 10 percent.

Of course, the benefits of this hip-pocket reuse would show up as a slight increase in whatever productivity metric the organization might have been using. The point to note is that no one had to try to figure out what the *effective* size of the reusable code fragment was.

Reuse from a Repository

One day an inspired manager thought to himself, Why not gather all this hip-pocket code together. Thus, the repository was born. Code fragments in the repository had a known size. Thus, in theory at least, that size (or some fraction of it) could either be subtracted from the system-size estimate or added to the new-code estimate. Managers could estimate effort and time on the basis of the now-reduced size of the proposed system.

Unfortunately for the success of this inspiration, there turned out to be a lot of costs associated with it.

Code acquisition. There is the cost of getting a code fragment—subsystem, program, object—into the repository in the first place. Within a single organization working in a common architecture, the code fragments at least fit within the pattern of that architecture. When a repository tries to spread its reach more broadly, it runs into architectural and interface discrepancies. That leads to the need for what has become domain or architectural analysis. It is necessary, but it is also a cost.

Code development. Organizations attempting reuse found by experience that the cost of developing a reusable component is about three times that of developing a similar component for a single application. That means other developers have to reuse the component at least two more times before it begins to pay off. In a single organization, that level of reuse is hard to achieve.

Repository operation. The repository itself has a cost of operation. It has to acquire components, store them, fix them when the original developers find flaws, update them as periodic releases arrive, find ways to describe them for potential users, and invoice users for using them. At first, covering all these costs adds up to a reuse charge comparable to what potential users would spend to develop the component themselves.

Start-up costs. Upper management has to finance the cost of starting a repository and carrying it for two or three years until the charges it can impose on projects cover its operating costs. In the typical software organization where the funds largely belong to the projects, the overhead money to finance a repository is hard to come by. Eventually, reuse lowers costs, but under this cost pattern, it is hard to get started.

Finding costs. A developer contemplating reuse has to find the reusable component. If there is little more in the repository than the code, the finding cost is high. If the reusable components are small— say, object-sized—they are hardly worth the trouble of finding them.

Modification costs. The using project has to bear the cost of adapting the supposedly reusable component to the special circumstances of its application. If the programmer has to decipher code to make this modification, the cost begins to approach that of developing a new component, especially if it is small.

Verification costs. The using project has to verify that the reusable component works in its new setting. If it can do this by black-box testing, that is, without having to understand the code in the component, that verification is inexpensive. If it has to resort to white-box testing, that is, getting into the component code, costs mount.

You can imagine that in the early stages of a reuse, these costs to the using project can add up to as much as, or even more than, the cost of developing the components themselves. In time, with additional reuse, the cost would come down. There is little incentive in the first stages of reuse for projects to reuse. In a repository restricted to a single software organization, it turned out that there was little likelihood of getting up to the three reuses at which reuse would turn profitable. So, although the repository approach to reuse had a little success here and there, on the whole, it did not solve the reuse problem.

Product-Line Reuse

Advocates of reuse have believed, at least since the early 1980's, that a line of products put out by a single company division provided opportunities to reuse the software from one of the products in later products of the same line. A number of companies have had success with this approach, and, in *Software Reuse: Architecture, Process, and Organization for Business Success,* authors Jacobson, Griss, and Jonsson recount some of their experiences.[1] A product-line manufacturer, of course, has control over the line's architecture and interfaces. It can specify the procedures or the content of the tables in a component that enables reusers to adapt it to a later product in the same line. It can run its own repository, usually nothing more elaborate than the engineering drawing number system it already has.

In practice, even product-line reuse was not quite that simple. The groups working on different products in the same line already existed and tended to resist the architectural and interface uniformity into which reusable components could efficiently fit. A new organization that Jacobson, Griss, and Jonsson called "the reuse business" had to be created in each product-line division. That took upper-management support. It took financing for three years or so before reuse began to pay for itself.

One Hewlett-Packard study of two applications, for example, reported the following:

- productivity (in non-commented source statements per engineering month) increased by nearly 50 percent (new plus reused code compared to new code only),

---

[1]Ivar Jacobson, Martin Griss, and Patrik Jonsson, *Software Reuse: Architecture, Process, and Organization for Business Success* (Reading, Mass.: Addison-Wesley, 1997).

- time to market (estimated for one of the products) fell 42 percent,
- defect density dropped 75 percent, and
- return on investment ranged from 215 percent for one of the developments to 410 percent for the other.[2]

Numbers like these are very attractive, but Hewlett-Packard spent more than a decade getting there from zero. A good many companies lack perseverance on that scale. Once again, reuse scored some successes here and there, but it did not lodge everywhere.

ERP Systems Are a Form of Reuse

Enterprise Resource Planning (ERP) systems, available from vendors such as SAP, Oracle, and J.D. Edwards, provide software packages that implement the administrative functions common to many businesses. All businesses are alike in broad terms, but at the level specific to any one company, they differ. Hence, the ERP packages are adaptable to the special needs of each installation. Making this adaptation is not simple, so an industry of consultants has sprung up to assist client companies. At the core of ERP, however, are the reusable packages.

Where initially the categories of reuse were largely restricted to one company or even one division of a larger company, ERP systems—and a second class of reusable systems that fall in this category, the business-to-business and business-to-customer interfaces to the Internet—are spreading to many companies. That spread, however, increases installation difficulty. The basic software has to be adapted to many applications. That means the application has to be analyzed and the more-or-less reusable packages have to be adapted to the different needs the analysts find. The task is further complicated by the fact that the business is often being reengineered (or perhaps engineered for the first time).

Architecture-Wide Reuse

The final stage in the evolution of reuse appears to be components that are reusable throughout the extent of a given architecture, or sometimes throughout many architectures. This stage is called component-based software engineering or component-based development.[3] In this stage, relatively little new code needs to be developed. The costs of the reusable components are known because they are for sale in the mar-

---

[2]Wayne C. Lim, "Effects of Reuse on Quality, Productivity, and Economics," *IEEE Software* (Sept.–Oct. 1994) pp. 23–30.

[3]W. Kozaczynski and G. Booch, "Component-Based Software Engineering," *IEEE Software* (Sept.–Oct. 1998), pp. 34–36.

ketplace. The finding costs are low because means such as catalogs and widely understood drawings have been developed to inform reusers. The modification costs are minimal because the reusable components have been developed to fit within established architectural, interface, and variation standards.

Because the reusable components are being sold to a number of customers, the initial development cost is soon recovered. Prices tend to fall to the level needed to cover the reusable-component company's running, updating, and marketing costs. This level would be much less than the cost to a project of developing its own version. This savings provides a substantial incentive to users to employ reusable components.

Reusable components at this level would fit an architecture and interfaces and would be readily adaptable to the project's variables through an accessible variation mechanism. In consequence, the project cost of making use of such a reusable component would be small. Figure 20-1 illustrates the evolution of reuse through these stages.

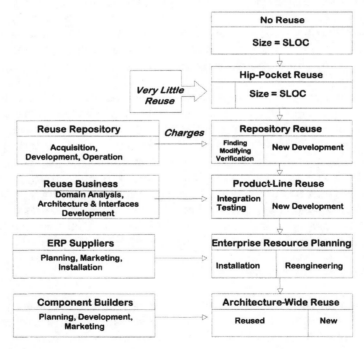

Figure 20-1:   *Software reuse has been evolving through a series of stages. Its evolution is now entering the age of architecture-wide reuse, in which companies specializing in component-building will supply reusable artifacts to companies building systems.*

What Are the Essential Supports for Reuse?

On the face of it, reuse seems to be an obvious idea. It can reduce time to market, effort, and development cost. It can improve quality and reduce defects. Yet it has come into use only slowly. This slow pace is due to the general lack of the elements needed to support reuse:

- architecture
- interfaces
- variation mechanism
- process
- modeling language
- tools

Of course, these six elements exist, but they exist in a great variety to which it is difficult to match reusable components. The supports must be standardized or, if not fully standardized, made more common. That way, the six supporting technologies can vitalize component-based software engineering, as suggested in Figure 20-2, and bring reuse to a higher level of application.

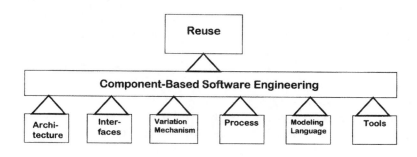

Figure 20-2:   *Six supporting technologies underlie the new art of component-based software engineering.*

Architecture Accommodates Components

Components are not widely malleable. They fit into particular kinds of applications, but not all applications. In other words, components fit a particular software architecture. The software industry already has a number of architectures for which it has prepared reusable components.

For example, J2EE (Java 2 Enterprise Edition) is, in effect, an architectural pattern into which components called Applets, Servlets, and Java beans fit. The industry will undoubtedly specify additional architectures into which categories of new components will fit. However, if a project wants to strike off into a totally new and different architecture, the existing reusable components won't necessarily fit in it.

Interfaces Enable Inter-Component Communication

Components communicate with other components. A reusable component, therefore, must have an interface that matches the interfaces of other components within the same architecture. Each interface consists of two elements: message-passing capability and message-content understandability.

The interfaces within a given architecture need to be consistent, but not between architectures. The interfaces in a real-time system may be quite different from those in a business system.

Variation Mechanisms Multiply Adaptability

It is unlikely that standardization will ever become so complete that reusable components will always fit a new application without modification. To overcome this limitation without multiplying the number of reusable components unmercifully, developers should be able to vary a component in some simple, easy-to-understand way. This way is called a variation point or variation mechanism. For instance, this mechanism may be a table in which developers list the constants pertinent to the application.

The variation mechanisms should be relatively standardized so that, first, users can understand them without studying manuals and, second, users need not understand the interior code of the component. Above all, a user should never have to recode the interior of the component. In addition to the cost to the user that recoding would entail, it might make the component incompatible with future changes or releases the vendor makes.

Process Provides Locations for Selection

People complain that there cannot be any one software development process because every software problem is different, every organization is different, and so on. Obviously, that is true. On the other hand, every sizable project has to, or ought to, go through the four phases.

Within those phases, certain workflows ought to occur: requirements capture, analysis and architecture, design, implementation, and test.

The Unified Process has helped to clarify this pattern.[4] One of the reasons for having a consistent process is to have a pattern within which the selection of reusable components can take place. It is comparatively easy to select a reusable component at the architectural level, but it is very difficult to make this selection at the code level. Code is difficult to understand, and few in the industry can do it. In the past, the fact that reuse selection had to take place largely at the code level greatly hindered the adoption of reuse.

Modeling Language Provides the Means

With a process in place, the software industry can have a drawing language similar in capability to the blueprints on which the engineering professions have long depended. In general, the earlier engineering fields depicted actual physical objects—resistors and capacitors, for instance—in their drawings. Software developers have only immaterial ideas to show, at least until the execution code turns a conceptual bit into a packet of electrons that operates a transistor. Software people are working with a series of models before they get to that little burst of electrons—hence, the term, modeling language rather than engineering drawing. But the two serve a similar purpose. That purpose, in the case of the modeling language, is to express the progress of software development through the series of workflows. To fill this gap, the Object Management Group standardized the Unified Modeling Language (UML) in 1997.[5]

For reuse, a widely understandable modeling language enables someone other than the original programmer to comprehend what is there. After all, if you don't know what is there, how can you reuse it? UML enables you to find a reusable component at the point in the workflow process where you are currently working. The architect, for example, working in a specified architecture, can pencil in reusable components at that point. Analysts and designers can firm up the selection from their models.

---

[4]Ivar Jacobson, Grady Booch, and James Rumbaugh, *The Unified Software Development Process* (Reading, Mass.: Addison-Wesley, 1999).

[5]The Object Management Group, founded in 1989, is a consortium of hundreds of companies in the United States, Europe, eastern Asia, and the rest of the world, dedicated to the evolution of standards for the development of software. A standard is proposed by a member company or a small group of member companies, considered by a task force of other member companies, passed by the overall Technical Committee, and ultimately approved by the OMG Board of Directors. The OMG does not produce computer products, only standards. One of its best-known standards is CORBA (Common Object Request Broker Architecture).

Tools Implement These Needs

With a process implemented in a modeling language, a large market for software tools comes into existence. It becomes financially feasible for tool builders to provide high-quality tools, further reducing the time and effort consumed by software development.

The Unified Process and the Unified Modeling Language are now in place. Architecture, interfaces, and variation mechanisms need much further work. Tools have to be adapted to what will come. The way forward seems clear.

Internet-Hosted Services

At present, the code that constitutes a software tool resides on the licensee's computer equipment. As the Internet reaches higher speeds and reliability, tools might reside on a host site and be downloaded as needed by software development organizations. The site might also host reusable components. They might be represented in some standard fashion, such as the Unified Modeling Language, enabling developers to select a component at the point in the development process (architecture, analysis, design, and so forth) at which they are working.

Estimating in the Age of Reuse

The macro-estimating methodologies currently in use grew up in the age of little or no reuse. In that age, it was possible to express the amount of functionality a project was to encounter in metrics such as source lines of code or function points. As the percentage of reuse increases, these metrics are no longer proportional to the amount of work—time and effort—that projects encounter. In the absence of reuse, there are no reusable components coming in from the side to complicate the SLOC count and, in consequence, to confound the estimate.

Similarly, in the case of informal, hip-pocket reuse, estimators and managers have no formal knowledge of how much of it there is. So they try to estimate the size corresponding to the total functionality. If the hip-pocket reusers then do a little better because they make some use of code they used elsewhere, that increased efficiency simply shows up in a slightly higher process-productivity value. Then, on the next project, these experienced programmers continue to make use of their hip-pocket code. The slightly higher process-productivity value remains valid for that project. The metric point is: No one has to try to figure out what the *effective* size of the reusable code was.

Components from a Repository

In the case of reusable components from a repository, their size is known. However, the actual size is not a reliable guide to time and effort estimating because the programmer would almost certainly have to modify the code in using it again. Modification involves all those costs of repository code that we enumerated earlier in this chapter. The repository could offset the first three—code acquisition, code development, and start-up costs—with the charge it makes for the reusable component. The second three—finding, modification, and verification—are project costs the project would have to estimate.

Product-Line and ERP Reuse

In the case of product-line reuse, the product-line manufacturer controls both the reuse business and the projects. The manufacturer is still faced with the same problem: how to estimate the cost of reusing a component.

In the case of ERP systems, the amount of new code is usually small, compared to the amount coming in ERP components. Both elements—ERP code and new code—have to be put together and the amount of work involved in doing that has to be estimated. In the next section, we describe one approach to making that estimate.

Any Metric Measuring Functionality Will Do

Let us begin with first principles. What we are really after in software development estimating is some metric that is proportional to the amount of work to be done. In the early days of software development, that metric was source lines of code and, later, function points. After a time, estimators found that they could convert the function-point count into a source-code count by multiplying function points by a *gearing* factor. For example, that factor was around 100 for the common third-generation procedural programming languages like COBOL and FORTRAN. In other words, one function point was typically programmed by about a hundred instructions.

Finding That Metric

The ultimate objective is to find some metric that measures functionality, whether it's SLOC, function points, or something else. In Chapter 5, for instance, we recounted our experience in using as a metric the number of requirements to be implemented in successive releases. At the QSM Users' Conference in October, 2000, Anthony Hemens, Dominik Letkiewicz, and Rob Ward gave an oral report on their initial efforts to relate metrics of ERP functionality to time and effort.

In brief, they obtained data on three installations from SAP and three from J.D. Edwards. For each company, the data consisted of project metrics describing functionality with the corresponding time and effort for each project. J.D. Edwards supplied seven functionality metrics for each project, such as new versions, unique event rules, and objects selected. The SAP functionality data was principally the number of implementation guidelines. For each ERP company, the investigators summed the functional metrics. Then, they found the statistical relationship between the functional metrics and the time and effort data on each project. They found essentially the same nonlinear relationship that QSM had found relating size in SLOC to time and effort.

However, these relationships were not in the same data range as the SLOC relationship. The next step, therefore, was to find a gearing factor that would enable them to run these ERP metrics on the QSM estimating software, which was designed to operate on SLOC as the measure of functionality.

Other metrics, of course, are just as valid as measures of functionality, but they must be converted into their SLOC equivalents in order to use the existing estimating software. This conversion is accomplished by multiplying the newly chosen metric by a gearing factor to convert it to a SLOC equivalent. To make this conversion, the experimenters first had to assume that these six projects had been executed at some process productivity level. They chose the level of the mean process productivity of the QSM business database. On this assumption, they found the gearing factor to be 50. The principle is the same as the gearing factor mentioned above, around 100, that is necessary to relate function points to third-generation procedural SLOC.

Calibration to the Rescue

This work is very preliminary. Hemens and his colleagues had data from only six projects. More data will likely change the details, but the principle is clear. Metrics related to ERP functionality can be related to the resulting time and effort. Holding the gearing factor constant at 50, the resulting process productivity value will give the relative productivity of each installation. With a process productivity value and an estimate of the metrics associated with the functionality to be installed, estimators can reach a more reliable value of time and effort for ERP installations.

Fundamental Principle Reinforced

This initial work with ERP estimating reinforces a fundamental principle. Knowledge work, at least knowledge work directed to an objective, as software development or ERP development is, can be represented by the equation first introduced in Chapter 7:

$$\textit{Functionality} \text{ metric at some } \textit{Quality} =$$
$$\textit{Effort}^a \text{ x } \textit{Time}^b \text{ x } \textit{Process Productivity}$$

Any metric or set of metrics that measures the functionality to be embodied in the product can be employed. The resulting relationship can be brought into the range of QSM's original work, expressed in SLOC, by finding the corresponding gearing factor. That results in process productivity numbers in the range originally established.

Basically, this methodology appears to be applicable to any kind of project work. Norden's original studies in the 1950's, for example, were based on hardware development. We can estimate the time and effort required by what we now call "knowledge work" in this way. There are, however, two prerequisites:

- The knowledge work to be estimated has to be organized as a project subject to economic limitations. A lone scholar, living on inherited wealth, pursuing personal growth in a library, for instance, does not constitute a project subject to economic principles.
- We have to find a metric (or combination of metrics) that measures the functionality of the intended product. Finding that metric and relating it to the project variables (time, effort, defects) requires some organizations to keep project records of time, effort, defects, and the functionality metric on a sufficient number of projects for the statistical analysis to be reliable.

It is evident that software reuse, or component-based development, falls within these parameters. It is also evident that much work remains to develop appropriate functionality metrics and the corresponding relationships. Moreover, much of this work, of necessity, must await the further development of architecture-wide reuse.

Architecture-Wide Components Increase Reuse

In the case of architecture-wide reusable components, most of the costs are greatly reduced and the remaining costs are known. Because the reusable components are being sold to a number of customers, the initial development cost is soon recovered. Prices fall to the level needed to cover the reusable-component company's running costs. Those prices will be policed by the market. This level will be much less than the cost to a project of developing its own version, providing users a substantial incentive to employ reusable components.

Because reusable components at this level will fit an architecture and its interfaces and will be readily adaptable to the project's variables through an accessible variation mechanism, the project cost of making use of such a reusable component will be small. When architecture-wide reuse is fully developed, this cost might be so low as to be buried in overhead.

Initially, it might be 10 to 20 percent of the cost of developing the component on the project. In other words, for estimating and bidding purposes, the effective size of the component might be entered into estimating relationships at 10 to 20 percent of its code size. We'll find out what the actual percentage is when we get there.

A rough indication of increasing reuse is contained in Figure 20-3. It is clear that past practice employed all new code and that, at some time in the future, the percentage of component reuse will be very high. In some current applications, reuse is already exceeding 90 percent. In between these extremes, the proportion of reuse will gradually increase as the practice spreads.

It is apparent that reuse reduces not the actual size of a proposed system, but the portion of that size that the project is actually going to work on. It is this effective size that is to be used in estimating. Since this effective size is less than the actual size, the estimating outputs—time, effort, defects—can be reduced accordingly.

Functionality or Process Productivity?

The problem the industry currently faces is that reusable components have not yet completely reduced the effective system size by the amount of their actual size. Time and effort are still needed by the project to find the component, to determine what it can do, to modify its interface to fit those on the project, and often to modify what the component does to fit the needs of the project.

Type of Reuse   Percentage of Source Code

```
                     0   10   20   30   40   50   60   70   80   90  100
Past Practice, No Reuse
     New             _____
     Reused          ...
Hip-pocket Reuse
     New             _____
     Reused          ... (None counted)
Repository
     New             _____
     Reused          _____
Product line
     New             _____
     Reused          _____
ERP
     New             _____
     Reused          _____
Architecture-wide
   At first
     New             _____
     Reused          _____
   Later
     New             ____
     Reused          _____
```

Figure 20-3:   *As reuse becomes more widely established, we expect the percentage of new code in projects to decline and the percentage of reused code (and artifacts generally) to increase. The cost of development will depend increasingly on the cost of producing, marketing, and inserting reusable components and verifying their operation in the new setting.*

Moreover, a modified component requires extensive integration and system testing—potentially a substantial cost. In fact, at the current state of the art, even a component used *as is* might need considerable testing in its new home. It might not have been adequately tested in its original application for the different demands of the new application.

As we reported in earlier chapters, estimating effort and time rests primarily on the following relationship:

$$(\text{Effort}/\beta)^{(1/3)} \times \text{Time}^{(4/3)} = \text{Size (at Quality Level)} / \text{Process Productivity}$$

It follows, then, that we can accommodate effort and time estimating in the presence of reuse in two ways. The first is by adjusting the estimated size of the proposed product, as we have been implying in the preceding sections. The second is by adjusting process productivity.

Size Adjustment Seeks "Effective" Size

The size term estimators seek is the effective size of the entire product. This size, for estimating purposes, would be something less than the actual final size, because some advantage would be gained by reusing components or COTS (commercial off-the-shelf). To obtain this effective size, many organizations have chosen the path of increasing their estimate of the new-code portion by adding *virtual code* to it. Virtual code is their estimate in size terms of the amount of work reusing a component would entail.

Contrariwise, an organization might add up its estimate of new code and the actual code count of reusable components to obtain the total size of both. It could then subtract a fraction of each reusable component's code count, to reflect the amount of work that it estimates will be saved by reuse. For example, a component contains 10,000 SLOC. The developers expect to incorporate it in the system product with about a quarter as much work as developing a new component would entail. So, the estimator subtracts three quarters of the component size, 7,500 SLOC, from his overall size estimate.

The effective-size approach disposes of only the estimating task. Projects would still have to use actual size—an estimate of new code plus actual size of reused code—to control progress during the Main Build Phase. In practice, the actual count during Construction is going to be just that: actual. Code completed will be counted automatically. Similarly, the projected code count (against which the actual code is to be compared) has to be of the total code.

Second Approach Adjusts Process Productivity

As the software equation cited above shows, estimators can increase the estimate of effort and time (needed to accommodate reusable components) by adjusting process productivity downward. The first step in this approach is to find the value of process productivity that is to be adjusted.

It is preferable to obtain this value by calibration from data recorded on completed projects, and that is the approach we have emphasized earlier in the book. However, many software organizations have little or no record of core metrics on past projects. Thus, when they first begin to employ the core-metrics approach to estimate new projects, they have to estimate the value of their process productivity. To aid them in this effort, we provide a set of questions for estimators to answer. They can score the answers to obtain an approximate value of process productivity.

When the matter of revising process productivity to accommodate reuse began to arise, we extended this set-of-questions approach to reuse applications. Following is this second set of criteria. Note that each one is phrased in terms of percent, degree, number, or some other value, capable of being numerically scored.

1. percentage of reused software in the system under consideration
2. degree of complexity of integrating reusable components with new code
3. degree of experience of the development team with the reusable components or with existing code proposed for reuse
4. number of functional interfaces in the reusable components and/or the existing code
5. percent of these functional interfaces to be used
6. degree of complexity of the functional interfaces to be used
7. time needed to select reusable products
8. amount of analysis effort required to assess impact on existing code
9. adequacy of documentation supplied with reusable components
10. adequacy of support provided by component builder
11. amount of effort required to document reusable components
12. percent of total testing to be devoted to regression testing of reusable components

These are the kinds of practical criteria that people considering reuse can assess. Each item is scored on a scale of 0 to 10.

For the size term to use in applying the software equation set forth above to the reuse application, estimators employ their best estimate of actual new and modified code. To estimate the value of process productivity to use in a reuse application, the estimators start with a value of process productivity obtained from calibration, if past data is available, or from the responses to the first set of questions. Then, from the scoring of the twelve questions in the reuse set, the estimators adjust the value of process productivity initially obtained downward. The value has to go down because the project needs more time and effort to do the work of integrating and sometimes modifying the COTS and reuse components. From this point on, estimating and project control proceed in the established way.

The ultimate answer, so far as reuse is concerned, is to get to architecture-wide reuse. At that point, the reusable components are so good that, aside from the price put upon them by component-supplying businesses, there is little or no cost to the project in using them. The effective size of the work—the functionality—to be estimated is the amount of new and modified code. That, of course, is the ideal. It still seems to be quite a ways in the future.

Chapter 21
Metrics
Backstop Negotiation

At one highly successful software company . . . the protocols [to be observed in preparing for and conducting negotiations] include . . . using a set of objective criteria to shape the discussion.

—Danny Ertel[1]

Objective criteria—there's a fine phrase. Included within it would be the criteria that can be measured, such as the five core metrics. Without objective criteria, negotiation sessions degenerate into back-and-forth contention in which the most forceful participants tend to dominate. And force often rests more on executive rank than on knowledge of the objective criteria. Aside from rank, "Without metrics, you're just another person with a different opinion," as Stephan Leschka of Hewlett-Packard nut-shelled it, as quoted in an article by Michael Mah.[2]

Research in negotiation scenarios finds that: "An identical situation, given to 20 or more pairs of negotiators to resolve, often results in no two outcomes being alike." The lesson seems to be that the out-

---

[1]Danny Ertel, "Turning Negotiation into a Corporate Capability," *Harvard Business Review* (May–June 1999), p. 58.
[2]Michael Mah, "Metrics and the Seven Elements of Negotiation," *IT Metric Strategies* (April 2001), p. 3.

come "has as much to do with the interaction between the parties themselves" as with " the substantive issues that are 'on the table.'"[3]

Unfortunately, basing negotiation on objective criteria presents two difficulties to decision-makers. First, the criteria may not be available at all. To have them, someone has to have established them long before, collected and analyzed the underlying data, and made it available to the decision-makers. Second, the decision-makers have to have the inclination and time to acquire this data.

As Peter Keen observed long ago, "Under pressure, decision makers discard information, avoid bringing in expertise and exploring new alternatives; they simplify a problem to the point where it becomes manageable."[4] That is, manageable in their immediate time frame. If they have oversimplified what has to be done, the manageable problem turns sour.

If there are no metrics on which the parties to a negotiation can base their discussion, their inevitable disagreements revert to shouting matches. Shouting leads to anger. Anger leads to the attorneys. Attorneys lead to court. Now, let us call in, as *our* expert witness, the expert witness in software litigation Tom DeMarco: "Corporate litigations are enormously expensive, typically costing the two parties a total in legal fees that dwarfs whatever settlement is finally imposed. Neither side wins, everybody loses."[5]

While the years-long process of litigation is dragging out, the software itself, very likely badly needed by the client, is stalled. What might have been is not there to do the job, and the company suffers accordingly in the marketplace.

"Every company today exists in a complex web of relationships, and the shape of that web is formed, one thread at a time, through negotiations," according to Danny Ertel.[6] Software development itself functions within a web of relationships.

Negotiation Bridges Gaps

There are always at least two parties, users and developers, involved in a software project. Often there are many more. In the negotiations that bridge the gaps between the parties, users may be represented by experts in software applications. They, in turn, may have to work

---

[3]Michael Mah, "The Multiple Dimensions of Metrics: Metrics and the Learning Organization," *IT Metric Strategies* (Feb. 2000), p.11.

[4]Peter Keen, "Information Systems and Organizational Change," *Communications of the ACM* (Jan. 1981).

[5]Tom DeMarco, *Slack: Creating Room in Your Company for Profits and Growth* (New York: Broadway Books, 2001), pp. 83–84.

[6]Ertel, op. cit., p. 55.

through the company's purchasing agents. On the development side, the people who will actually work on the project may be represented by their company's marketing organization or by various levels of executives, as suggested by Figure 21-1.

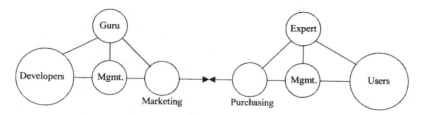

Figure 21-1:   There are many relationships in the software development scene where negotiation may take place, some of them suggested by this diagram.

For in-house applications, various layers of managers may separate the users and developers. Between a client and an outsourcing organization, the channels of communication may be quite formal; a change in or addition to an existing program goes through paperwork and managerial approvals on both sides.

On either side of these gaps, the managers along the way may be fine citizens, long experienced in their own line of work. The record shows, however, that many of them have little grasp of the complexities of software development. Yet these gap-fillers, often without either user or developer experience, are responsible for conducting the negotiations. They need the objective criteria.

Objective criteria fall into two categories: those that can be measured and those that must be appraised. This book is concerned primarily with criteria that are measurable, in particular, with the five core metrics. That is not to say that other criteria are not of great importance. They are, but they must be evaluated, not just measured, by appropriately experienced people.

In Chapter 13, for example, we referred to the practice of establishing criteria that a project should meet at each review point. Some of these criteria would be measurable. Others would be less numerically oriented, such as identifying critical and significant risks (discussed in Chapters 9 and 10). Once a risk has been identified, it can be put on a list and tracked. Developers can count the number of risks currently on the active list. But the initial identification and the later determination that the risk has been mitigated entail judgmental activities other than measurement. These activities, in general, rest upon a professional background in software development.

The Principal Gaps

In the early phases, the two parties have to establish that a particular system is feasible both technically and financially. Technical feasibility rests upon professional judgment, but the business case rests, in part, on an estimate of the size of the proposed system. Disagreement between the parties over these judgments constitutes a gap to be bridged by negotiation.

Then, at some point before the Main Build Phase, the developers have to firm up the size to support the estimate and bid. During the Main Build, the developers may encounter trouble; for example:

- The estimate, bid, and the plan based on them may not have been realistic.
- The plan may have been fairly good at the time it was promulgated, but the project has now run into problems the parties did not anticipate.
- The client has learned that the product as currently specified does not meet its real needs.

Again, the size has to be revised and the remainder of the project has to be replanned and reestimated, as discussed in Chapter 15.

The next gap is the one between a release and the subsequent one. The final gap in this sequence is the one between the final release in this generation of the product and the first of the next generation. With each release, the work to be done has to be analyzed, estimated, bid, and planned. At each point, the parties have to negotiate their way across the gap.

In organizations where business engineering is under way, emphasis is moving from software systems, each specialized to a stovepipe department, to a single customer-oriented software system that cuts across the stovepipes. That leaves gaps requiring negotiation between the stovepipe managers and the business-engineering advocates.

A still more encompassing gap is the one between a client and an outsourcing company. They must negotiate the contract that governs their relationship. Then, during the relationship, they must negotiate each new issue that arises. And finally, they must negotiate their ultimate separation. Nothing lasts forever.

Different Interests at Stake

The organizations and people on either side of these gaps have different goals in mind. These interests are legitimate, but they do differ:

- A software contractor tends to focus on getting as much time for a project as it can, at a high price and a low quality or reliability requirement. Seems logical, right? The client, of course, wants the opposite. Also logical. Unfortunately, if either party succeeds in pushing the other too far into its hole, the result is not what either one wants. It looks like there is a difference between immediate interest and long-term interest.
- Within a stovepipe organization, the separate interests of the various departments may conflict with what is best for customers. The CEO's (and the business's) overall interest conflicts with the parochial interests of the stovepipe vice presidents. Again, the difference is between the immediate and the long term.
- A visionary executive's lofty view of what would be nice to have, such as a computer-operated manufacturing plant, conflicts with lesser officials' understanding of what is technically or financially feasible.
- At the time of overrun of a software project, the client might believe it has a contractual right to expect the project to be completed. The software organization might have reason to believe that more time and funds are legitimate. For example, in the view of the developers, the client might have been changing its mind frivolously (resulting in requirements creep). But, in the view of the client, the changes, arising from work on the project, were necessary.

A Job for Negotiation Man!

Marketing and executive types often feel that their commissions, bonuses, and stock options depend on getting the lowest (highest) price and the quickest (slowest) delivery. Each side wants to get the best deal on the work at hand. They feel less pressure, at least at the point of making the deal, to produce software of high quality and reliability, or to meet the needs of the users. Under these pressures, it is not unusual for the terms of the deal to be flawed, that is, for the eventual outcome of the project not to satisfy either organization.

Partway through a project, or near its end, blaming the client for not providing enough time or effort (money) in the original deal does not get the product finished. Similarly, blaming the software developer for being slow does not get the product out the door. What is needed is not performance-judging, not blaming, not emotionalism, not a fight—what is needed when trouble looms is a problem-solving approach. What are the facts at that point? The problem-solving approach replans the project on the basis of the then-current reality.

It is often possible for one of the parties to a software transaction to get lopsided terms in the immediate deal. If the eventual result is one of the software disasters that are so common, the long-term relationship is deep-sixed. The client fails to get the software it needs to support its business—this is not good. The software supplier loses money, a client, and status—not good. It is in the interest of both parties to have a long-term relationship that works. The challenge is to be able to work on the immediate problem while maintaining the harmony of the long-term relationship.

"When Eastman Kodak transferred its data center operations to IBM, the two companies struggled to balance the deal and the relationship," Ertel reported.[7] Their solution was to work out together the issues that pertained to individual deals and the issues that governed the larger, longer relationship between the two companies. "Trouble with a lack of trust or poor communication—relationship issues—could not, for example, be solved through changes in pricing, software licensing terms, or other deal-related issues."

To avoid a failed project, a severed long-term relationship or, at best, a bumpy course, a certain amount of *hard* bargaining is in order at the point of establishing the initial relationship between the parties. They should negotiate the relationship to satisfy the needs of both. Later, when the two parties are operating under the terms of their agreement, individual projects will still run into troubles. But at that point, the parties will realize they have long-term interests in common. Their bargaining should then go into *soft* mode. It should focus on problem-solving, not blaming.

The Core Metrics Support Negotiation

There are many metrics and each one may undergird some aspect of some negotiation. However, the five core metrics are central to most

---

[7]Ertel, op. cit., p. 64.

economic negotiations. Moreover, providing the appropriate econom-ics—time and effort—underlies getting the functionality right. That, in turn, leads to a reasonable estimate of size. Size, together with process productivity, underlies time and effort (cost) estimates. With these four metrics, we can project the defect rate, one indicator of product quality.

Both the client and the software organization want a successful outcome of the immediate project (the deal) and of many projects to come (the relationship). Success on the project at hand includes achieving results on the five core metrics:

- working within the *time* and *effort* (cost) limitations of the bid
- realizing the *size* that provides the functionality needed
- achieving the expected reliability level (*defect rate* or MTTD)
- working at the *process productivity* level that reaches these goals

Successful accomplishment of a series of projects (the long-term rela-tionship) depends on concluding each project (deal) successfully. Some of the participants at the deal level may be fixated on the project at hand. Marketing people, for instance, may obtain commissions based on the immediate deal. They may be less concerned with follow-on relationships, which they see as largely out of their control. They may view long-term success as being dependent on the capabilities of the existing software organization (of which they may have, privately, a low opinion).

Software executives and project managers may place so much pressure on developers to complete a project within the limitations of a poor deal that morale falls, fatigue rises, and staff departures material-ize—hardly precursors of long-term success.

Figure 21-2 summarizes what we have been saying in this chapter. We have to have some metrics if negotiators are to make use of them. We have to lodge them in a usable database so the negotiators and others concerned can get at them when they need them. We have to enable negotiators and others to understand the metrics and how to use them in some depth. Then we, as either the development organi-zation or the client, have to make use of the measurements to control development, to overcome deviations from plan, and to replan a project when the facts point in that direction. Moreover, the results of replan-ning have to be recorded in a formal change order. The change order has to be issued at the time of replanning, when the circumstances are

clear to all concerned. That is much better than negotiating dimly
remembered circumstances, months after they have ceased to exist.

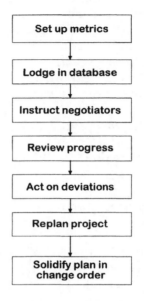

Figure 21-2:   *The use of metrics to plan and control software
development provides negotiators with a solid
base on which to work.*

Software Development Depends on Negotiation

Unfortunately, negotiation has been confused by some with the sleazy
tactics of the stereotyped lawyer. Like it or not, interests of competing
parties do differ. In the helter-skelter world of "devil take the hind-
most," there is always a strong temptation to take the immediate
bucks and move on to the next sucker. That is negotiation (if you can
even call it that) at its worst. That mind-set does not wear well in the
difficult arena of software development.

Rather, negotiation should be the process through which two parties reach mutually beneficial commitment. It divides the interests of
both sides into the short-term, affecting the immediate deal, and the
long-term, maintaining their relationship. It builds momentum on
both sides toward changes in attitude.

Negotiation Depends Upon Metrics

Both clients and developers need to depend upon objective facts—the five core metrics—as the central focus in organizing and operating software development.

They must link their negotiators' priorities to their company priorities—namely, a successful project in a series of successful projects. Accomplishment takes precedence over penny-ante stuff.

Finally, not every deal is preordained, not every relationship is blessed by heaven. In Ertel's view, top executives "make their negotiators feel comfortable walking away from a deal that is not in the company's overall best interest."[8] It is hard to walk away from money, but sometimes the core metrics leave the negotiators with no alternative. But other times, the core metrics provide the factual base that saves the negotiation.

Take-home thought . . .

> Blaming feels good
> Like software should.
> Litigation feels better,
> If only software could.

---

[8]Ertel, op. cit., p. 56.

Chapter 22
Motivating Participants In the Software Development Process

The participants in the software development process tend to be highly motivated—or at least they start out that way. Some studied software engineering or computer science in college. Some majored in other areas but have gravitated to software development because it interested them. Once in the field, they find it interesting. What they turn out, software to run the world, has for many years been a center of attention. For this work, they have gained psychic rewards and economic emoluments, sometimes high, but seldom stingy.

Similarly, the several levels of supervision and management over the software development process are also highly motivated, in part by the same factors that animate the staff—the intrinsic value of the work. Added to these factors is a greater economic reward. Even beyond these two elements is a third: the satisfaction offered by providing a quality product, on time and within budget.

Indeed, the participants in the software development process can be highly motivated. Yet, all too often, they are not. This negative feeling seems to have fed back even into the colleges. *The Wall Street Journal* reports, "While U.S. colleges awarded 18% more bachelor's degrees in 1997 than in 1987, they awarded 37% fewer degrees in computer science, 24% fewer in math, 16% fewer in engineering, and 2% fewer in physical sciences, the National Science Foundation says."[1]

---

[1]David Wessel, "Professor Romer Goes to Washington," *The Wall Street Journal* (Jan. 25, 2001), p. A1.

What caused this decline in the inclination to pursue these tough subjects? Some people believe that the blame falls on the colleges. For instance, Paul Romer, a Stanford University economist cited in the same article, is badgering Washington to offer financial incentives to the universities to increase the number of science majors.

No doubt there are many reasons for this decline in science enroll-ments—of which the one in computer science seems to be the deepest. One reason, we think, is that word is getting back to the students that development projects are not being well managed. Surveys report that a considerable fraction of projects fail altogether. Other fractions grossly exceed their budget, run way over schedule, and lead to dozens of hours per week of uncompensated overtime. Failure after failure drains motivation, and the word gets back.

Then there are those who get into software development in their youth. In their twenties, they enthusiastically work the long hours. It is exciting and spiced by the likelihood of advancement. In their thirties, they have lawns to mow, children to play with, and wives or husbands to placate. The long, frustrating hours are no longer so inviting. In their forties, they seek other lines of work.

So, the motivation was once there. To the extent that poor man-agement attenuated it, good management can reinvigorate it. For, in software development, success depends on people.

People Are the Ultimate Resource

People solve problems, not estimating methodologies, processes, stan-dards, or tools, as we emphasized early in this book (Chapter 3). How-ever, software development is, at best, difficult. People have to sur-mount these difficulties. Therefore, to develop successfully, manage-ment, with the thoughtful support of clients, has to provide the setting in which people can work effectively. The estimating methodology, working within the framework provided by processes, standards, and tools, provides this setting. Still, within this setting, people solve the problems. That brings us to the question: How do you acquire, lead, and keep people?

Hire Good People

Innocent bystanders often say that the trick is to hire good people. It's a good thought, of course, but it is not so easy to implement. If you have a successful enterprise, you will attract good people. You will have the funds to pay above-average salaries, bonuses, and perhaps stock options. Still, you have to select the good people from among the many who apply—some of whom are not so good.

The usual outcome is that the *average* software organization pays *average* salaries and attracts *average* people. Perhaps you can do a little better, but you can't count on it. Half of us are going to be below average—that's a statistical fact!

Build Organizations

All is not lost at this point. One of the strengths of the organizing principle is that it takes *average* people and makes *superior* organizations out of them. The techniques are known, though not always practiced, particularly in software organizations. Broadly speaking, the techniques are something along these lines:

- Divide the work into staffing categories, so that not everybody has to know everything. In software, we have managers, requirements analysts, architects, high-level designers, detail designers, test planners, programmers, and testers, as well as specialties such as metrics staff, estimating staff, and process-improvement staff.
- Set up a process that enables the many people in these several categories to know where their piece of the work fits into the whole.
- Standardize the pattern in which the results produced at the various stages of the process are presented, enabling these different staffing categories to communicate with each other, as well as with the stakeholders.
- Draw off the repetitive parts of the process, such as making drawings, into tools, enabling the people to spend more time on the creative parts, less time on the routine parts.
- Set up repetitively used elements as standard components.

Keep People

People may be *average* when they are hired, but if they hang around awhile they become *above-average* performers. They become familiar with your process, drawings, tools, and the technical content of your business and its software. So, building a world-class software organization requires having people hang around.

Most of what people learn is learned on the job, not in formal training programs. It is hard to match training to what people need in order to do what comes up next week. We do not mean to discourage training. Have as much of it as you can. Try to relate it to the current work as well as you can. But since people learn by doing, try to keep your people (except the duds) for as long as you can.

What keeps people? Well, nice offices, competitive salaries, and benefits—all the paraphernalia of personnel practices play a part. But we want to draw special attention to the working situation. Basically, projects should be well managed. Above all, the time and effort allocated to a project should be realistic. People don't like to work on impossible projects, projects that fail, projects that require excessive and long-enduring overtime, and so on. People don't like to be scheduled so tightly that they have no time to recover when a task takes a little longer than expected.

Give People Time

Despite the help of job specialization, processes, standards, modeling languages, and tools, the work actually involved in software development is still very difficult. Addressing that difficulty falls to the people. In fact, as we sort out the simple work and automate it to various degrees, the remaining work, left for the people, becomes, on the average, even more difficult.

There is no evidence that people's brains are working any faster today than they did ten thousand years ago, during the hunter-gatherer stage of human evolution. In fact, to avoid the lions and tigers at the birthplace of the human race, in Africa, those brains had to work fast. The point we are moving toward is that accomplishing difficult knowledge-work takes human brain-time. In each project, there is difficult work left for the staff, despite whatever process, drawing programs, and tools we can provide. That work takes time. If management doesn't provide that time, whatever it is, the project goes awry.

Time is one of the gifts afforded us by mastery of a formal estimating methodology. Time is essential for human brains to do the work that is left for them. If an organization doesn't provide time on that scale, the human brains become discouraged and move on, to other organizations, sometimes out of the field altogether. Then you are not "keeping your people." Your potentially superior organization declines. Trouble looms!

Five Essential Motivating Factors

Successful projects rely upon the presence of five factors:

1. They get something done . . .
2. at a quality suited to the application . . .
3. in a limited time . . .
4. with limited effort . . .
5. at a competitive productivity level.

There are other factors, of course, but these five are the inescapable minimum that good management has to provide. In this final chapter, it should come as no surprise to you that the first step toward good management is to manage functionality (size), quality (reliability or defects), time (schedule), effort (cost), and productivity (process), as we have detailed in Parts II and III. Management of these five factors rests in turn upon establishing a metric relationship between them. There must be one; it must be reasonably accurate; and management must use it, as we discussed at length in Chapter 11.

Extending Estimating Wisdom More Widely

Even without the aid of formal estimating methodologies, project managers often realize that the time and effort figures being bandied about by marketing and executive managers in their own companies are short of what they need. They observe that executives in internal client departments or in other companies often have even less knowledge of software schedules and costs. Yet these executives have a large voice in setting the time and effort within which project managers must operate.

Of course, there is no easy answer to this dilemma. There are hard answers, however:

- All of us must try to communicate not only to software managers, but also to their superiors and clients, that there are reasonably accurate estimating methodologies that can provide the time and effort under which the Construction Phase is to operate. The first two phases, prior to the Main Build, should be carried far enough to get a good handle on the proposed product's functionality and, hence, its size (from which estimating starts).
- Moreover, project managers must learn to negotiate *hard* the terms of the relationship with clients, before

the contract is cast in bronze. It is at this point in time that they can win reasonable allowances of time and effort.

- Unfortunately, the initial contract is often not the last word. This contract cannot foresee every adverse circumstance that may come up during the Main Build. Project managers may have to renegotiate the plan and the time and effort projections to accommodate these unanticipated problems. At this point, both developers and clients have a common interest in a successful development. They must now learn to negotiate *soft* the differences that arise during the course of development. (For more on hard and soft negotiation, see Chapter 21.)

Both outsourcers and clients must become much more proficient in negotiating their differences. Only through better negotiation skills can they avoid the horrendous costs of conflict as well as the disastrous business effects of poor, or even failing, software.

In an interview that can be viewed in its entirety on line, Michael Mah[2] puts the relationship between client and outsourcer this way: "We have to teach people the difference between hardball negotiation before the deal is signed and a completely different kind of negotiation after the companies are 'married.' . . . The negotiation tactics that most companies use to get to a signed deal can create negative aftereffects in the relationship after the deal is signed, especially if one party is left feeling exploited."[3]

Mah notes that application development projects, especially the more innovative ones, have a large research-and-development component that requires special attention. "Most companies, regardless of the project, structure their contract as though they were a manufacturer contracting with a factory—that's an unrecognized flaw. You start the relationship on the wrong foot because the performance levels and the balance scorecards don't reflect R&D mechanics.

"You don't want to focus on overweighting cost reduction at the expense of other desirable goals," Mah goes on to say. "You want to balance time and effort with quality, reliability, and defect rate. After all, IT solutions that are poor quality are of very little use."

---

[2]Michael C. Mah is a principal with QSM Associates, a consultant with the Cutter Consortium, and a former editor of Cutter's *IT Metric Strategies*. He currently specializes in software-dispute resolution.
[3]These comments appear in an interview posted on the Cutter Consortium Website: www.cutter.com/consortium.

Ten Great Truths

The truth is, everyone has had trouble with software development. The sad truth behind this first truth is that we, as individuals, as managers, as organizations, have had trouble facing up to this truth. In recent years, however, many organizations are overcoming these troubles. Others are not yet so successful. Successful organizations have found that it is the intelligence behind successful software management that makes the difference. The first step toward identifying that intelligence rests on the effective application of simple metrics to manage software development.

The Five Great Truths About Metrics

First, there must be *an accurate way* to represent in metric terms what goes on in software development:[4]

- Establish a measure of functionality beforehand.
- Establish a measure of the productivity of your software process.
- From this functionality, given this productivity, estimate time, effort, and defect rate.

The feature that distinguishes the accurate way from other ways is the realization that time and effort are *multiplicatively* intertwined; they are interdependent; they cannot, with accuracy, be planned independently of each other. Every estimate is a time-effort pair, an effort with an associated time.

Second, we need this accurate way to underpin estimating, bidding, project control, and the relations between client and developer or client and outsourcer.

Third, we need this accurate way, not only for these business reasons, but because it is the only way to provide development people in appropriate numbers (effort) with enough time (schedule) to do the work at the quality and reliability levels needed by the client's application.

Fourth, we need this accurate way to provide a satisfactory working situation. The accurate way is the only way to keep staff around long enough to grow a superior organization.

---

[4]By "accurate" we do not mean "accurate to several decimal places." Software development, after all, is a human process, not a physics constant. The multiplicative relationship between effort and time gets enough accuracy so that management can manage to it. Nevertheless, there is still a lot of uncertainty present. For more on this point, see Appendix A.

Fifth, we need this accurate way to measure a software organization's competitive standing. This measure—process productivity—tells management and staff not only that they are on the right track for improving their organization, but also that they can endure for the substantial time it takes to grow a superior organization.

The Five Great Truths About Software Development

Metric truths are of great importance, but their further consequence is to make possible the realization of the five great truths about the field of software development as a whole.

First, there must be *an activity* to which to apply the five core metrics. That activity is the *process*. A software organization must have a way of doing its work. That way may be informal or it may be as concrete as the Unified Process. At the very least, it has to be repeatable, if estimates of time, effort, and process productivity are to have any meaning.

Second, there must be some *standards* and there have been—a lot of them, from programming languages to text editors. In recent years, the standards idea has moved on to the Unified Process and the Unified Modeling Language.

Third, there must be *reuse* of previously developed software to reduce the effort and time needed to develop the new product. There is considerable reuse already, under the general name component-based development. The pre-existence of process and standards is a prerequisite to more extensive reuse.

Fourth, there must be *software tools* to take over the routine tasks of software development. For example, there is no reason to make a developer hand-draw the rectangles, ovals, lines, arrowheads, and other features of UML when he or she can command a software tool to do so. Note, however, that first the modeling features have to be standardized before developing and marketing the tool becomes economic. As Jacobson, Booch, and Rumbaugh have noted, "Successful development of process automation (tools) cannot be achieved without the parallel development of the process framework in which the tools are to function."[5]

Fifth, there must be a means of bringing to the developer the *procedural knowledge* he or she needs to accomplish the task immediately at hand. This need arises out of the reality that the volume of knowledge applicable to software development is now overwhelming, with one example alone amounting to more than 20,000 pages. Mere

---

[5]Ivar Jacobson, Grady Booch, and James Rumbaugh, *The Unified Software Development Process* (Reading, Mass.: Addison-Wesley, 1999), p. 29.

humans need an automated tool to guide them to what they need when they need it.

These five truths about software development still leave it to people to cope with the creative side. That takes people in *sufficient* numbers for a time *sufficient* to produce a *sufficient* product at a productivity level *sufficient* to survive in a competitive environment.

The real beauty of these ten truths about metrics and software development is in how they work together—we get enough accuracy from the first set and enough effectiveness from the second set to make software development work most of the time. Coming full circle, it is the intelligence of the metrics that underlies the broader intelligence underlying software development.

Appendix A
Good Enough Is Better Than Floundering

There is a lot of variability (or uncertainty or noise) in the core-metric data produced by software development projects. To narrow this range of variability, we stratified the data. By stratify, we mean to sort out the data into classes; in Figure 17-1, for example, we sorted the data into three main classes: information systems, engineering systems, and real-time systems. Sorted in this way, the data points fall in three strata. To gain still greater precision for some purposes, we have gone beyond these three categories and stratified data into nine subcategories: microcode/firmware, real time, avionic, system software, command and control, telecommunications and message switching, scientific, process control, and business systems. Despite categorization, there is still a lot of noise, even in common applications within the same organization, even within the same development group. Why?

Well, the teams have different skill sets. Particular applications, even within the same application type, have different complexities. Management teams differ in the capabilities they bring to the scene. Customers differ in the amount of interaction they have with the software organization and their influence on the development team. And so it goes, on and on. These factors all contribute to the noise in the data.

Statisticians, engineers, and scientists have a name for processes that generate this kind of data—stochastic. Each data item is considered to be a sample from somewhere on a probability distribution; for example, the distribution provided by the statistical normal curve. Each sample may come from anywhere along such a curve. As a result, the series of samples, when they are plotted or subjected to statistical analysis, does not fit smoothly along distribution curves, such as the Rayleigh curve. The curve representing the stochastic data is rather jagged.

What is remarkable about this picture is that despite this ever-present noise, log-log regression gives us fits *good enough* to make the resulting functions useful. The functions are not precise like the speed of light reported by physicists: 299,792,458 meters per second. They are *good enough* for software management purposes.

Management wants functions that predict effort, time, and defects for the estimates that underlie their bids. They want predictions of these same three metrics over the course of the project to serve as the control side of plan-to-actual comparisons. They want a comparative baseline within the same application area with which to study improvements over time and comparisons (in a gross sense) between organizations. For all these purposes, they don't need decimal-point precision. They just need *good enough*.

Fortunately, we *can* see through the noise well enough to do decent engineering estimates and analysis.

We do encounter lots of noise in the time-varying behavior of individual projects. For example, when we plot SLOC generated per month versus time, we see a buildup, a peak, and then a fall-off in the magnitude of the code produced, as time moves on. However, the curve through the data points will not be a smooth one. Rather, it will be ragged—a noisy plot. The general pattern (in the software case) is Rayleigh-like. It can be handled mathematically by the Rayleigh-curve equation. A number of other up-down curves and their corresponding algebraic representations would also fit this jagged data just as well.

Plots of staffing (effort) or defects month-by-month show the same noisy result. These patterns must result from stochastic noise that is inherent in the software development process. This noise cannot be avoided. We must accept it as a fact of software life.

We can, however, model this behavior as a statistical process. We can map those uncertainties through algorithms (such as the software equation)[1] to give us useful measures of the uncertainties in the estimated management parameters (schedule, staffing, effort/cost, defects).

You haven't found much on these statistical complications earlier in this book. That is because we are writing for software people who

---

[1] Please refer to Chapter 7 for the development of the software equation.

know from practical experience that data on software projects is uncertain or, in statistical language, who already accept quasi-deterministic solutions based on expected values. We are addressing readers who want to develop software in an intelligent manner, not to master stochastic statistics. That would take another turn at college and, attractive as those years were, you don't have time to go through them again. After all, your real purpose (and ours) is to get good estimates (not perfect ones). *Good enough* to plan, estimate, bid, and control expensive software projects. *Good enough* to get projects done on time, within budget, and with decent reliability.

Keep in mind that the results reported in this book are not only statistically valid, they are also operationally established. We have been applying them (or helping people like you apply them) in business, industry, and government worldwide for more than twenty-five years. The list of users includes sophisticated organizations in the United States, Europe, and Japan. Throughout, we've kept one key idea uppermost:

Simple enough to use; sophisticated enough to work.

Appendix B
Behavior of the Core Metrics

The core metrics of the 6,300 projects reported to the QSM database between 1983 and 2000 exhibit two interesting behaviors. First, these metrics, summed in six periods of three years, conform to the pattern established by the software equation first developed in Chapter 7. Second, they show general improvement during the first five periods (Jan. 1, 1983, to Jan. 1, 1997) and a reversal during the final three years (1997 to 2000).[1]

Of course, the validity of the equation has been confirmed thousands of times in individual applications, both in forecasting the behavior of a coming project and in the actual behavior of a completed project. Nevertheless, it is gratifying that the behavior of the entire database is consistent with the pattern discovered in the 1970's, as described in the Introduction to this book.

The sources of the projects are worldwide—North America, Europe, and the Far East. The projects contain more than 200 million lines of code in more than 100 development languages. They embody 55,000 person-years of effort. The largest category of application is information technology, though engineering and real-time systems are also present.

---

[1]Douglas T. Putnam, QSM's vice president of professional services, prepared the analysis on which this Appendix is based.

The study divided the core-metric data from the 6,300 projects into six three-year segments. Analysis on a yearly basis had revealed a certain amount of fluctuation from year to year. Analysis in three-year increments, however, smoothed out these variations and better revealed the long-term trend.

As a reminder, the five core metrics relate to each other in the software equation:

Work product (at a *Reliability* level) =
Effort over a *Time* interval at a *Productivity* level

In this relationship, *work* product is measured by a *size* metric. In addition, the database provides *staff* for each project.

Study Results

Table B-1 summarizes the results. The behavior of each metric is set forth in the figures that follow, listed here in the second column.

Metric	Figure	First Five Periods	Last Period
Size	B-1	Declined	Big Jump
Effort	B-2	Declined	Big Increase
Time	B-3	Declined	Small Increase
Staff	B-4	Steady	Big Increase
Process Productivity	B-5	Increased	Declined
Mean Time To Defect	B-6	Slow Improvement	Big Jump

Table B-1:   *During the first five periods (1983 to 1997), declining effort and time led to increased process productivity. Circumstances reversed in the final period (1997 to 2000): As effort and time increased, process productivity declined.*

Size

Project size is based on a count of new code produced on a project plus an estimate of the new-code equivalent of reused functionality that was worked on during development. The trend through the 1980's and the first half of the 1990's was a consistent reduction in project size, measured in this way. However, in the 1997-to-2000 time frame, a marked increase in size occurred, as shown in Figure B-1. Average project size doubled.

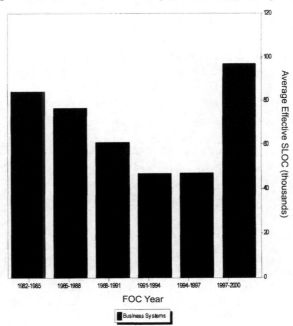

Average Effective SLOC vs. Full Operational Capability Year

Figure B-1:   *After a steady reduction in project size for more than a decade, sizes reported to the QSM database more than doubled as new software applications came into play.*

Effort

In Figure B-2, we can see that project effort declined from 165 person-months to 60 person-months during the first five three-year periods, a dramatic decline. In the final period, however, effort nearly doubled, to more than 100 person-months, following the same path as effective size.

Average Life Effort (PM) vs. Full Operational Capability Year

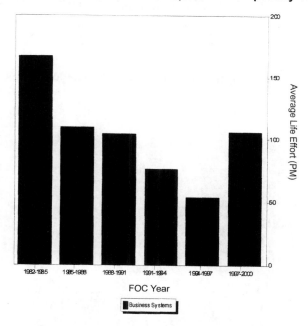

FOC Year

Business Systems

Figure B-2:   *During the first five periods, effort per project declined steadily—a result much to be desired. However, the events of the last three years of the twentieth century markedly reversed this pattern.*

Time

Figure B-3 shows a schedule pattern similar to the effort pattern of Figure B-2. Schedules declined at a rather rapid rate during the first five periods, dropping from two-and-a-half years in 1982 to eight months, in 1997. Then in the sixth period, the schedule gains reversed. This reversal seems to have taken place in spite of the great emphasis placed on Internet time in the late 1990's. The implication, we suspect, is that the realities of software development (and of the software equation) countered the fond hopes of this period. In short, difficult software development does take time! The software equation translates an increase in schedule time to a decline in process productivity, and that is what happened, as shown later, in Figure B-5.

Average Life Duration (Months) vs. Full Operational Capability Year

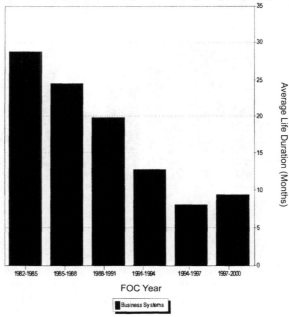

FOC Year

Business Systems

Figure B-3:   *During the first five periods, schedule duration declined at a rather consistent rate. The decline reversed itself in the final period, despite the competitive need in recent years to get projects up and running.*

Staff

Project staffing levels were consistent at six or seven people during the first five periods, as Figure B-4 shows. Then the staff size jumped to about nine people in the final period. A possible explanation is that management, striving to operate in Internet time, added more staff. Another possibility is that a shortage of experienced staff led to the use of more (inexperienced) people. However, it appears that adding people, by itself, does not improve the other core metrics. The historical data adds support to our analysis described in Chapter 7, to Fred Brooks's experience a generation earlier, and to Peter Norden's observations before Brooks's, namely, that just adding people, without regard to the other factors, is not enough.

Average Main Build Average Staff vs. Full Operational Capability Year

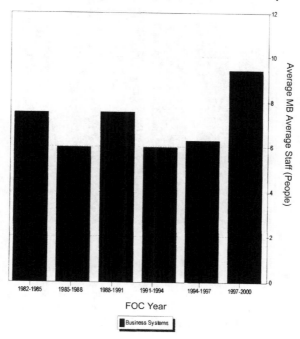

Figure B-4:   *A substantial increase in staffing during the final period had a negative effect on the other core metrics: Process productivity declined while time and effort increased.*

Process Productivity

Figure B-5 shows that process productivity increased over the first five periods and then declined during the last. That was the first decline (of any magnitude) of process productivity during the six periods. According to the software equation, process productivity drops when the product of effort and time increases or when size declines. The diagrams show that effort and time both increased during the final period. However, size also increased substantially. The net effect of these changes in the aggregate data was a small decline in process productivity.

Average Productivity Index vs. Full Operational Capability Year

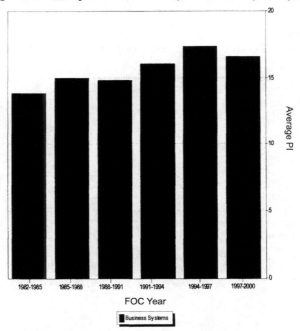

Figure B-5:   *Projects completed in each three-year period show a steady growth in process productivity until the last three years of the twentieth century.*

The possibility that the process productivity level may continue to decline is alarming. The decline in the late twentieth century may be attributed in part to the three great influences discussed in Chapter 1—Year 2000 corrections, Internet commerce, and large-scale applications. This increase in size and complexity may have outrun the methodologies and tools that were in wide use at the end of the century. The improved processes and tools now spreading rapidly offer the promise—used intelligently—of reversing the negative trend in productivity.

Mean Time To Defect

In Figure B-6, we come to some good news. The record shows that during the first month after delivery, MTTD has been steadily increasing for the last twelve years.

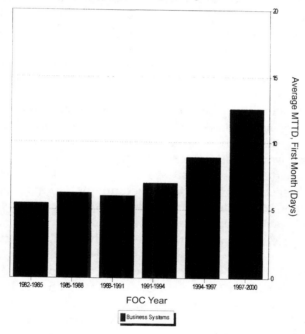

**Average Mean Time To Defect, First Month (Days), vs.
Full Operational Capability Year**

FOC Year

Business Systems

Figure B-6:   *Software organizations reporting to QSM
steadily improved the reliability of their products
during the last decade of the twentieth century.*

The jump in the last three-year period was especially marked—from about nine days to twelve-and-a-half days. We can only assume that software development organizations—at least those reporting to the QSM database—are taking reliability with great seriousness. We may speculate further that the greater complexity resulting from the growth of business-to-business and business-to-consumer Internet relationships and the replacement of stovepipe organization patterns places greater emphasis on avoiding defects in the implementing software. Metrics non-users, lacking data to report, are likely doing worse!

Will the Next Period Reverse Again?

As always, the future remains unknowable. No one can say for sure. However, we can *speculate*.

1. *Size:* During the latter part of the 1990's, software development was entering new fields—Internet, e-commerce, Web development. There were few reusable components available. Entire systems had to be built from scratch, increasing the size reported to our database. As these new areas settle down, as reusable components become available, as new tools facilitate the work, the reduction in the effective size of individual projects may resume.

   Obviously, projects will not fall to zero size or even to very small sizes. But the size of individual projects may remain fairly small, even as the overall magnitude of software applications is bound to grow. The trend we outlined in Chapter 20—toward standard architectures, interfaces, and variation mechanisms, supporting component-based development and making reuse effective— is a growing force toward smaller effective size.

2. *Effort:* On the one hand, relatively small project size, supported by component-based development, is a force toward less effort per project. Also, improved process productivity, a goal certainly within reach, leads to less effort. On the other hand, many negative factors, ranging from poor education to overwork, that we need hardly enumerate in detail, are forces toward increased effort.

3. *Time:* As the software equation demonstrates, time is hardly an independent variable that may be set wherever higher management levels wish. If all goes well in the future—that is, if process productivity increases, if project size is small, and so on—then schedules may be a bit shorter. At best, however, they must be long enough not only to get the work done but also to meet

the needs of the application at the requisite level of quality and reliability.

4. *Staff:* The data indicates that a relatively small staff, on the order of five people, is more effective than a larger staff of nine to twenty, as discussed in Chapter 11. The number of staff members is not an arbitrary number that can be set at will. It is the outcome of effort and time projections that in turn depend upon the amount of functionality to be built, the process productivity achieved, and the quality needed. The arbitrary addition of staff to complete a project at high speed or to get to market "fastest with the mostest" is feasible only to a limited degree. Therefore, it is likely that project staff will decline only to the extent that large applications can be factored into small projects that small staffs can work on almost independently.

5. *Productivity:* The influence of factors such as increasingly complex projects may discourage a rise in productivity. On the plus side, of course, we now know a good deal more about improving development productivity (see Chapter 19).

6. *MTTD:* The factors to watch include gains in process productivity, which lead generally to better reliability, and an emphasis on system availability, such as 24/7 operation. The need for almost continuous uptime puts pressure on executives to pay more attention to quality.

Still, while the future continues, as always, to be uncertain,

- If an organization adopts the elements that lead to better development—phases and iterations, model drawings, component-based development, the tools that implement them, and
- If it embraces metrics-based management to keep these elements in focus,
- Then, it will reduce effort, staff, schedule, and effective size (for a needed functionality) and improve process productivity and quality.

Bibliography

Bassett, Paul B. *Framing Software Reuse: Lessons from the Real World.* Upper Saddle River, N.J.: Prentice Hall, 1996.

Booch, Grady, James Rumbaugh, and Ivar Jacobson. *The Unified Modeling Language User Guide.* Reading, Mass.: Addison-Wesley, 1999.

Brooks, Jr., Frederick P. *The Mythical Man-Month: Essays on Software Engineering.* Reading, Mass.: Addison-Wesley, 1975.

Charting the Seas of Information Technology. The Standish Group International. Dennis, Mass.: 1994.

Clark, Elisabeth K. Bailey, et al. "Mission-Critical and Mission-Support Software: A Preliminary Maintenance Characterization." *Crosstalk* (June 1999), pp. 17–22.

DeMarco, Tom. *Slack: Creating Room in Your Company for Profits and Growth.* New York: Broadway Books, 2001.

Drucker, Peter F. *Managing in a Time of Great Change.* New York: Dutton/Penguin Group, 1995.

Elton, Jeffrey, and Justin Roe. "Bringing Discipline to Project Management." *Harvard Business Review* (March–April 1998), pp. 153–59.

Ertel, Danny. "Turning Negotiation into a Corporate Capability." *Harvard Business Review* (May–June 1999), pp. 55–70.

Gabig, Jr., Jerome S. "Software Source Selection," *Guidelines for Successful Acquisition and Management of Software-Intensive Systems*, Version 3.0, pp. 822–94. Software Technology Support Center, Department of the Air Force. Hill AFB, Utah: 2000.

Glass, Robert L. *Software Runaways*. Upper Saddle River, N.J.: Prentice Hall, 1998.

Gottesdiener, Ellen. "OO Methodologies: Process & Product Patterns." *Component Strategies* (Nov. 1998), pp. 34–44.

Gross, Neil, et al. "Software Hell." *Business Week* (Nov. 6, 1999), pp. 104–18.

Grove, Andrew S. *Only the Paranoid Survive*. New York: Bantam Doubleday Dell Publishing Group, 1996.

Guidelines for Successful Acquisition and Management of Software-Intensive Systems. U.S. Department of Defense, Software Technology Support Center, Department of the Air Force, Version 3.0. Hill AFB, Utah: 2000.

Hammer, Michael, and Steven Stanton. "How Process Enterprises Really Work." *Harvard Business Review* (Nov.–Dec. 1999), pp. 108–18.

Heemstra, F.J., W.J.A Siskens, and H. van der Stelt. "Kostenbeheersing Bij Automatiseringsprojecten: Een Empirisch Onderzoek." *Informatie*, Vol. 31, No. 1 (1989), pp. 34–43.

Humphrey, Watts S. *A Discipline for Software Engineering*. Reading, Mass.: Addison-Wesley, 1995.

———. *Introduction to the Team Software Process*. Reading, Mass.: Addison-Wesley, 2000.

———. *Managing the Software Process*. Reading, Mass.: Addison-Wesley, 1989.

———. "The Personal Software Process: Status and Trends." *IEEE Software* (Nov.–Dec. 2000), pp. 71–75.

———. "Using a Defined and Measured Personal Software Process." *IEEE Software* (May 1996), pp. 77–88.

Jacobson, Ivar, Grady Booch, and James Rumbaugh. *The Unified Software Development Process*. Reading, Mass.: Addison-Wesley, 1999.

Jacobson, Ivar, Martin Griss, and Patrik Jonsson. *Software Reuse: Architecture, Process, and Organization for Business Success.* Reading, Mass.: Addison-Wesley, 1997.

Johnson, Donna L., and Judith G. Brodman. "Applying CMM Project Planning Practices to Diverse Environments." *IEEE Software* (July–Aug. 2000), pp. 40–47.

Keen, Peter. "Information Systems and Organizational Change." *Communications of the ACM* (Jan. 1981), pp. 24–35.

Kozaczynski, Wojitek, and Grady Booch. "Component-Based Software Engineering." *IEEE Software* (Sept.–Oct. 1998), pp. 34–36.

Lim, Wayne C. "Effects of Reuse on Quality, Productivity, and Economics." *IEEE Software* (Sept.–Oct. 1994), pp. 23–30.

Mah, Michael C. "Metrics and the Seven Elements of Negotiation." *IT Metric Strategies* (April 2001), pp. 1–10.

———. "The Multiple Dimensions of Metrics: Metrics and the Learning Organization." *IT Metric Strategies* (Feb. 2000), pp. 1–16.

McConnell, Steve. "The Best Influences on Software Engineering." *IEEE Software* (Jan.–Feb. 2000), pp. 10–17.

Mosemann II, Lloyd K. "Did We Lose Our Religion?" *Crosstalk* (August 2002), pp. 22–25.

Norden, Peter V. "Useful Tools for Project Management," *Operations Research in Research and Development,* ed. B.V. Dean. New York: John Wiley & Sons, 1963.

Paige, Jr., Emmett. "Predictable Software: Order Out of Chaos." *Crosstalk* (June 1994), pp. 2–5.

Paulk, Mark C. "Software Process Proverbs." *Crosstalk* (Jan. 1998), pp. 4–7.

Process Maturity Profile of the Software Community 2000 Year-End Update. Software Engineering Institute, Carnegie Mellon University. Pittsburgh: 2000.

Putnam, Lawrence H. *Software Cost Estimating and Life-Cycle Control: Getting the Software Numbers.* Los Alamitos, Calif.: IEEE Computer Society, 1980.

———, and Ware Myers. *Executive Briefing: Controlling Software Development.* Los Alamitos, Calif.: IEEE Computer Society, 1996.

———. *Industrial Strength Software: Effective Management Using Measurement.* Los Alamitos, Calif.: IEEE Computer Society, 1997.

———. *Measures for Excellence: Reliable Software on Time, Within Budget.* Englewood Cliffs, N.J.: Prentice Hall, 1992.

———. "QSM Database Shows Drop in Productivity." *IT Metric Strategies* (May 1998), pp. 13–16.

Reifer, Donald J. "Software Management's Seven Deadly Sins." *IEEE Software* (March–April 2001), pp. 12–15.

Royce, Winston W. "Managing the Development of Large Software Systems." *Proceedings, IEEE WESCON* (Aug. 1970), pp. 1–9.

Rubin, Howard. "The 1997 Worldwide Benchmark Project: Worldwide Software Engineering Performance Summary." *IT Metric Strategies* (April 1998), pp. 1–12.

Shannon, Claude E. "The Mathematical Theory of Communication." *Bell System Technical Journal,* Vol. 27 (1948), pp. 279–423, 623–56. Also, University of Illinois Press, 1949.

Walston, C.E., and C.P. Felix. "A Method of Programming Measurement and Estimation." *IBM Systems Journal,* Vol. 16, No. 1 (1977), pp. 54–73.

Wessel, David. "Professor Romer Goes to Washington." *The Wall Street Journal* (Jan. 25, 2001), p. A1.

Index